Ancient Mycenae

THE CAPITAL CITY OF AGAMEMNON

THE PAGE-BARBOUR LECTURES FOR 1955
AT THE UNIVERSITY OF VIRGINIA

Ancient Mycenae

THE CAPITAL CITY OF

AGAMEMNON

BY GEORGE E. MYLONAS

PRINCETON, NEW JERSEY

PRINCETON UNIVERSITY PRESS

1957

▣

GEORGE E. MYLONAS is Professor and Chairman of the Department of Art and Archaeology at Washington University. He also holds the honorary title of Professor of Archaeology at the University of Athens.

Dr. Mylonas took an active part in the excavations conducted at Mycenae in 1952-1954, when the second and new Grave Circle (discovered in 1951) was explored. The rich finds of this Grave Circle, enclosing graves of the ruling families of the 17th and 16th centuries B.C., are described and illustrated in this book.

The vignette on the title-page is from an engraving on a Mycenaean gem found in 1954, which originally seems to have been deposited as a gift or offering in the Tomb of Clytemnestra. It represents the great Mycenaean goddess riding through the ether on her mythical animal. See page 95 and plate 35. It dates from the thirteenth century B.C.

▣

Printed in the United States of America by Princeton University Press, Princeton, New Jersey Illustrations printed by the Meriden Gravure Company, Meriden, Connecticut

TO

CHRESTOS TSOUNTAS
DISCOVERER OF THE PALACE OF AGAMEMNON
AT MYCENAE

ΜΝΗΜΟΣΥΝΟΝ

PREFACE

THE discovery of the new Grave Circle gave me the privilege of working at Mycenae, one of the renowned centers of the mythical world of Greece. For that privilege I am deeply grateful to the Council of the Greek Archaeological Society and to its secretary, Professor Anastasios Orlandos. I am also grateful to Dr. John Papademetriou, the ephor of the district, for his invitation to join him in this work. For three memorable summers, 1952, 1953, and 1954, we lived in the shadow of the Citadel of Agamemnon and collaborated in the task of unearthing the remains of the ancestors of the great king. Our exploration of the new shaft graves and the long discussions we had in the quiet of night, often with the magic Mycenaean full moon looking down on us from the top of Zara, will be remembered long and with affection.

When I was asked, in 1954, to give the Page-Barbour Lectures at the University of Virginia, I felt that Mycenae and her new shaft graves should be my subject. This book is based on these lectures, delivered at Charlottesville on March 29, 30, and 31, 1955. To the Page-Barbour Committee of the University of Virginia and to its chairman, Professor Edward Younger, I am grateful for their invitation and for the friendship and indeed Homeric hospitality which they extended to me during my stay in their fair city. To my friend of long standing, Professor A. D. Frazer, whose sudden death is mourned by classicists the world over, I am grateful for his many courtesies, for the reading of the manuscript, and for valuable suggestions.

It is a pleasure to acknowledge my indebtedness to the American Philosophical Society, the State Department, the Fulbright Committee, and the John Simon Guggenheim Foundation for grants which made it possible for me to return to Greece and take an active part in the work. To Washington University and its administration, and especially to Chancellors Arthur H. Compton and Ethan A. H. Shepley and to Deans Carl Tolman and Thomas S. Hall, I am grateful for their encouragement and interest in my work and for the leaves of absence granted me in 1951-1952, 1954, and 1955-1956. To the Institute for Advanced Study in Princeton I am also indebted for my residence at the Institute, during which time I undertook the final revision of my text. Thanks are also due to Professor A. Orlandos and Dr. E. Stikas, of Athens, for the photographs and drawings of the work of restoration carried out under their direction and for their permission to use them. My indebtedness to the work of Schliemann, Tsountas, and Wace, the three immortals of Mycenae, will become evident in the pages to follow. But I am especially grateful to Professor Wace for the drawings and photograph of Figs. 21, 23, and 29. All photographs, unless otherwise stated, are by V. and N. Tombazis, of Athens, to whom I am indebted for excellent work, constant help, and eager participation in our efforts. To Princeton University Press and especially to Miss R. Miriam Brokaw and Miss Harriet Anderson I am grateful for their efficient work, ever-ready help, and valuable suggestions. Lastly, I want to express my gratitude to Mrs. George E. Mylonas for her ever-ready help, encouragement, and inspiration.

The original title of the Page-Barbour Lectures, *Mycenae: The Capital City of Agamemnon*, has been changed to the present title, *Ancient Mycenae: the Capital City of Agamemnon*, to differentiate this volume from Professor Wace's fundamental book *Mycenae: an Archaeological History and Guide*, also published by Princeton University Press.

This contribution to the story of Mycenae is humbly dedicated to my teacher, Chrestos Tsountas, Professor of Archaeology at the University of Athens, in grateful appreciation of his deeds and of his teaching, which have inspired so many generations of students to follow the path of devotion to scholarship and duty.

G. E. M.

Washington University
October 24, 1956

CONTENTS

Ancient Mycenae

THE CAPITAL CITY OF AGAMEMNON

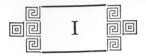

MYCENAE: LEGENDS AND HISTORY

MORE than three quarters of a century have passed since the day (November 28, 1876) when Heinrich Schliemann sent his famous telegram to King George of Greece, announcing the discovery of the grave of Agamemnon, the storied leader of the Greek expedition against Troy. That telegram heralded one of the great archaeological discoveries in Greece—the discovery of the Grave Circle of Mycenae and the royal shaft graves within her Citadel—and brought the famous site back to the attention of the world and to a popularity unparalleled in her long history. People of varied tongues and nationalities began to talk of her glories, immeasurably more people than the chosen aristocrats in whose courts the bards used to sing the κλέα ἀνδρῶν, the achievements of her great king. The excavations which followed Schliemann's discoveries brought to light chapters in the life of Mycenae which were unknown even to Agamemnon and his followers.

The literary traditions of the site are not many, because the days of Mycenae's greatness and leadership were over when the classical Greek authors were recording in their poems, dramas, histories, and orations the activities of the cities of Hellas, and when records of public events were inscribed upon stone stelai. The few references are centered around Agamemnon, the members of his family, and the fateful destiny of the Pelopids, beloved and at the same time hateful to the gods. Beyond his time and that of his Pelopid ancestors, tradition will take us back but a few generations, and to the legendary founder of Mycenae, to Perseus the son of Danaë and Zeus. Apollodoros tells us how the hero, distressed because of the accidental death of his grandfather Acrisios, a calamity which had been predicted by an oracle, did not return to "Argos to claim the inheritance of him who had died by his hand," but "went to Megapenthes, son of Proetos, at Tiryns and offered an exchange with him, surrendering Argos into his hand. So Megapenthes reigned over the Argives, and Perseus reigned over Tiryns, after fortifying also Midea and Mycenae."[1]

[1] Apollodoros, II, 4, 4. Ed. Heyne; transl. Sir J. G. Frazer.

Pausanias repeats the story and explains how the site was chosen and how it received its name.[2] According to his version, Mycenae was founded on the site it occupies "because in that site the cap [*mykes*] of his [Perseus'] scabbard had fallen off and he regarded this as a sign to found a city." To this he added: "I have also heard that being thirsty he chanced to take up a mushroom [*mykes*] and that water flowing from it he drank, and being pleased gave the place the name of Mycenae." A copious spring at a short distance to the east of the Citadel, known as Perseia, was pointed out in antiquity as the one revealed by the plucking of the mushroom. In our day it still provides the village of Mycenae with a good supply of excellent water. A third derivation of the name from that of a woman named Mycene is discarded by Pausanias.[3] However, the other two possibilities are surely etiological and resulted from the similarity of the first part of the name of the site to the word *mykes*. Whatever might have been the reason which prompted the choice of the site and its name, the fact remains that Perseus is the acknowledged founder of Mycenae, and as such he was venerated to the time of Pausanias.[4] For the construction of its walls Perseus is reported to have used the Cyclopes, the legendary builders of Tiryns,[5] and to this tradition Euripides refers when he calls the walls of Mycenae Cyclopean and Mycenae herself a Cyclopean city.[6]

The dynasty established at Mycenae by Perseus is known as the Perseid, the earliest known to tradition. It was followed by the Pelopid dynasty established by Atreus, the son of Pelops. Tradition has preserved the story of the change but says little about the length of time during which Perseus and his descendants ruled over Mycenae. We learn from Apollodoros that in Mycenae Perseus had five sons and a daughter by Andromeda: "Alcaeos and Sthenelos and Heleus and Mestor and Electryon and a daughter Gorgophone, whom Perieres married."[7] It is not stated how many of these sons and their descendants ruled over Mycenae and for how long. We

---

[2] Pausanias, II, 16, 3f. Ed. and transl. Frazer.   [3] Cf. *Odyssey*, 2, 120.

[4] In II, 18, 1 he states: "On the way from Mycenae to Argos is a shrine of the hero Perseus beside the road on the left." See also the archaic inscription found by Tsountas in the neighborhood of the Perseia fountain, *Ephemeris*, 1892, 67, and *IG* IV, 493.

[5] Pausanias, II, 16, 6.

[6] Euripides, *Electra*, 1158; *Troades*, 1087-1088; *Iphig. Aul.*, 265, 534, 1501; *Iphig. Taur.*, 845.

[7] Apollodoros, II, 4, 5, and II, 4, 6.

hear that Electryon and Sthenelos ruled over Mycenae after the death of Perseus and that through the latter the Pelopids came to the site. For Sthenelos married Nikippe, the daughter of Pelops, and to her at Mycenae her brothers Atreus and Thyestes went when they found themselves in disagreement with their father Pelops. Eurystheus, the son and successor of Sthenelos, known as the master for whom Heracles performed his exploits, was killed in Attica, whereupon the people of Mycenae elected Atreus to rule over them.[8] In this manner, according to tradition, occurred the change of dynasties, and in a peaceful way the Pelopids succeeded the Perseids.

In the *Iliad* we find the story of the succession of the Pelopid dynasty down to the days of Agamemnon.[9] Atreus was succeeded by his brother Thyestes, and he in turn by Agamemnon, the leader of the Greek expedition against Troy. In the days of the Perseid dynasty the rulers of Mycenae apparently controlled the Argolid and its cities of Argos, Tiryns, and Midea. Their power was increased during the reign of the Pelopids and seems to have reached its zenith in the days of Agamemnon. The picture preserved in the *Iliad* is one of great power and prosperity, of a state dominating the southern section of Greece. Agamemnon is not only the ruler of Mycenae, "the well-built citadel," but also of "wealthy Corinth and well-built Cleonae," of those who "dwelt in Orneiae and lovely Araethyrea and Sicyon, . . ." of those "that held Hyperesia and steep Gonoessa and Pellene," and of those "that dwelt about Aegium and throughout all Aegialos, and about broad Helice." In other words, Agamemnon was supposed to rule over the northeastern corner of the Peloponnesos. Furthermore, he was the "lord of many isles and of Argos."[10] It is true that Diomedes is stated in the "Catalogue of Ships" to have been the ruler of the Argives,[11] but the behavior of that hero seems to indicate that he was under the suzerainty of Agamemnon. Then, too, we may recall how Agamemnon promised to give Achilles seven well-peopled cities, if only the hero would relent and again join the sorely pressed Achaeans. All seven cities were located "by the sea, in the uttermost border of sandy Pylos,"[12] on the southwestern coast of the Peloponnesos. Thus the epic tradition pictures Agamemnon as the suzerain of a large section of the Peloponnesos and of the islands by its eastern

[8] Thucydides, I, 9; Hellanicos *apud schol. Iliad*, II, 105; Strabo, VIII, 6, 19 (377).
[9] II, 102-108.
[10] II, 569-575, and II, 108.
[11] II, 559-564.
[12] IX, 149-153.

coast. Because of his domain he is the leader of the expedition and is acknowledged as βασιλεύτατος πάντων, the most kingly of all. His power extended not only over land but also over the seas; this is proved by his contingent of one hundred ships in the expedition, the largest contingent mentioned, and by his lending sixty additional galleys to the Arcadians, who, being an inland people, lacked ships.[13]

The tragic fate which awaited Agamemnon on his return to Mycenae has been exploited by the tragedians and has become one of the better known stories of the ancient world. Agamemnon was murdered by Clytemnestra and her paramour, Aegisthos. Seven years later both were killed by Orestes, who apparently became the king of Mycenae.[14] During the reign of his son Tisamenos, it seems that the power of Mycenae collapsed under the impact of the invading Dorian tribes, and her Citadel was destroyed. Though the destruction may have failed to extinguish life completely, it succeeded in eliminating Mycenae from a role of importance. The suzerainty of the Argolid, her power and prestige, passed over to the city of Argos, while Mycenae became a secluded village. The sources quoted and the available literary evidence from the tragedians (whose value is doubtful because of their exploitation of the original tale) seem to indicate that the life history of Mycenae in the prehistoric age was rather short, limited to seven or eight generations, three or four of which belonged to the Perseid dynasty and four to the Pelopid.

According to tradition, the coming of the final waves of the Dorians, and the consequent destruction of Mycenaean supremacy, occurred towards the end of the twelfth century. For centuries after that event Mycenae remains unrecorded. We next hear of her when another menace hangs over Greece, when the Persian armies threaten to flood the Hellenic mainland. A contingent of eighty Mycenaeans is recorded as having joined the small force of Leonidas entrusted with the defense of Thermopylae.[15] A year or so later Mycenae, along with Tiryns, contributed her men to the campaign of Plataea[16] and had the privilege of inscribing her name on the bronze serpents supporting the trophy placed by the Greeks at Delphi. The honors

---

[13] II, 610-613. [14] *Odyssey*, 1, 28-43, and 3, 303-308.

[15] Pausanias, II, 16, 5.

[16] Four hundred men were contributed by both cities. See Herodotos, IX, 28. The relative size of both cities can be conceived of when we consider that the city of Corinth contributed 5,000 men; Orchomenos in Arcadia, 600; Sicyon, 3,000; Epidauros, 800; Phlious, 1,000; etc.

conferred on the Mycenaeans, their refusal to accept the supremacy
of the Argives, and their demand for a leading role in the direction
of the affairs of the temple of Hera and of the Nemean games, increased the envy and hatred of the people of Argos. Taking advantage of the preoccupation of the Spartans with the Helots and
the Messenians, the Argives suddenly and without provocation attacked Mycenae and succeeded in destroying her, c. 468 B.C.[17] This
second destruction which Mycenae suffered in the course of her history was so great that at least two ancient authors maintain that the
site never recovered from the blow. "Mycenae remained uninhabited
until our day," states Diodoros, while Strabo writes that "not a trace
of the city was to be seen" in his time.[18] Evidently Strabo never
actually visited the site, because the ruins of Mycenae were to be
seen later. When Pausanias, in the middle of the second century A.D.,
visited the site he saw parts of the circuit wall with the Lion Gate,
the underground "treasuries of Atreus and his children," the graves
of Atreus, Agamemnon, and those who were massacred with him
on their return from Troy, the graves of Aegisthos and Clytemnestra
beyond the walls (for they were not considered worthy to be buried
along with Agamemnon within the Citadel), and the Perseia fountain
among the ruins of Mycenae.[19] Since there is good reason to believe
that the graves which Pausanias identified as those of Agamemnon
and his followers were completely covered and invisible at the time
of his visit, it seems possible from his statement to conclude that he
obtained his information from people who lived on the site and who
cherished her traditions; in other words, it seems likely that Mycenae
in the days of Pausanias was still inhabited, though completely deprived of her importance and glory. A few shepherds may have been
the only occupants, and the important historic role which she played
in the past had become tradition and myth.

Pausanias is the latest of the ancient authors who mentions Mycenae. After him, the site passed into oblivion until late in the period
of the Turkish occupation of Greece. Then it was noted by a number
of early travelers and became the object of pilfering by art collectors
and purveyors. Lord Sligo, Lord Elgin, and Veli, the Pasha of
Nauplia, are three of Mycenae's known despoilers.[20] After the lib-

---

[17] Pausanias II, 16, 5. The story is dramatically told by Diodoros XI, 65.
[18] Strabo, VIII, 6, 10 (372).   [19] Pausanias, II, 16, 5-7.
[20] For the early travelers and the spoliation of Mycenae, cf. Wace, A. J. B., BSA,
25 (1921-1923), pp. 283ff.

eration of Greece, especially after 1833, such open depredations came to an end and shortly afterward the site came under the protecting care of the newly formed Greek Archaeological Society of Athens. In 1840 the Society started the investigation of her antiquities by undertaking the clearing of the Lion Gate, which throughout the ages stood in full view of the visitors of the site.[21]

Mycenae was, however, forcibly brought to the attention of the world by Heinrich Schliemann. After discovering the site of Troy, Schliemann decided to follow the leaders of the expedition to their homes and attempt to bring to light their palaces and their graves. Mycenae naturally attracted him, and in 1874 he dug some exploratory trenches in the Citadel, without important results. In 1876, guided by Pausanias' account, he resumed his exploration and this time he excavated the area to the south of the Lion Gate. Before long he disclosed to an astonished world of scholars and of interested laymen the famous Grave Circle of Mycenae with its royal shaft graves, filled with objects of art and of gold. Five graves were cleared within four weeks, the richest find in archaeological research to that date.[22] The epic term "Mycenae rich in gold" received a new and real meaning, and the Citadel guarded by its lions became a center of unparalleled activity. In the five shafts he cleared Schliemann recognized the graves mentioned by Pausanias, and he stopped his exploration of the Grave Circle after the fifth grave was investigated. In 1877 Stamatakes discovered a sixth shaft grave. Later investigations proved that Schliemann's identification of the graves as those of Agamemnon was not correct, but this did not diminish the importance of his discovery, for his shaft graves not only yielded a multitude of objects of art, but also proved that the mythical age of Greece was a reality and that beyond her historic era stretched a period whose importance and meaning had previously been unsuspected. Schliemann's discoveries opened up a new horizon to research, a horizon which is still absorbing the attention of many scholars, and his writings on Mycenae and Tiryns conjured up vistas of romantic explorations and of fabulous discoveries.

Schliemann's work was followed, as has been noted, by Stamatakes'

[21] Pittakes undertook the clearing of the gate. See *PAE*, 1840-1841, pp. 136-138.
[22] His account of the discovery appeared first in German and then in English with a preface by Gladstone: *Mycenae*, London, 1878. A better organized account of Schliemann's discoveries was published a few years later by C. Schuchardt (English translation by Eugènie Sellers), *Schliemann's Excavations*, London, 1891.

with chapters in the life of Mycenae unknown to literary tradition.[33] We have seen that the Perseid and Pelopid dynasties comprise but seven or eight generations; that the last scion of the Pelopid dynasty was overthrown when Mycenae was destroyed by the traditional Dorians. The date of that destruction can be placed c. 1100 B.C.,[34] a date preserved by tradition. Eight generations before that date will take us, at the earliest, to the middle or to the beginning of the fourteenth century B.C. Beyond that date, tradition has nothing to contribute. After all, according to tradition, Mycenae was founded by Perseus, the originator of the Perseid dynasty.

Modern excavations take us beyond that date and to the beginning of the Bronze Age.[35] They prove that the site was inhabited in the Early Bronze Age—the Early Helladic period, as it is now known to scholars—c. 2500-1900 B.C. The only remains thus far found from that period of occupation are sherds and pots. They were found around the Grave Circle and the adjoining South House. Comparatively few sherds came to light on top of the Citadel itself and below the foundations and floors of its Palace, and some were discovered in the area of the hill known as Kalkani at a short distance from the Citadel. No architectural remains have been uncovered thus far, but we have to remember that a good part of the Citadel has not been completely excavated and that what has been explored was rebuilt so many times as to make almost impossible the survival of older architectural remains. In spite of this lack, the conclusion is inevitable that the site was inhabited in Early Helladic times.

The site was also inhabited during the Middle Bronze Age—the Middle Helladic period (c. 1900-1580 B.C.). But, again, the greater part of this period is represented by pottery. A few walls here and there have been found, but no complete or nearly complete structures. From the few revealed remains, we can assume that the uppermost terrace of the Citadel was occupied by houses in Middle Helladic times, perhaps by the dwelling of the ruler, and that it was surrounded by a fortification wall, only scanty remains of which seem

---

[33] For a discussion of the evidence regarding the Bronze Age remains of Mycenae, see Wace, *BSA*, 25 (1921-1923); *Mycenae, An Archaeological History and Guide*, pp. 20-25.

[34] Thucydides, I, XII, 3-4, states that eighty years after the Trojan war (ending according to tradition c. 1183 B.C.) occurred the "Return of the Heracleidai," our "Dorian invasion."

[35] Three sherds, possibly of the Neolithic period, were found in the course of the excavation of Circle B and one was known from the site before the latest excavation.

---

brief efforts in 1877-1878, in the course of which he found the sixth shaft grave and cleared the so-called Treasury of Atreus from its debris.[23] Interest in the site was kept alive by the further efforts of the Greek Archaeological Society and its representative, Chrestos Tsountas. The then young but highly gifted Greek scholar placed the exploration of the site on a scientific basis, and in successive campaigns from 1886 to 1902 brought to light the remains of the prehistoric palace and the historic temple on the very top of the Citadel, the foundations of houses within the circuit walls, and the amazing underground cistern. In addition Tsountas explored a good many Mycenaean graves, including some tholos tombs, beyond the Citadel.[24] Tsountas supplemented the model publication of the reports of his excavations by his Μυκῆναι καὶ Μυκηναῖος πολιτισμός (1893), a work which has proved of fundamental importance to the study of the civilization of the late Bronze Age of Greece.[25]

For about twenty years after Tsountas' excavations Mycenae remained in the background while Crete and the epoch-making discoveries of Sir Arthur Evans dominated the scene of Greek archaeological research. Sporadic and minor investigations were undertaken by Professor D. Evangelides in 1909, by Professor A. Keramopoullos in 1917, and by Professor G. Rodenwaldt in 1911,[26] but the effort to uncover the famous site completely was abandoned. Attention was again directed to Mycenae when Professor A. J. B. Wace and the British School of Archaeology at Athens resumed large-scale investigations on the site in 1920 and continued them to 1923. In the course of these excavations the remains in the Citadel uncovered by Schliemann and Tsountas were further cleared and studied, and evidence was obtained which enabled Professor Wace to draw a reasoned picture of the history and structural phases of Mycenae and to give a clearer view of the successive periods of the culture developed there. In addition, during the course of these investigations, a number of

---

[23] *PAE*, 1878, pp. 16-17.

[24] See Tsountas, Chr., in almost every volume of *PAE*, 1886-1899 (*PAE*, 1886, pp. 19, 59-79; 1887, pp. 11-65; 1888, pp. 28-29; 1889, pp. 18-21; 1890, pp. 35-36; 1891, pp. 19-20; 1892, pp. 56-58; 1893, pp. 8-9; 1895, pp. 23-25; 1896, pp. 29-31; 1897, pp. 24-27; 1899, pp. 15, 102-103). See also *Jahrbuch*, 1895, pp. 143-151; *Ephemeris*, 1887, pp. 155ff.; 1888, pp. 119ff.; 1891, pp. 1ff.; 1897, pp. 97ff.; 1902, pp. 1ff.

[25] An English translation by J. I. Manatt, *The Mycenaean Age*, was published in 1897 in Boston.

[26] *PAE*, 1909, pp. 27, 63; *Ephemeris*, 1912, pp. 127ff.; 1918, pp. 52ff.; *Ath. Mitt.*, 36 (1911), pp. 221ff.; 1918, pp. 129ff.; *Jahrbuch*, 34 (1919), pp. 87ff.

chamber tombs were explored, and the tholos tombs were studied and for the first time published in a scientific manner.[27] The observations made also cleared up some problems connected with Schliemann's discoveries and established the burial customs of the Mycenaean world.

Professor Wace's work was brought to an end at the conclusion of the 1923 campaign by the decision of the executive committee of the British School of Archaeology,[28] but fortunately this proved to be a mere interruption; in 1939, though only for a brief period, he was back at Mycenae and hopes were revived for the continuation of the exploration on a large scale.[29] These hopes were shattered by the Second World War, but they were revived in 1950 when Professor Wace returned to the site and resumed the exploration of the houses of the Lower City and the cemetery to which the shaft graves belonged. At the same time, the Greek Archaeological Society, through Dr. John Papademetriou, renewed its interest in the site and in 1950 began the exploration of the remains of a house on the slopes of the north hill.[30] The year 1951 was marked by the successful restoration of the so-called Tomb of Clytemnestra by the Department of Restoration and Preservation of Antiquities under the direction of Professor A. Orlandos and Dr. E. Stikas. The year before, Dr. Papademetriou had placed two blocks in their original position in the famous relieving triangle of the Lion Gate and had thus restored the frame within which the well-known relief has to be viewed.

Intense archaeological activity characterized the years 1952, 1953, and 1954. Professor Wace and his associates continued to investigate the prehistoric cemetery by the Cyclopean walls, and disclosed and cleared the remains of a number of Mycenaean houses in the lower city.[31] In 1952 the Greek Archaeological Society began the investigation of a new Grave Circle which was accidentally discovered by Professor A. Orlandos' technicians at the completion of their restoration of the Tomb of Clytemnestra.[32] The exploration of the houses in the

[27] Wace, A. J. B., *et al.*, *BSA*, 25 (1921-1923). Wace, "Chamber Tombs at Mycenae," *Archaeologia*, 82 (1932), pp. 1-232.
[28] *BSA*, 25 (1921-1923), p. 5.   [29] Cf. *BSA*, 45 (1950), pp. 204ff.
[30] *BSA*, 48 (1953), pp. 3-93. *PAE*, 1950, pp. 203ff. For the work of restoration, see *Ephemeris*, 1948-1949, "Chronika," pp. 43-48.
[31] Wace, A. J. B., *et al.*, "Mycenae 1939-1952," *BSA*, 48 (1953), pp. 3-93. Wace, "Mycenae," *JHS*, 74 (1954), pp. 170-171.
[32] Mylonas, G. E., and J. Papademetriou, "The New Shaft Graves of Mycenae," *Archaeology*, 5 (1952), pp. 194-200; Papademetriou, *PAE*, 1952, pp. 427-472.

Lower City and of the new shaft graves of Mycenae recalled in ma ways the great days of Schliemann and Tsountas and revived wor interest in the site. It also proved wrong the notions current amo students of archaeology and among experts that Mycenae had co pletely yielded its treasures to Schliemann and Tsountas, and th no further great discoveries and surprises were to be expected ther Furthermore, the exploration raised hopes of continued large-sca investigations in the years to come. To this record of archaeologic: research must be added the work of the Greek Service for the Resto ration and Preservation of Ancient Monuments in 1954. In that yea it undertook and successfully began the restoration of the falle: parts of the circuit wall of Mycenae, the preservation and restoratio of the remains of the Palace on top of the Citadel, and of the inter esting and partially excavated tholos tomb known as the Tomb o Aegisthos.

A survey of the literary and traditional information regarding Mycenae and of the efforts of archaeologists to bring to light the remains and the cultural activities of that site raises a natural question. Is it possible to correlate the information gleaned from tradition with results obtained by the excavators? Do they agree, do they supplement each other, or are they at variance? Certainly modern excavations have proved the accuracy of the epithets bestowed on Mycenae by Homer and the tragic poets. The visitor standing before the Lion Gate or on the upper terrace of the Citadel amid the ruins of her vast Palace, below which like a rich and colorful mosaic spreads the Argive plain, surrounded by crystalline mountains, and trying to visualize the extent of the site and its importance on the basis of the ruins and of the works of art they contained, will find himself repeating unconsciously the words of the poets: "Mycenae, the well-built citadel"; "Mycenae, the broad-wayed"; "Mycenae, rich in gold."

The correspondence goes beyond this. The excavations have proved that the site was an important center of culture in the days of the Perseid and the Pelopid dynasties, that it was of lesser importance in the days of the Persian wars, that it was a mere village after the destruction of 468 B.C. However, the excavations have provided us

Marinatos, Sp., "On the New Shaft Graves of Mycenae," *Geras in Honor of A. Keramopoullos*, pp. 54-86 (in Greek).

to have survived.[86] The second half of the period is further represented by a number of graves which seem to have formed a large
cemetery in the area later occupied by the Lion Gate and the circuit
wall to the southwest, a cemetery the use of which continued into the
Late Helladic or Mycenaean period. As a matter of fact, Schliemann's
Grave Circle originally formed part of that cemetery. To the end of
the same period seem to belong the construction and the beginning of
the use of the new Grave Circle found only ten meters to the west
of the apex of the tholos of the so-called Tomb of Clytemnestra.
This new Grave Circle we shall call Grave Circle B, following the
suggestion made by Professor Marinatos,[37] while that discovered by
Schliemann within the Citadel we shall hereafter call Grave Circle A.
From the graves of the period we learn that the importance of
Mycenae and the prosperity of her people gradually increased until it
reached quite a high state toward the beginning of the sixteenth
century—toward the end of the period; that her contacts with the
outside world, and especially with Crete, gradually increased and that
in the closing years of the period her people were in close contact not
only with Crete but even with Egypt.

It seems that the prosperity and importance of Mycenae increased
during the first subdivision of the Late Bronze Age, known as the
Late Helladic I or Mycenean I period (1580-1500). To that period
belong the shaft graves found by Schliemann and Stamatakes, and
their surprising contents form an eloquent demonstration of the
prosperity and power of Mycenae. It seems that a palace was constructed on top of the hill while in the adjacent hills rock-hewn
chamber tombs were excavated for the burial of the people. Prosperity
and an expansion of influence continued in the Late Helladic II or
Mycenaean II period (c. 1500-1400 B.C.). By then, in addition to
rock-hewn chamber tombs, we find in regular use a new type of royal
grave, the tholos tomb. With the Late Helladic III or Mycenaean III
period (c. 1400-1100 B.C.)[38] we enter the last era of prosperity and

---

[86] I am deeply indebted to Professor Wace, who was kind enough to let me read
the proof of his report on these remains, which were investigated again during the
summer of 1954.

[37] Marinatos, op.cit., p. 57, n. 2.

[38] For the dates of the Late Helladic subdivisions, see Furumark, A., Chronology
of the Mycenaean Pottery, and Wace, BSA, 48 (1953), p. 15, n. 22. Of course, the
division of Mycenae's life and activities into periods and subperiods is somewhat
arbitrary and there cannot be any certainty as to the exactness of the dates given, but
for this study we shall have to follow the divisions, the dates, and the terminology

activity of the site. Most of the visible remains of the Citadel as well as the two most advanced tholos tombs—the so-called Treasury of Atreus and the so-called Tomb of Clytemnestra—belong to this period.[39] Their riches reflect the position of leadership and importance assigned to the site by epic poetry. With Crete no longer an artistic and cultural center (since her sites were destroyed around 1400 B.C.), Mycenae developed into the main artistic, religious, and cultural center of the Aegean world and the focal point from which radiated great activity in all directions, even to Syria and Egypt, to the coast of Asia Minor, and to Sicily. It remained such until *c.* 1100 B.C., when a great catastrophe overtook the site.

Is it possible to recognize in one of the periods disclosed by the spade of the excavators of Mycenae the era of the dynasties known from tradition, the Perseid and Pelopid? Tsountas was the first to suggest that the shaft graves of Mycenae represented one dynasty, the tholos tombs another, and to attribute the former to the Danaans and the latter to the Achaeans.[40] Professor Wace suggested two dynasties which he named the "shaft graves dynasty" and the "tholos tombs dynasty" without identifying them with people or heroes known from tradition.[41] Others equated the Perseid dynasty with the Danaans of Tsountas, and related it to the shaft graves; and the Pelopid dynasty with the Achaeans, and attributed to it the tholos tombs, which continued to be constructed to the end of the Mycenaean Age, i.e., to the end of the Pelopid rule.

I should like to think that the distinction between the shaft graves and the tholos tombs is not as clearcut as it is presumed to be, and that it should be attributed to other reasons which have nothing to do with a change in dynasty. In the chapter dealing with the tholos tombs, I suggest that in the Grave Circles we may have the prototype of the tholos tomb, in which case the use of the latter cannot indicate a change in dynasty. But, on chronological grounds, we can exclude at once the equation of the Perseid and Pelopid dynasties with the

now current, with the hope that someday, after more evidence is unearthed, we shall be able to treat the question in detail and independently.

[39] It is now generally accepted that these two impressive monuments were neither the Treasury of Atreus nor the Tomb of Clytemnestra; rather, they are the graves of rulers of Mycenae who remain unknown and unnamed. The names, however, have been retained by scholars as convenient labels and they will be used here as such without the continual use of the modifying "so-called."

[40] *The Mycenaean Age*, pp. 249-251, 343-346.

[41] *BSA*, 25 (1921-1923), pp. 119-120. *Mycenae*, p. 22.

shaft graves and early tholos tombs. With the discovery at Mycenae of the new shaft graves, the upper chronological limit of this type of sepulcher is pushed into the seventeenth century B.C., and we have seen that only some seven or eight generations separate Perseus from the end of the Mycenaean supremacy, c. 1100 B.C. Again, the oldest of the tholos tombs have been dated by Professor Wace at about 1510 B.C.[42] We could never attribute these graves to the Pelopids, since Atreus, the founder of that dynasty, is only four generations away from the destruction of 1100 B.C.

Although we cannot equate the legendary kings of Mycenae with the shaft graves and with the older tholos tombs, we can, I believe, associate them with a good section of the Cyclopean walls and with the Palace on the Citadel. It would seem that the first great period of the Palace dates from the middle of the fourteenth century; the south section of the Cyclopean wall of Mycenae served as a retaining wall for the terrace on which the southwest wing of the Palace was constructed. Consequently, a good part, perhaps the main part, of the Cyclopean walls of Mycenae must have existed by that date.[43] The construction of the walls and Palace must have been a memorable event, which would have formed an important part of the traditions handed down from father to son through the long generations. We have seen that according to the Mycenaean tradition Perseus was the founder of Mycenae. Perseus ruled over the site he built some seven or eight generations before its destruction c. 1100 B.C. If we figure thirty years to each generation, we shall have to place the beginning of Perseus' rule at c. 1310 or 1340 B.C., at about the middle of the fourteenth century B.C.

If we now turn to the *Marmor Parium*, where traditional dates have been preserved, we find that Heracles is supposed to have visited Athens, and perhaps to have been initiated in the Lesser Mysteries at Agra, during the reign of Aegeus, i.e., c. 1307/6–1295/4 B.C.[44]

[42] *Mycenae*, p. 16.

[43] *Ibid.*, pp. 22, 133. For our views on the construction of the walls of Mycenae and their dates, see Chapter II of this book.

[44] Jacoby, *Das Marmor Parium*, pp. 8 and 9. *The Marmor Parium* dates the Trojan War c. 1209 B.C., i.e., some 25 years earlier than the date given by Eratosthenes, c. 1183 B.C. This difference should be kept in mind in any attempt to suggest the years of Eurystheus' and Atreus' rule. Also, we should bear in mind that ancient sources vary somewhat in their dates of the event: cf. *Cambridge Ancient History*, II, p. 497. Professor Berard, *Recherches sur la chronologie de l'époque mycenienne*, has recently maintained that the Trojan War took place some time between 1410 and 1375 B.C., but see Wace in *Gnomon*, 1955, pp. 523-525. Broneer, "Athens in the

Heracles was the contemporary of Eurystheus, whose reign is thus placed by tradition toward the end of the fourteenth and the beginning of the thirteenth century B.C. Eurystheus of course was the grandson of Perseus. Again, we hear that in the reign of Theseus, Aegeus' son and successor, the fated expedition of the "Seven Against Thebes" took place. The *Marmor Parium* gives 1251/0 as the date of that event. According to tradition, that expedition was one generation before the Trojan War, since the sons of the leaders killed in front of the walls of Thebes took part in the expedition against Troy. Thus the Theban War must have occurred in the days of Atreus and Thyestes, the successors of Eurystheus and predecessors of Agamemnon. The rule of the latter must be placed around 1200 B.C., since 1183 B.C. is the traditional date for the fall of Troy. Hence, Atreus' rule must be placed between 1250 and 1220 B.C., for Thyestes succeeded him to the throne of Mycenae.

Of course we cannot admit the dates preserved in the *Marmor Parium* as the true and exact dates of events which took place in the Heroic Age of Greece, but they certainly should be considered at least as indications which may substantiate conclusions reached through traditional or other channels. The traditional evidence would thus place Perseus, the builder of the Cyclopean walls of Mycenae, in the fourteenth century, since after him and to the days of Agamemnon (*c.* 1200 B.C.) at least five kings ruled over Mycenae and since his grandson Eurystheus was the king in the first half of the thirteenth century. A date about the middle of the fourteenth century B.C. will be appropriate for the beginning of Perseus' rule, a date which was also suggested for the construction of the main part of the Cyclopean walls of Mycenae.

There is another indication, arising from tradition, that Perseus may have lived long after the first tholos tombs were constructed in the Argolid. According to the legend of his birth, Acrisios, his grandfather, informed by the oracle that his grandson was destined to kill him, in an effort to avert this evil fate, "built a bronze chamber underground in the courtyard of his house, and there he put his daughter

Late Bronze Age," *Antiquity*, 30 (1956), pp. 9-18, suggests a revision of the date of the war. However, the destruction of some Mycenaean palaces may be attributed to the Herakleidai, who, according to Thucydides I, 9, 2, were a power to be feared in the days of Eurystheus. On the other hand, the archaeological evidence is not so complete as to permit at present a change of Eratosthenes' traditional date. We shall maintain therefore the traditional date as preserved by Eratosthenes.

Danaë and her nurse and kept her there so that she might not bear a son."[45] Long ago, Helbig suggested that in Danaë's underground structure we have a structure reminiscent of a tholos tomb, of a building like the Treasury of Atreus, whose walls were decorated with bronze rosettes and friezes.[46] This tradition seems to indicate that structures similar to the tholos tombs were being constructed long before the birth of Perseus.

The evidence obtained by excavation not only verified the tradition and transformed its vague myths into an impressive reality, but also extended our knowledge of the life history of Mycenae from the fourteenth century B.C. to the first half of the third millennium B.C. The contribution of the excavations to our knowledge of the life and activities of Mycenae of the historic era is also considerable.

The destruction of Mycenae's power, c. 1100 B.C., is not recorded in the writings of any ancient author, nor do we find any mention of her until the days of the Persian wars. But the story of her activities can be illustrated by the remains uncovered. The lack of remains makes it impossible for us to know what followed her destruction and how the transition from the Bronze to the Iron Age was accomplished. In the centuries that are usually included in the Geometric period, i.e., from 1000 to 700 B.C., the Citadel was again inhabited. Remains of houses were found even in the Palace area, and graves of the period have been disclosed in various parts of the Lower City. The remains indicate that a small and unimportant settlement was established at the site apparently by the descendants of those who survived the destruction of 1100 B.C. They seem to have been more prosperous in the Archaic period, 700-500 B.C., or prosperous enough to construct a temple, ornamented with sculptured metopes, on top of the Citadel. The era of the Persian wars followed, and soon after that, the destruction of Mycenae by the people of Argos c. 486 B.C. That calamity, according to Diodoros and Strabo, brought to an end Mycenae's life history.

The excavations, however, prove otherwise. They prove that in the third century B.C. the people of Argos established on the hill of Mycenae a koma or fortified village. It was then that the Cyclopean walls of its enceinte were rehabilitated. Within the Citadel a good

---

[45] Apollodoros, II, 4, 1. Cf. Sophocles, Antigone, 944ff., Pausanias, II, 23, 7, and Horace, Odes, III, 16, 1.

[46] Das homerische Epos aus den Denkmälern erläutert, 2nd ed., p. 440.

number of houses were built and the temple on top of the hill was rebuilt on a larger scale. Part of the ridge to the west of the Citadel was enclosed by walls and transformed into a Lower City. Of the public buildings in the Lower City, the remains of the Perseia fountain, not far from the Lion Gate and alongside the modern road which leads to it, were cleared by Professor Wace in 1952[47] and the remains of a small theater were revealed, built obliquely across the dromos of the Tomb of Clytemnestra, a tholos tomb which was completely buried and invisible in classical times. Fragments of two inscriptions found give us some idea of the government of the village and the information that the Spartan king Nabis carried off to captivity in Sparta the ephebes of Mycenae.[48] In Plutarch we find that in 235 B.C. the Argive tyrant Aristippos, after an unsuccessful attack on Cleonae, was killed at Mycenae.[49]

How long the village continued to be inhabited is not certain. But a fragment of a grave stele and the discovery of a few graves seem to indicate that the site was still inhabited in Roman Imperial times, though sparsely. On his visit in the middle of the second century A.D., Pausanias must have found a small and dwindling hamlet, with the houses of even the Hellenistic village in ruins; and so he wrote: "In the ruins of Mycenae there is a fountain called Perseia and underground buildings of Atreus and his sons where their treasuries were." These underground buildings are located in the area of the Lower City of the Hellenistic village and, as we have seen, the remains of the Perseia fountain were uncovered in that same Lower City and belong to the Hellenistic era. Originally, the fountain must have been surrounded by Hellenistic houses, and the ruins of these were apparently seen by Pausanias. The recent discovery, in the Lower City and above the ruins of the "Cyclopean Terrace Building" of fragments of lamps "which cannot be dated earlier than about the third or fourth century A.D." seems to indicate that Mycenae was still inhabited in those centuries.[50] After the third century of our era, Mycenae faded away into oblivion and only the tales of her glory were vaguely remembered by the literate few. The striking discoveries of Schliemann and Tsountas brought her back to life. Their work, as well as

---

[47] Wace, Holland, and Hood, *BSA*, 48 (1953), pp. 19, 27.

[48] The inscriptions date from 195/194 B.C. and are decrees honoring Protinos and Panormos, who took care of the Mycenaean youths in Sparta. See Boethius, C. A., in *BSA*, 25 (1921-1923), pp. 408ff. and 422ff.

[49] *Aratus*, 29.   [50] Wace, *BSA*, 48 (1953), p. 17.

that of Professor Wace and many another scholar, has made possible
the tracing of her history and her culture and has proved that her
Golden Age belongs to the prehistoric era and especially to the Late
Helladic period. To the study of the remains of that period, we shall
devote our efforts in the following pages.

II

MYCENAE AND HER WALLS

To THOSE OF US who are fortunate enough to have the privilege of exploring her soil, Mycenae's visitors are a constant cause of wonder. People by the hundreds, people of varied tongues and backgrounds from all over the world, wind their way each year to the top of her Acropolis, braving the burning sun's rays in the summer and the icy blasts of the north wind in the winter, with a determination which is amazing. For some, the visit is a pilgrimage filled with the memories of the Trojan War and of the feud of Atreus and Thyestes which resulted in the bloody deeds of Aegisthos and Clytemnestra. For others, it is a quest after the unusual and the mythical. For others still, it is a trip which was recommended to them. No matter by what motive they were prompted to undertake the trip, seldom do the visitors depart disappointed. From Mycenae's fallen walls, her burned-out Palace, and her vaulted tombs, the memories of the past arise to haunt and enfold the visitor. The quietude of the rugged and barren mountains, the wild impressiveness of the gorges leading to the multicolored Argive plain, the evidence of past power and splendor met at every step, fill the human soul with awe and bring to the lips of the initiated the prophetic words of Priam spoken for a rival city:[1]

ἔσσεται ἦμαρ, ὅτ ἄν ποτ᾽ ὀλώλῃ Ἴλιος ἱρὴ
καὶ Πρίαμος καὶ λαὸς ἐϋμμελίω Πριάμοιο

As in her life, so in her fall Mycenae was fortunate. For, as Tsountas remarked long ago, it was the good fortune of the capital of Agamemnon to be destroyed while it still enjoyed prosperity and power and to remain undisturbed for generations until the spade of the excavators—Schliemann's, Tsountas', and Wace's—revived her glories.[2] By a strange twist of fate, the catastrophe which brought to an end her great cultural mission and her role as the leader of the Hellenic world in the dawn of history has preserved for us an almost perfect example of a Mycenaean fortified city.

[1] *Iliad*, IV, 164-165: "The day shall come when sacred Ilios shall be laid low, and Priam and the people of Priam with good spear and ash" (transl. A. T. Murray).
[2] *Mycenaean Age*, pp. 25-43.

Mycenae's location in southern Greece and in the northeastern section of the Peloponnesos, some eighty-five miles from Athens, was strategic and fortunate. Mycenae was a city hidden in the folds of mountains and hills which close the northeastern corner of the Argive plain (Fig. 1). So situated, ἐν μυχῷ Ἄργεος ἱπποβότοιο,[3] the city dominated the approaches to that plain from the north and could control the deep, sheltered bay of Nauplia, some nine miles to the south of its Citadel. That Citadel stands in front of the gentle saddle connecting Prophet Elias and Zara, two huge masses of stone that rise in sharp, sloping lines to a height of 805 meters (2,645 feet) and 660 meters (2,170 feet) respectively (Fig. 2). A deep gorge with precipitous sides and a narrow white-pebbled torrent at the bottom, known as the Chaos or Chavos to the natives, separates the Citadel from Zara like an immense moat, offering little encouragement for scaling it from that side. A smaller ravine, known as Kokoretsa, with gentle sloping sides, now planted with olive trees, separates the north side of the Citadel from Prophet Elias. To the east and toward the saddle, the approach is easy, while to the west and toward the Argive plain the ground slopes comfortably to a depression traversed by a long and low ridge on top of which perhaps in prehistoric days was located the main street of the Lower City of Mycenae (Fig. 3).

The Citadel, a tableland, roughly triangular in shape, now known as the *kastro* or castle, rises to a top strongly defined by ancient terracing, 280 meters (912 feet) above sea level. Its slopes are surrounded by fortification walls, the famous Cyclopean walls. In spite of its height and its walls, the site seems lost in the folds of mountains, hills, and ravines, and only the experienced eye can detect it from the main highway which connects Argos with Corinth and which emerges into the Argive plain from the picturesque pass of Tretos. Until recently, even when the visitor approached the site on the narrow road which passes through the modern village of Mycenae, the Citadel was not easily defined and its fortification walls seemed lost beneath the mounds of earth poured along its long western side by the early excavators of the site.[4]

The greater part of the fortification walls of Mycenae is built in

---

[3] *Odyssey*, 3, 263: "in the nook of horse-pasturing Argos."

[4] This earth is now being removed by the Greek Service for the Restoration and Preservation of Ancient Monuments and by Professor Wace. The Cyclopean walls of Mycenae will once more become the conspicuous landmark they were in antiquity and will give the site the impressiveness which characterized it in the past.

the well-known Cyclopean fashion. The walls consist, in other words, of large limestone blocks, roughly dressed with the hammer or completely unwrought, of different sizes piled on top of one another with their interstices filled with clay and small stone (Fig. 4). Pausanias, in writing of the walls of Tiryns, offers an interesting description of this type of construction: "Nothing is left of the ruins of Tiryns except the wall, which is the work of the Cyclopes, and is made of unwrought stones, each stone so large that a pair of mules could not even stir the smallest of them. In ancient times small stones have been filled in so as to bind together the large stones."[5] These large stones, however, form but the inner and outer faces of the wall; the space between them, the width of the wall, is filled in with smaller stones and earth.

A smaller part of the circuit is built in ashlar masonry. The conglomerate used is shaped by means of hammer and saw in rectangular blocks which are placed in horizontal, more or less even, courses without regard to the proper lining of joints (Figs. 5 and 6). Blocks used are as a rule smaller than those in the Cyclopean construction, and the interstices were apparently filled with clay. This ashlar construction, however, formed but a facing, at the back of which the wall was constructed in the Cyclopean fashion. The ashlar system was used for the construction of the main gate of Mycenae, the Lion Gate, and its bastion; for the Postern Gate; and for the erection of a rectangular tower at the southeastern edge of the *enceinte* and below the terrace of the "House of Columns." There is a difference of opinion as to the date of the two types of construction. Some believe that the ashlar construction is later than the Cyclopean, while Tsountas and Professor Wace believe that they could be contemporary. Pointing out that ashlar was used in the construction of the dromos and the façade of the Treasury of Atreus, they conclude that it was used because it gave the feeling of greater strength to the wall, offered no foothold to an escalading foe, and lent an impressive appearance to the gates. The need of additional strength will also explain the use of ashlar in the construction of the tower which blocked the way to the Palace from the east, formed a lookout post of great value, and dominated the precipitous Chavos. We believe that the two forms of Mycenaean construction could have been contemporary regardless of the problem

[5] Pausanias, II, 25, 8, transl. Frazer. For the walls in general, see Wace, *Mycenae*, pp. 49-54.

connected with the date of the different parts of the fortification walls.

A third system of wall construction is apparent today. Small and well-cut stones of polygonal shapes were used and were fitted in position to form a wall of solidity and good appearance. In the days of Schliemann this wall caused a good deal of speculation, but now we know that the polygonal construction belongs to the Hellenistic period and that it was employed to fill the gaps in the Cyclopean walls caused by the destruction of 486 B.C. The most conspicuous piece of polygonal construction is to be seen at the Lion Gate. It was used to round off the northwest corner of its bastion (Fig. 5). Part of the Cyclopean wall forming the bulge to the south of the Lion Gate was also repaired in the polygonal style as well as the so-called "polygonal tower" farther to the south. The latter is built mainly of conglomerate blocks; it is actually a wall erected to bridge a gap in the Cyclopean wall.

The circuit wall of Mycenae has a total length of some 900 meters; it encloses an area roughly triangular in shape, of some 30,000 square meters (Fig. 7). The wall is preserved almost in its entire length; only a small part in the bulge which goes around the Grave Circle, the part faced by the "polygonal tower," and a section on its south side, apparently swept down into the precipitous gorge by landslides, are missing. The wall averages 6 meters in thickness, although in places it reaches a maximum of 8 to 10 meters. The greatest thickness is to be found along its northern line and in the eastern half of the south side. It was once believed that the increased thickness concealed galleries like the ones found at Tiryns, but the complete investigation of the wall has proved that such galleries do not exist at Mycenae; the greater width of the wall should be attributed to an effort to strengthen lines which were considered vulnerable. A small room, covered by a saddle roof, halfway between the Lion and the Postern Gates, was built alongside the wall and not in it; consequently this room should not be considered a gallery. The original height of the wall cannot be determined, nor is it possible to know whether or not mud-brick palisades or other protective parapets were erected over the stone part. Usually the height of the Hellenistic "polygonal tower," 18 meters above the rocky ground upon which it stands, is taken as an indication of the original height of the circuit wall, but we cannot be certain even as to that. As is usual in Mycenaean times, the circuit wall follows the contour of the ground, is founded upon rock wherever possible, and often the rock formation is used in its construction. A very good example of this is to be seen on the eastern stretch of the wall to the left as we approach the Lion Gate, but other examples, especially on the north side, are also visible.

The *enceinte* was entered by two gates, a main and a postern. The former is the famous Lion Gate (Fig. 6). Here terminated the main road of the Lower City, transformed at its extreme end into a gradually ascending ramp, retained by a wall, remains of which are to be seen below the modern ramp to the Lion Gate. That gate was defended by a long stretch of ashlar wall on the east side and by a rectangular bastion 14.80 meters in length and 7.23 meters in width (Figs. 6 and 7-A). Between them was formed a long and rather narrow court, some 15 meters in length and 7 meters in width, at the road level, which served to reduce the number of an attacking army that could possibly maneuver in front of the gate. While the invading army's right or unprotected side was exposed to the defenders of the bastion, its entire force was exposed to the missiles—perhaps huge rocks—which could be hurled from the top of the east line of the wall.

The Lion Gate itself is of massive and imposing construction. Four huge monoliths of conglomerate, Schliemann's *breccia*, known to the inhabitants of the district as "almond stone," hammer-dressed in the main, formed the two door jambs, the threshold, and the lintel.[6] The gate is almost as wide as high, and measures 3.10 meters high and 2.95 meters wide at the threshold. It narrows somewhat upward, measuring below the lintel 2.78 meters (Fig. 8). The opening was closed by a double door, as is proved by the pivot holes which are to be seen at each end of the threshold and the lintel.[7] The doors were mortised to a vertical beam acting as a pivot around which they revolved; the ends of this beam projected above and below and were fitted into the pivot holes cut in the threshold and lintel. Sockets, which served to receive a sliding bar or cross beam securing the doors when closed—an arrangement well known from the door of Tiryns— can be seen on the inner face of the sideposts; there were also oblong sockets into which the door handles would sink when the doors were

[6] The threshold measures 4.65 m. in length, 2.31 m. in width, and 0.88 m. in thickness at its western end. The lintel measures 4.50 m. in length, 1.98 m. in width, and 0.80 m. maximum height at its center. The door jambs measure 3.10 m. in height, 1.94 m. in width, and 0.54 m. in thickness at the inner end, while at the façade they measure 0.66 m.

[7] The pivot holes in the threshold have been altered; those in the lintel measure 0.15 to 0.16 m. in diameter.

kept wide open. The threshold has preserved equally eloquent traces of its life and use (Fig. 10). Along either end there is a rather broad and shallow depression, made by chariot or cart wheels; along its east end we have a deeper groove, some 26 centimeters wide, serving as a drain, while its surface was scored to provide a firm footing for man and animal alike. The rectangular socket in its center is taken to be of a later date since it does not line with the door arrangement,[8] but the round hole in its middle seems to belong to it and it could have served for a pole backing the door when it was securely closed.

The wall above the gate and its lintel is constructed so as to form an empty triangle, a feature characteristic of Mycenaean construction and known as the "relieving triangle." This empty area is blocked by a slab of stone bearing the famous relief from which the gate receives its name: the lion relief. The slab measures 3.90 meters at its broadest point a little above its base line, is 3.30 meters in height, and about 0.70 meters in thickness, and is of native hard limestone. Its base line is worked in a curve to fit the top of the lintel which bulges upwards. Since there is a tight fitting at the corners, the weight of the slab in the main is born by its extremities. In 1950 Dr. John Papademetriou identified and restored to their original position the two blocks at the right side of the triangle, almost completing it, and so the composition can now be seen in its original frame, gaining in clarity and vigor (Fig. 9).

The relief can be considered one of the earliest monumental pieces of sculpture of the Greek prehistoric world;[9] in spite of its exposure for so many centuries it is excellently preserved (Fig. 9). Its subject is well known. Two lions stand on either side of a column, tapering downward, bearing a symbolic entablature, and based firmly on top of two altars placed side by side and covered by plinths. The lions rest their front paws on these plinths and turn their heads toward the spectator approaching the gate; the heads were apparently made of different material and are now missing. Some believe that they were made of bronze and, as parallels, point to the "golden and silver dogs, which Hephaestos had fashioned with cunning skill to guard the

---

[8] However, one could suggest that in the rectangular cutting was secured a short post or peg against which rested the wooden doors. In that case, the cutting too could be conceived as contemporary to the gate.

[9] Of course the reliefs on the stelai from the shaft graves are much older, but their workmanship is so crude that one wonders whether it entitles them to the distinction of monumental sculpture.

palace of greathearted Alcinoos."[10] The dowel holes, however, used to secure the heads to their background, are so large and deep that they indicate, not bronze, but a heavier material, probably steatite.

The modeling of the relief is vigorous, and both the lions and the architectural details are rendered with clarity and precision. Of course, a good many anatomical details in the rendering of the lions have been omitted, but the effect is one of strength and of purpose well fitting the architectural character of the relief. The composition in general—in the symmetrical and heraldic arrangements of its units, in its broad base gradually working upward to a gathering point—is a happy one and appropriate to its position over the lintel of a doorway; it increases the architectural quality of the gate and adds to the feeling of stability and strength.

The design has a long line of predecessors. Heraldic designs make their appearance in the transitional period between Middle Minoan III and Late Minoan I A in Crete and are not uncommon in that island and in the Peloponnesos.[11] Scholars agree that the Lion Gate relief follows the traditional design, but they disagree as to its significance, if indeed it possesses any.

Tsountas long ago pointed out that the composition could be either symbolic or decorative, and inclined toward the latter.[12] Sir Arthur Evans believed in its religious and symbolic significance, and saw in the column the aniconic form of a deity and in the presence of the relief over the gate a symbol which placed the Citadel under the protection of the Great Mother Goddess who thus became the establisher of Mycenae.[13] Professor Wace, following Sir Arthur Evans, accepted the column as a sacred pillar, an aniconic form of a deity, a symbol of protection. According to his interpretation, the position of the relief showed that the gate and the walls of Mycenae were placed "under the protection of the divinity indicated by the pillar, perhaps the Great Mother Goddess, who is often associated with lions." However, he did not exclude the possibility of a heraldic

[10] *Odyssey*, 7, 91-93.

[11] Sir Arthur Evans, *JHS*, 21 (1901), pp. 153-169. Wace, *BSA*, 24 (1919-1921), p. 206. Nilsson, M. P., *The Minoan-Mycenaean Religion and Its Survival in Greek Religion*, 2nd ed., pp. 252ff. Long before Sir Arthur's suggestions, scholars saw in the columns a divine "symbol," but Adler, in *Archaeol. Zeitung*, 1865, p. 6, proved that this view was untenable. For the tools and methods employed in the carving of the relief, cf. Wace, *Mycenae*, p. 52, and Casson, S., *The Technique of Early Greek Sculpture*, pp. 23-41.

[12] *Mycenaean Age*, p. 31. [13] Sir Arthur Evans, *JHS*, 21 (1901), pp. 15ff.

interpretation of the composition, and added: "The lion was probably the badge of Mycenae and thus this relief may have a kind of heraldic as well as religious significance."[14]

I believe that the composition can have only a heraldic significance. The column in the center cannot be conceived of as the aniconic representation of a goddess because of its entablature which will indicate that it had a structural function.[15] Columns which may be accepted as the aniconic representation of a divinity are not unknown to the Minoan-Mycenaean world, but they are free-standing and bear no entablature.[16] On the other hand, columns with entablature standing in lieu of buildings are rather common. In rejecting Sir Arthur Evans' interpretation, Professor Nilsson has pointed out that signs to which religious significance could be imparted, such as the double axe, perhaps were used "to put the construction under divine protection and impart to it divine strength in addition to its material strength."[17] Such symbols, however, are not to be seen in our composition, and perhaps the Mycenaeans felt that the massiveness of their construction was sufficient to withstand enemy assaults. If it was customary to add to the natural strength of fortifications divine protection by means of a few easily provided symbols, then surely we ought to find such symbols in the contemporary circuit walls of Tiryns and Athens. But nowhere else have such symbols been detected and nowhere else do they exist.[18]

For the same reason we cannot accept Professor Nilsson's suggestion that the column with its entablature represented the shrine of Mycenae guarded by lions.[19] If a shrine were to be represented, then

[14] Wace, *BSA*, 25 (1921-1923), p. 16 and *Mycenae*, p. 53.

[15] Nilsson, M., *op.cit.*, p. 245.

[16] Cf. Mylonas, G. E., "Lykaian Altar of Zeus," *Classical Studies in Honor of William A. Oldfather*, pp. 124-127.

[17] Nilsson, *op.cit.*, p. 247.

[18] Professor Wace has pointed out that "Homer implies that the wall of the Greek camp at Troy was successfully breached by the Trojans because it was built without divine protection, *Iliad*, XII, 6-8." However, the poet specifically states that "for no long time did it abide unbroken," not because it was not placed under divine protection, but because "it was built against the will of the immortal gods." If a symbol or a relief could have added divine security to the strength of the wall, surely wise Nestor would have advised its addition. Poseidon's concern over the building of the wall was not over the failure of the Greeks to place it under the protection of the gods, but over his fear that the fame of that wall would "reach as far as the dawn spreadeth, and men will forget the wall that I and Phoebus Apollo built with toil for the warrior Laomedon," *Iliad*, VII, 451-453.

[19] Nilsson, *op.cit.*, p. 255, n. 74.

we should expect to find the emblems of the shrine on the column. In the well-known gold-leaf representations of shrines from the shaft graves of Mycenae, birds are represented perched on them or flying over them, and sacred horns are placed at the foot of their columns and on top of their entablatures. The amazing clay seal impression from the Rhyton Well of Mycenae, dating from Late Helladic III times, offers another striking example of the use of symbols, sacred horns, and a bird, to identify a shrine.[20] And if it was technically possible and compositionally essential for the gem cutter to include in the design on a small seal, measuring about 0.03 x 0.024 meters, the concomitant symbols of a shrine, certainly it would have been possible and essential to include these symbols in a monumental piece of sculpture to be set in a conspicuous place. The absence of these symbols from the lion relief will, I believe, exclude the possibility that a shrine is represented on it.

We should like to offer another interpretation. It seems to us that the column with its entablature could stand only for the Royal Palace, the Royal House of Mycenae. In close connection with a royal house stands, of course, the dynasty, the ruling family which abides in it. The column therefore could very well symbolize the palace and the dynasty, a palace and a dynasty guarded by lions, the guardians and companions of the Great Goddess herself. We may now note how the column is based on the altars and how it seems to grow from them, like a tree growing from the earth. This certainly indicates the close association of the royal house, of the dynasty, with religion and divinity, a characteristic feature of Minoan-Mycenaean beliefs and practices,[21] and implies that the dynasty it symbolizes stands upon, is founded upon, religion and upon the conception that its right to rule is based on and grows out of the divine will.

We believe that in the relief we have the artistic counterpart of the Homeric belief in the divine right of the kings, another close parallel between Homeric beliefs and Mycenaean practices. The relief over the main gate can be conceived of as the emblem, the coat of arms, of the διογενεῖς βασιλῆες, kings born of Zeus, the σκηπτοῦχοι, the scepter

---

[20] For the finds from the shaft graves, see Karo, G., *Die Schachtgräber von Mykenai*, pls. 18, 27, No. 26. For the impression from the Rhyton well, see Wace, *Mycenae*, fig. 110c.

[21] The fact that a section of the palace was used as a shrine will indicate the close association. Cf. *Odyssey*, 7, 81 and *Iliad*, 11, 547-549.

bearers, of Mycenae whose "honor," as Homer states, "is from Zeus, and "whom Zeus, God of Counsel, loveth."[22]

Professors Persson and Wace have suggested that the lions might be the badge of Mycenae.[23] Of course there is no way of proving this, but their use on the monumental relief seems to substantiate that suggestion. In Homeric poetry the comparison of a valiant warrior to a lion is not limited to Agamemnon alone, but is used for other leaders of the Greeks and Trojans. However, in one instance it seems as if the lion was associated only with the leaders of the Argive plain. When, in the tenth book of the *Iliad*, Agamemnon went out to rouse the leaders of the Greeks, he placed over his shoulders "the skin of a lion, fiery and great, a skin that reached his feet" (x, 23-4). Menelaos covered his broad shoulders with a leopard's skin (x, 29), while Nestor used a "purple cloak of double fold and wide, whereon the down was thick" (x, 133-134). Odysseus "cast about his shoulders a shield richly dight" (x, 149), but Diomedes, the leader of Argos, again used "the skin of a lion, fiery and great, that reached his feet" (x, 177). One can only wonder whether any special tradition connecting the lion with the rulers of Mycenae and their dependent princes is reflected in the action of Agamemnon and Diomedes. Of course, the lion seems to be the attendant of the Great Goddess; as such it could be borrowed by the great kings of Mycenae, the favorites of the gods, and used as the emblem of their site. I should like to think that the lions were the particular emblem of the Pelopids who came to Greece from Asia Minor, a country where the use of lions as emblems has a long history[24] and that the composition over the gate was the coat of arms of Atreus and his descendants. However that may be, it is certain that the relief was in position and that the lions had started their vigil over the site and its royal family when Agamemnon and his followers passed through the gate to start on their long and perilous expedition against Troy.

The Postern Gate is located in the north line of the circuit wall, some 250 meters east of the Lion Gate (Fig. 7-B). It is placed in a

[22] *Iliad*, II, 197; cf. II, 205-206, IX, 98-99. For the revealing story of Agamemnon's scepter, see *Iliad*, II, 100ff.

[23] Only recently, long after I had reached my conclusions, I found out that Axel Persson had suggested the lion as the badge of Mycenae; cf. *Dragma Martino P. Nilsson Dedicatum*, pp. 379ff.

[24] Cf. the old Phrygian theory of W. H. Ramsay as published in *JHS*, 3 (1882ff.) and listed by Frazer in his commentary on Pausanias, Vol. II, p. 103. *Mycenaean Age*, pp. 245ff.

set-back of the north wall, the east end of which is transformed into a bastion guarding the gate and so placed as to command the un-protected right side of anyone approaching from the north. Again, a small court is formed in front of the gate, but this time it is rather narrow, measuring only 2.30 meters in width and 7.80 meters in length, the length of the bastion. The gate is much smaller than the Lion Gate, but is constructed of conglomerate blocks in the same fashion, in ashlar style, and presents the same characteristics as the main entrance to the Citadel. Four large blocks are again used for the door posts, the lintel, and the threshold and frame an opening 2.29 meters high and 1.38 meters wide at the threshold. The opening narrows upward slightly, measuring 1.33 meters in width below the lintel. Two pivot holes in the lintel indicate that the gate was closed by a double door; when shut, this door was secured fast by a wooden beam that slid into well-cut sockets on the side of the door posts in a manner similar to that known from the Lion Gate and the inner gate of Tiryns.[25] Instead of a relieving triangle over the lintel, we have two rectangular slabs back to back, with an empty space between them of 0.20 to 0.26 meters. These carried the wall construction across and were so fitted as to carry the pressure to the sides.

The Postern Gate could be called the "water gate" of the Citadel because it is located near the northeastern corner of the original circuit wall and consequently near the springs on which the water supply of the Citadel depended. Here again, it is interesting to note the parallel between the Mycenaean remains and the Homeric tradition. At Mycenae, as was the case in Troy, the springs were beyond the walls but conveniently located so that they could be used even during a siege. Through the Postern Gate the road, a lane some 4 meters in width at its beginning and later reduced to 2.80 meters, brought one to the northwestern corner of the terrace on which stood the Palace. From the wider point of the lane another path branched off toward the east and the direction of the underground reservoir. Immediately within the gate and on the left-hand side as one enters is a small room. It has a triangular plan and measures 1.80 meters in maximum width by its entrance, 2 meters in maximum length, and 1.50 meters in height. Its dimensions would indicate that a watch dog rather than a guard was stationed there.

[25] The door jambs are monoliths measuring approximately 2.29 m. in height, 1.38 m. in width, and 0.48 m. in thickness, while the lintel, a single block, measures 2.80 m. in length, 1.39 m. in width, and 0.65 m. in maximum thickness.

The north wall of the *enceinte* originally terminated some 70 meters to the east of the gate (Fig. 7-C). But at a later period, perhaps the closing century of the Mycenaean era, it was extended to include a small area which now forms the eastern end of the Citadel. In that extension we find a third small opening known as the "Sally Port" and located at the extreme southeastern end of the circuit (Figs. 7-G and 11). It is actually a small and narrow passage through the Cyclopean wall, 7.10 meters in length (equalling the width of the wall), 1.05-1.18 meters in width, and 2.50 meters in height. It is roofed over by a corbel vault of the inverted *V* type, similar to those used in the galleries of Tiryns. Its dimensions and location seem to indicate that it served for sorties of the garrison aimed at an enemy who was attacking the Postern Gate. It does not seem to have been closed by a door, and of course it could be entered by an enemy whose scouts could have easily detected it. However, since it was so small and because it was placed in a rocky terrain, it could be easily defended by a small force. Besides, even if the passage was invaded, the attacking enemy after crossing it, would find itself in an enclosed area, measuring approximately 12 by 32 meters, and consequently in extreme danger.

On the northeastern corner of the enclosed area a Hellenistic cistern is located (Fig. 7-F), in its north wall a drain E, and in the northwestern corner, again in the north wall, we have the opening to an underground reservoir (Fig. 7-D). This is the most striking construction in the Citadel, a truly Cyclopean undertaking. It can be distinguished in three parts or sections.[26] Part one is composed of a descending stepped passage cut obliquely through the north wall (Fig. 12). Sixteen of the original steps are still preserved in the passage which takes us, by means of a well-constructed doorway, outside the wall and onto a small rectangular platform. Today the platform is open to the sky, but it was roofed over originally and so was safe from enemy attack. It was further defended by the north wall under whose shadow it was placed. On the southwest side of the platform we have the door opening of the second section: an underground stepped passage, with twenty preserved steps, leading westward and terminating in a landing some 2.80 meters below the level of the first. Three steps on the north side of the landing take us to the third

[26] For plans and a full description, see Karo, G., "Die Perseia von Mykenai," *AJA*, 38 (1934), pp. 123-127, pls. XII-XIII.

section of the passage, which now turns at right angles to the platforms and proceeds steeply toward the northeast. Some fifty-four steps below, and about 12 meters deeper, the passage terminates at a well-like reservoir about 1.60 by 0.70 meters and some 5 meters deep. The reservoir was kept filled with water through a large opening in its saddle roof,[27] at which ended a water conduit of terracotta pipes. The steps and the walls of the third section are covered with a thick coat of watertight plaster, and evidently part of the stepped passage acted as a reservoir (Fig. 13). The passages are roofed over either by the inverted V corbel vault, characteristic of late Mycenaean construction, or by its variation, the saddle roof, or by huge slabs placed horizontally across its walls. The first section is roofed over by the corbel vault and is about 4 meters high and 1.50 to 2 meters wide (Fig. 12). The platform at the foot of this section was apparently roofed by horizontal slabs and measures 1.60 by 2.50 meters. The roof of the second section is composed of horizontal slabs, while the third section presents both the corbel vault and the saddle type of roofing (Fig. 13). The roof immediately over the reservoir is of the saddle type, and at that point the passage is some 4 meters high, though only 2 meters at its beginning. Its width averages 1.60 meters, while that of the second section ranges from 1.40 to 1.60 meters. The steps average 0.15 meters in height and are made mostly of limestone slabs. The construction is truly Cyclopean and awe-inspiring, and the sight of anxious visitors descending into the dark depths of the earth holding lighted candles is unforgettable. The reservoir reminds one of that found by Oscar Broneer in the north slope of the Acropolis of Athens,[28] but unlike the Athenian example the underground reservoir of Mycenae is of monumental construction. It is perfectly preserved and, had Pausanias seen it, he would have declared it to be another wonder of the ancient world.

Tsountas' conclusions regarding the late date of the eastern extension and its cistern are universally accepted.[29] But the date of the rest of the peribolos of Mycenae is still to be established. The evidence

[27] In the saddle roof, the side walls again incline inwardly in the manner usual in the inverted V corbel vault, but they do not meet at the top. Instead, shortly before their meeting point the distance between them is covered by horizontal slabs. One could call the saddle roof a truncated inverted V corbel. It is a mistake to call such a construction a horizontal roof.

[28] Broneer, O., "A Mycenaean Fountain on the Athenian Acropolis," *Hesperia*, 8 (1939), pp. 317-429.

[29] "Zur einigen mykenischen Streitfragen," *Jahrbuch*, 1895, pp. 143ff.

available to date is very limited and it applies mostly to the Postern Gate, the Lion Gate, and the Cyclopean wall which swings to the south of that gate, forming the west side of the *enceinte*. The evidence was obtained by Professor Wace from trenches dug in front of the Lion Gate, under the threshold of the Postern Gate, and in two points between these gates; in the main it consists of a limited number of sherds.[30] It led the excavator to conclude that the Cyclopean walls, with the exception of those enclosing the northeastern end of the *enceinte*, and the Lion Gate belong to the same period and were constructed at the same time. That time was at first placed early in the fourteenth century.[31] A reexamination of the evidence led to the conclusion that the Cyclopean wall and the Lion Gate were built late in Late Helladic III A, about 1350-1330 B.C.[32] However, among the sherds found around the Lion Gate are included typical examples of Late Helladic III B ware. And the same is true in the case of sherds found in the retaining wall of Grave Circle A.[33] In addition, at least in one point among the broken stones which form the bedding on which the Cyclopean wall to the west of Grave Circle A was founded, three animal and eight human female terracotta figurines were discovered. Unfortunately, the types of these figurines are not stated, but they are identified merely as "of the usual L.H.III types."[34] Such figurines are considered characteristic products of the Late Helladic III B period.[35] Consequently the part of the Cyclopean wall built over the bedding containing the figurines must be somewhat later than the figurines, i.e., it must date from the advanced years of Late Helladic III B.

The date of the Late Helladic III B has now to be considered. Professor Blegen, who was the first to distinguish Late Helladic III B ware as an "intermediate phase" between the earlier and later products

[30] More pottery was found in 1955 during the reconstruction of the tower of the Lion Gate and the wall adjacent to it, but that pottery has as yet to be studied.

[31] *BSA*, 25 (1921-1923), p. 13.

[32] Wace, *Mycenae*, pp. 133-134.

[33] *BSA*, 25 (1921-1923), p. 22, fig. 6; p. 25, fig. 7 and pl. v. Cf. Mackeprang, M. B., "Late Mycenaean Vases," *AJA*, 42 (1938), pp. 537-559 and especially pp. 555-559.

[34] *BSA*, 25 (1921-1923), p. 106.

[35] Note that figurines were found in the lowest strata between the west wing of the Lion Gate and the east wall of the granary with typical and rather late Late Helladic III B sherds: *BSA*, 25 (1921-1923), pp. 23-27 and figs. 6 and 7. For the date, see Furumark, A., *The Chronology of Mycenaean Pottery*, pp. 86-89. Also Persson, *The Royal Tombs of Dendra*, p. 83, n. 1.

of the potter's art in Late Helladic III times,[36] did not fix the limits. The thirteenth in general was assumed to be the century contained by the Late Helladic III B period.[37] Professor Furumark, after comparison of its pottery with that from Syria and Egypt, concluded that the period covered the years from c. 1300 to 1230 B.C.[38] On the other hand, Professor Wace has recently suggested that the Late Helladic III B period must include the years from c. 1340 to c. 1210 B.C.[39] We may not agree with Furumark's minute subdivisions of the Late Helladic ware, based in the main on stylistic analysis and personal impression, but, until otherwise proved by stratified finds, his chronological limit for the beginning of the Late Helladic III B seems to be correct.[40] On the other hand, the lower limit of the period has to be placed around 1200 B.C. since the characteristic vases of its closing years present similarities to the Philistine ware which is now placed after 1200 B.C. The construction of the Lion Gate and the Cyclopean wall to the south and west, as far as our evidence goes to date, occurred in Late Helladic III B times, rather advanced times at that; we should be inclined therefore to date it between 1300 and 1200 B.C., and late rather than early within these limits, to c. 1250 B.C.[41]

The date suggested, c. 1250 B.C., will apply to the Lion Gate, to the lining of the Postern Gate, to the tower at the southeastern end of the *enceinte*, and to the west wall of the peribolos. We have no evidence which will help us even suggest a date for the north and south Cyclopean walls. They could have been contemporary, later, or earlier than the Lion Gate. No one has yet suggested that they were later. Professor Wace believes them to be contemporary. If they are contemporary, then the entire peribolos of Mycenae, minus the extension at the northeastern end, will have to be placed in Late Helladic III B times and to about 1250 B.C. However, can we believe that the Citadel of Mycenae was unfortified until that date, or that until 1250 B.C. it was surrounded only by negligible walls which have completely disappeared?[42]

---

[36] Blegen, *Zygouries*, pp. 28ff. and pp. 143ff. and especially p. 167.
[37] Mackeprang, *op.cit.*, pp. 552 and 555.
[38] *Chronology*, pp. 110-115.   [39] *BSA*, 48 (1953), p. 15.
[40] Cf. Blegen, "Preclassical Greece—A Survey," *BSA*, 46 (1951), pp. 23-24. Unfortunately, Professor Wace's change of dates is not based on evidence.
[41] The same date is suggested by Mackeprang. Daniels, *AJA*, 52 (1948), p. 108, suggests a slightly later date. For the Philistine ware, see Daniel, *AJA*, 44 (1940), p. 556, and Albright, *AASOR*, XII, pp. 53-58; XIII, pp. 94f.
[42] This will be impossible to maintain in view of the fact that the neighboring

Such a belief will find itself in conflict with tradition. There can be little doubt that the building of the Cyclopean walls of Mycenae, especially those around her north and south sides, was a memorable event which must have left a vivid impression on the conscience of her inhabitants, an impression which ultimately would have been crystallized in tradition. The name of the ruler responsible for their construction would have been closely associated with the event and would have survived in tradition. Perseus is the only ruler associated with the building of Mycenae: "that Perseus became the builder of Mycenae, the Greeks know," writes Pausanias (II, 15, 4). We have seen that the middle of the fourteenth century will perhaps be appropriate for the beginning of Perseus' rule.

This date, indicated by tradition, will be in conflict with the archaeological evidence if we accept Professor Wace's suggestion that the entire peribolos of Mycenae, minus the northeastern extension, was built at the same time. The available archaeological evidence will date the construction so assumed to around 1250 B.C. and the traditional date of Perseus seems to be around 1350 to 1330 B.C. It will also be in conflict with the assumption that the north and south walls are later than the Lion Gate. But it will be in agreement with actualities if we adopt Tsountas' suggestion that the peribolos of Mycenae must be divided into an earlier and a later section, the Lion Gate and the Cyclopean wall to the south being a later addition to the original north and south walls.[43]

Professor Wace rejected Tsountas' suggestion because wall H (Figs. 7-H and 8), which was supposed to be part of the earlier *enceinte*, appeared to him to be a retaining wall. He conceded, however, that additional excavations behind that wall were necessary to prove its real nature.[44] The study of wall H, which I undertook in June 1955, convinced me that it is a retaining wall built after the completion of the Lion Gate. Its construction, the fact that it has only an outer face, the way it abuts against the wall of the inner court of the Lion Gate, definitely prove its character. It must have been built to protect the inner court of the Lion Gate and the roadway to the ramp from

---

Tiryns possessed Cyclopean walls by 1400 B.C. Cf. Mueller, K., *Tiryns*, III and *Ath. Mitt.* 38 (1913), pp. 79ff.; *AA*, 1927, pp. 366ff.

[43] *Mycenaean Age*, p. 113.

[44] *BSA*, 25 (1921-1923), p. 62. Wall H is No. 9 in Wace's plans. Wall H can be seen through the Lion Gate of our Fig. 8. As a matter of fact, it was restored to its present state by Balanos.

landslides and from matter brought down the slope of the hill by rain water after those parts were finally arranged and after experience proved the necessity for such a wall. However, wall H is not essential to Tsountas' suggestion.

During the summer of 1955, the Greek Service for the Restoration and Preservation of Ancient Monuments began the reconstruction of the east wall of the outer court of the Lion Gate. I was able to follow that work for a while and to study the stretch of wall marked AA in Fig. 7.[45] It became evident then that the ashlar masonry of conglomerate which forms the outer face of that wall is a mere curtain or lining behind which we have a Cyclopean fill of limestone. It was apparent when one looked at the wall from above that the conglomerate curtain has a different direction from that of the inner limestone fill, especially at its southern end; that the ashlar facing immediately to the north of the Lion Gate runs obliquely to the body of the Cyclopean wall. In addition, the ends of some of the conglomerate blocks of the facing are resting on the limestone blocks of the fill and the latter were prepared to receive the former. It is generally believed that in a Cyclopean construction the fill was added after the inner and outer faces of the wall were completed. In other words, the outer and the inner faces of a Cyclopean wall were constructed first and then the distance between the two was filled with stones and earth. Consequently, the direction of the fill has to be the same as that of the faces if they belong together; furthermore, some of the stones of the fill would rest on top of the projections of the blocks forming the faces. In our case, the direction of the fill seems to be different, and projections of the stones of the outer face are lying on top of stones of the fill. These peculiarities can be explained only if we assume that the fill of limestone and the face in conglomerate did not belong together originally; that the former belonged to an earlier wall which for a distance and at a later time was faced with ashlar masonry.

Again, I noted that wall AA at its southwestern end does not terminate in the way indicated in the published plans; it is not brought into relation with the wall of the inner court of the Lion Gate. Preliminary clearing done at that end seems to indicate that the wall today ends irregularly, with stones jutting here and there as if its

[45] To Professor A. Orlandos and Dr. E. Stikas, in charge of the work of restoration, I am deeply indebted for the facilities placed at my disposal which made possible my study of the wall.

end was destroyed intentionally and its stones were removed. The stones indeed seem to suggest that wall AA once continued its course beyond the Lion Gate and its inner court. Of course, only proper excavation of the area will definitely prove this point.

An examination of the terrain will disclose that, up to the Lion Gate, the builders of the north line of the Cyclopean wall followed the contour of the rocky foundation of the hill—so much so that shortly to the east of the north projection of wall AA the peribolos forms a small almost rectangular recess (Fig. 7-z) which certainly has no meaning, but which was imposed by the formation of the rock. At the gate they abandoned the contour to sweep southward and to enclose an additional area within the circuit. The suggested continuation to the south of wall AA and its extension, along letters I and I', to the Chavos, as suggested by the dotted line in Fig. 7, would follow all along the rocky contour until the gorge was reached near point J.

Because of these observations, I believe that Tsountas' suggestion that wall AA originally extended to the Chavos is correct. The remnants of a wall marked in Steffen's plan as "kyklop. Maurreste" seem to have formed part of that wall. The ramp leading to the Palace may have formed the approach to an early gate, remnants of which were noticed by Tsountas. The Lion Gate and the existing west wall are a later extension of the peribolos. The section of wall AAII'J, which does not exist today, apparently was pulled down at the time of the construction of the Lion Gate and its stones employed for the building of the wall extending to the south of that Gate and forming the west side of the extended peribolos. Since the west wall was now much longer than the older one which it replaced, the limestone blocks from the latter were not sufficient; consequently, blocks of conglomerate were also employed for the construction of the former.

Summarizing our discussion, we may state that the available evidence, both archaeological and traditional, makes it necessary to distinguish three periods in the history of the fortifications of Mycenae. To the *First Period* belong the existing north wall, A to C, the east wall C, the south wall from C to point J and the wall AAII'J, which was destroyed when the extension to the west was made and whose end we have behind the Lion Gate and its inner court (Fig. 7). To this period also belongs the Cyclopean construction retaining the ramp which later led to the Palace. The area enclosed by these walls could have been the original Late Helladic III Citadel.

To the *Second Period* belong the Lion Gate, the Cyclopean wall to the south, sweeping around the Grave Circle, and the existing west wall to point J. Their construction added a large area to the original *enceinte* (Fig. 7). At the same time, the greater part of the older wall closing the west side (wall AA-J) was destroyed, with only the ramp to the older gate left and used as the avenue to the Palace. Furthermore, it was in this period that the Postern Gate, B, was lined with ashlar masonry and that the so-called tower, Q, at the southeastern corner of the peribolos was built (Fig. 7). The additions, especially the arrangement around the Lion Gate, mark an important advance in military tactics. Then was put into practice the principle of forcing an enemy to approach the main gate with his unprotected side turned to its defenders, a principle used at Tiryns and Athens at a late period, and certainly developed after some experience in fortification work of the Cyclopean style. Such experience could have been provided by the construction of the first period.

To the *Third Period* belongs the existing northeastern projection of the *enceinte*, EFGC, including the subterranean cistern and the Sally Port. This gradual expansion of the Citadel of Mycenae will agree well with Late Helladic practice, as illustrated by the fortifications of Tiryns and of the Acropolis of Athens.[46]

When we turn from the main division into periods to establish their chronology we realize how inadequate is our evidence. We have no definite evidence for the earlier period. The Second Period could be placed with some reservation, since Professor Wace does not agree, around 1250 B.C. For the Third Period we can only state that it is later than either one of the other two, but we have no clear-cut chronology for it. We hope that subsequent exploration of the walls (undertaken while this book was in press) will yield evidence which will make possible the accurate dating of their construction. Meanwhile, we may point out that the evidence which can be obtained from the study of the Palace and especially of its southwest wing[47] indicates the middle of the fourteenth century as the time of the construction of the early Cyclopean walls; this date is also indicated by the Perseus tradition. We can suggest that date for our First Period until more reliable evidence is forthcoming. The Second Period, including the

---

[46] Müller, K., *Tiryns*, III, p. 208 and pl. 4; Burg I, II, III; *AA*, 1927, pp. 366ff. For the walls of Athens, see Kolbe, W., *AA*, 1939, col. 227-236; Broneer, O., *AJA*, 52 (1948), pp. 111-114.

[47] *Infra*, pp. 65-66.

Lion Gate, we can place around 1250 B.C., while the Third Period should perhaps be placed after the fall of Troy and the return of Agamemnon, i.e. shortly after 1183 B.C.

We would like further to suggest a correlation of these periods of construction with the known legendary leaders of Mycenae. To the reputed founder of Mycenae, to Perseus, we may attribute the construction of the first peribolos wall; after all, that wall marks the real construction of the Citadel. Also, the traditional date of Perseus seems to agree with the one suggested for that peribolos. The Lion Gate, with its coat of arms and the Cyclopean wall which now forms the west line of the fortifications, could be conceived as the work of Atreus. We could credit his descendants, perhaps Orestes, with the construction of the northeastern section with its subterranean cistern. The civil disturbances which must have followed the feud involving Agamemnon, Aegisthos, and Orestes could be considered responsible for the construction of the subterranean cistern and its inclusion in the fortified area; thus the vulnerability of the acropolis of Mycenae could have been remedied.

The Lower City of Mycenae in prehistoric times occupied an open area unprotected by walls. The fortifications known to have enclosed a Lower City, which were marked by Steffen on his plan and which can easily be seen today, belong to the Hellenistic period and have no relation to the city of Agamemnon and his predecessors. As a matter of fact, there can be some doubt as to whether a Lower City, as we understand it today and as it existed in Hellenistic times, did exist in the Late Helladic period. Tsountas long ago seems to have proved that the citizens of Mycenae lived κωμηδόν, in small detached groups at a short distance from each other, with the graves of their ancestors surrounding their dwellings and with roads and lanes connecting their small subdivisions with each other and with the Citadel,[48] a system known to have been used in Sparta in the historic period and reflected in the ancient demes of Athens. In the Citadel lived only the ruling family, its friends and relatives, and perhaps some of the other leaders of the community; the other inhabitants seem to have lived beyond the walls and in small groups dictated by family ties.

Before we leave the discussion of the Citadel, we must note that a network of roads connected it with the northeastern coast of the Peloponnesos and with the surrounding territory of the Argolid.

[48] *Mycenaean Age*, p. 33.

Steffen has mapped out these roads in his monumental work,[49] and more have been detected since his time. Remains of a viaduct over the Chavos are still apparent at a short distance to the west of the Citadel and the roads leading to Corinthia, the area which epic poetry places under the domain of Agamemnon, can easily be detected. These roads are narrow, meant only for pedestrians and beasts of burden, and average some five feet in width. It seems that at advantageous points small forts and lookout posts were built and maintained for the safety of the traveler. The most interesting Mycenaean lookout post has been located on top of the mount of Prophet Elias, where in Hellenistic times a small fort was established.[50] The view from that post is magnificent in all directions, and from it an approaching enemy could have been easily detected long before he reached the perimeter of Mycenae. There can be little doubt that on top of that mountain the famous fire signals of Mycenae were lighted, and that the fall of Troy was signaled to the people of Mycenae from that mountaintop by means of fire.[51] When, in the hot summer day, we turn our eyes to the top of Prophet Elias, the words of the poets and the tragedians come tumbling into our minds and the fate of the Pelopids stands out as clearly as if it had happened but yesteryear.

[49] Steffen, *Karten von Mykenai*, pp. 8-12 and pl. I.
[50] *Mycenaean Age*, p. 38; BSA, 25 (1921-1923), pp. 429-434.
[51] In Aeschylos' *Agamemnon*, 281ff., we find the famous description of the "fire signals." There, Clytemnestra states that the final fire was lighted on the peak of Mount Arachnaeos.

III

THE PALACE AND THE HOUSES
OF THE CITADEL

THE AREA enclosed by the Cyclopean walls is in the form of a large equilateral triangle, the apex of which is turned to the northeast and to the saddle between Mounts Zara and Prophet Elias and the base toward the plain to the southwest of the Citadel. In the base of the triangle and near the northwest corner of the *enceinte* is the Lion Gate, the main entrance to the Citadel. On clearing that entrance, we find a small wall-enclosed and evidently roofed court some 4 meters square, and in the eastern wall of this a small chamber known as the "Guard Room." Its small size, however—1.85 meters maximum length, 1.30 meters width, and 1.50 meters height—will indicate that it was perhaps used for a watchdog. To the south, the court opens into a well-constructed road, some 4.50 meters broad at its beginning, artificially graded to lead to a ramp (Figs. 7-1 and 8), the north end of which is met at a distance of 27 meters from the south end of the court. Its west edge is supported by a well-constructed Cyclopean retaining wall, while its eastern side is limited by another wall which can be traced beyond the ramp to the north and to the Lion Gate.

The ramp apparently marks the beginning of the avenue which, in the second period of wall construction, led to the top of the Citadel and to the Palace. It is carefully and precisely constructed; over a first layer of stones and earth a second layer of larger stones was placed, over which a third made up of pebbles, and that in turn was covered with hard-pressed earth which forms the surface layer. The ramp ranges in width from 4.10 to 5.75 meters and is preserved to a length of 24 meters. At its south end it breaks abruptly, and apparently the break was caused by later construction. It is generally assumed that at that point the ramp, or the avenue which replaced it, turned at right angles to the east, proceeded for some distance up the western slope, and finally forked in two directions. One of the branches gradually ascended the slope in a northeasterly direction and led to the northwestern entrance of the palace, while the other proceeded along the slope in a southeasterly direction to terminate at the southwestern corner of the palace-area and in front of the Grand Stairway. In 1895 Tsountas detected the road just below that stairway, retained at that point by a Cyclopean wall.

The extent of the Palace to the north, west, and south is clearly defined.[1] There can be little doubt that the south Cyclopean wall of the *enceinte* acted as a retaining wall for its terrace in that direction;[2] a retaining wall marks its northern limit, while a well-preserved retaining wall with frequent setbacks can be seen along the entire length of its west side. The east side alone is undetermined and, according to Tsountas, it is in the eastern area of the Palace that the domestic quarters seem to have been located. The area covered by the Palace is considerable; its remains can be seen in an area at least 60 meters from north to south and 55 meters from east to west, but its original extent must have been even larger. The Palace was constructed on uneven ground and on different levels, on top of the hill and along its sloping sides to the west and south; and so it must have presented a stepped or terraced appearance. Its important sections were built in two main levels: the first high up on the top of the hill and, some 5.50 meters below it, the second formed by an artificial terrace, constructed in the main against its southwestern slope. Between them we have two long corridors, running roughly from west to east and known as the South and North Corridors respectively, with storage rooms opening from them.

The part of the Palace on the upper level was completely destroyed when the site was used for the construction of a temple, perhaps a temple dedicated to Athena, first in the sixth century and again in Hellenistic times. (The plan of the Hellenistic temple is indicated in dotted lines in Fig. 14.) Scanty remains of walls or floors left here and there tell of the existence of important units on that level. Three column-bases in the foundations of the Hellenistic temple seem to indicate that a large colonnaded hall formed part of the Palace on the very top of the hill.

The units of the southwestern lower level are better preserved and fortunately belong to an important wing of the Palace. That wing stood on an artificial terrace, filled in with loose stones, and ultimately retained by the southern line of the Cyclopean circuit wall. To it led

---

[1] For the excavations and remains of the Palace, see especially Tsountas, *PAE*, 1886, pp. 59ff., and Wace, *Mycenae*, pp. 69-90.

[2] That wall would belong to the first and older structural period in the history of the Cyclopean fortification walls; see *supra*, pp. 37-38.

the broad avenue from the Lion Gate. The avenue actually ended in front of a small structure serving the Grand Stairway which gave access to the southwest wing. A broad doorway led into a small vestibule, measuring 2.67 by 2.63 meters, whose floor was covered with lime cement. To the west of this vestibule opened a compartment known as the "West Lobby" (Fig. 14-A), against the north and west walls of which run a low bench of stone and clay, originally covered with stucco, 0.35 to 0.45 meters in height and 0.45 meters in width. The bench is reminiscent of the Homeric:[3]

ἐν δὲ θρόνοι περὶ τοῖχον ἐρηρέδατ' ἔνθα καὶ ἔνθα,
ἐς μυχὸν ἐξ αὐδοῖο διαμπερές

and of the polished stones,

οἳ οἱ ἔσαν προπάροιθι θυράων ὑψηλάων
λευκοί, ἀποστίλβοντες ἀλείφατος.

The northern half of the Lobby gives access to the Grand Stairway, an impressive and comfortable rising which lent dignity to the approach to the Palace (Figs. 14-A and 15). It is composed of twenty-two steps, low and of wide tread, 0.35 to 0.45 meters in width (excepting the sixth step, which has a width of 0.84 meters) and 0.10 to 0.12 meters in height, made of small pieces of sandstone well fitted and covered with white stucco. The frequent repair of this stucco is evident in many places. The width of the stairway is 2.40 meters.

Along its north side, a good wall is preserved to a considerable height, acting somewhat as a curtain and as a retaining wall for the terrace to the north, while its southern side is closed by a low balustrade partially preserved (Fig. 16). At the western extremity of that balustrade may have been a column which helped to support the landing over the Lobby. The first flight of steps apparently ended in a rectangular landing platform, at right angles to which a second flight of perhaps seventeen or eighteen steps must have led to a second landing directly above the Lobby. No trace of the second flight of steps has been preserved. Below those steps and on the ground level, two rooms were revealed to the east of the vestibule (Figs. 14, B-C and 16), indicating the existence of a landing platform above the innermost small compartment, c. The entire complex of the

---

[3] *Odyssey*, VII, 95-96, "Within, seats were fixed along the wall on either hand, from the threshold to the innermost chamber," and III, 406-408, "which were before his lofty doors, white and glistening as with oils." (Transl. Murray.)

stairway is clear and impressive and can easily be reconstructed, at least up to the top of the first flight of steps. Professor Wace believes that the second flight of steps and the whole complex of the stairway was roofed over and that the upper structure rose above the floor level of the Court. However, there is no evidence indicating that the complex was roofed, and perhaps we must restore the second flight open to the sky and leading to the second platform, which was also open. Instead of a wall on the south side to support a roof, we must continue the balustrade of the first flight to the second landing platform through which access to the terrace of the southwest wing was obtained. The north wall too would have ended in a similar balustrade.

The Grand Stairway led to a small Forecourt, of an irregular quadrilateral form, with a well-cemented floor (Fig. 14-D). The existence of a small drain running through its east wall seems to indicate that this Forecourt was open to the sky. That east wall separates the Forecourt from the Main Court of the wing. A red sandstone threshold still *in situ* at the north end of its east wall, of a total length of 1.90 meters, is part of a doorway 1.20 meters in width, and indicates an opening to that Court. But apparently a second and wider doorway at the south end of the east wall formed the main entrance to the Court. To that belonged a threshold block, preserved to a length of 1.62 meters with a width of 1.18 meters; it was removed by Tsountas because it projected dangerously above the north wall of the stairway.

To the north side of the Forecourt opens an almost Square Room (Fig. 14-E), the door opening of which is indicated by two threshold blocks still *in situ*. Professor Wace believes that a pier of rubble masonry perhaps divided this opening in two. No traces of a pivot hole are to be seen on the easternmost threshold block, but on the western we have the impression of a revolving pole. This is usually referred to as a "pivot hole," but certainly it is not like the pivot holes cut in Mycenaean thresholds. At best, the impression will indicate that for a brief period a light and perhaps a temporary door was used to close the west half of the doorway which originally was open. The room has an almost square shape and measures 5.50 meters from north to south and 6.20 meters from east to west. Its floor was covered with painted stucco, surviving only along the edges of the walls, and immediately below this Tsountas found a drain made of tile and running from west to east. Unfortunately, only a small section of that drain was investigated. Against the north wall of the Square Room

Tsountas found a rectangular area, 0.80 by 1.07 meters, rising from the floor about 0.05 meters and perhaps higher. When Professor Wace cleared that rectangular area, he found that a rim made of plaster rose 0.02 to 0.03 meters above the floor level while the oblong was actually sunk 0.015 meters below it. Its surface was found covered with plaster, only small parts of which were missing. A painted border, composed of a blue strip between red lines, offset the oblong from the rest of the painted floor, while red color covered the wall behind it. Elsewhere, the wall seems to have been white with a dark stripe below.

Tsountas compared this rectangular space to the hearths which can be seen today in the huts of peasants, and accepted it as such. Professor Wace, on the other hand, took the oblong to have been the base on which stood a throne, the throne of the ruler of Mycenae, and consequently called the square apartment the Throne Room, where audiences were granted and visitors were received.[4] Indeed its position is excellent for such a purpose, since a visitor of distinction on ascending to the Palace by means of the Grand Staircase would find himself in the Forecourt right in front of the audience room where he would be officially received.

However, in the palace of Tiryns and now also of Pylos, the throne of the ruler was located in the *domos* (main room) of the Megaron to the right of a person entering. At Mycenae it is no longer to be seen there since that side of the Megaron has not been preserved. The Megaron seems to be indicated by our literary evidence as the place where visitors were received, and its *domos* with its wall paintings, its hearth, and its tall columns, was an impressive setting for a mighty king.[5] Of course, on the analogy of the Palace of Knossos, we could suppose that a special throne room existed in the palace of the most eminent of mainland rulers. To do so we have first to prove that the throne room of Knossos was indeed an audience room, and then we have to assume that the Minoan tradition was remembered at least two generations after the Palace of Knossos was destroyed. Besides, at Mycenae we do not have the side benches which characterize the Knossian example nor the sunk area. Other reasons also add to the difficulty of accepting the identification.

Holland was the first to point out that the Square Room was so

---

[4] Tsountas, *PAE*, 1886, p. 68; Wace, *BSA*, 25 (1921-1923), pp. 187-188.
[5] See *infra*, pp. 53-55.

large that interior supports of some kind were necessary for its ceiling and the second story over it. And, although he believed that "a single column in the center would be excellent from the structural point of view," he rejected this solution in favor of two columns because a single column "would come directly in front of the throne—rather a preposterous arrangement."[6] A preposterous arrangement, if the room were indeed a throne room, but the best arrangement if the room did not fill that function. That a lone support could be used in those days and in the mainland is indicated by the single column which apparently was employed to support the structure over the existing flight of stairs of the Grand Staircase, and by the single column of the outer portico of the northwest Propylon. Now we find it employed in the Propylon of the Palace of Pylos, cleared in the campaign of 1954, and in a spacious room in the southwest section of the same palace, cleared in the summer of 1953.[7] Again, two columns placed in a room of the size of the one under consideration would have deprived it of its impressiveness.

Let us now turn our attention to the rectangular raised area itself. To Tsountas it suggested a hearth. A hearth of a rectangular shape and almost of the same dimensions (1.10 by 0.88 by 0.09 meters) was found in the so-called "House of Tsountas," although there it is located in the center of the room and not against its wall. In the Palace of Nestor a slightly raised rectangular platform was found against the wall and to the side of the entrance of the *aethousa* (portico) to the *prodomos* (vestibule) of the Megaron. A second similar platform was found against the wall and to the right of the entrance from the *prodomos* to the *domos*. It is scarcely possible to believe that these platforms in their particular position supported thrones, since we have the throne area within the *domos*. A third "slightly raised stucco platform" was found in the "spacious room" of the southwestern section of the Pylos Palace where a single column was used for support. There again it was found by a doorway "on the right as one goes out." Professor Blegen states that as yet it is not clear whether these platforms were used for a "seat, or a stand for a sentry or a servant," and considers them "as a peculiarity of the palace of Epano Englianos."[8] I believe that in these raised platforms we have parallels to the example found at Mycenae. They bring to mind

[6] *BSA*, 25 (1921-1923), p. 276.
[7] Blegen, *AJA*, 58 (1954), p. 29, pl. 4, fig. 2; and *AJA* 59 (1955), p. 32, pl. 24.
[8] *AJA*, 58 (1954), p. 29.

[46]

two passages in our epic poetry, which may suggest their possible use. In the *Iliad*, when Phoenix described his predicament in the house of his father, he told how his relatives kept watch over him and how fires were kept burning:[9]

ὑπ' αἰθούσῃ εὐερκέος αὐλῆς, . . .
ἐνὶ προδόμῳ, πρόσθεν θαλάμοιο θυράων

One wonders whether the fires were lit in fireplaces of the shape and type of the platforms of Pylos and Mycenae.

The other passage is to be found in the seventh book of the *Odyssey*, 84-102, and describes a detail in the Palace of Alcinoos. On entering its premises, Odysseus admires the gardens, the high-roofed *doma*, the bronze walls decorated by a cornice of cyanus, the doors, doorposts, and lintels made of gold, silver, and bronze, the gold and silver dogs which guarded the palace, and finally, within, "golden youths," who "stood on well-built pedestals, holding lighted torches in their hands to give light by night to the banqueters in the hall." The position of the platforms of Pylos beside door openings is appropriate for such stands used in the lighting of the interior of the palace at night. And we may imagine that the raised platform in the room of Mycenae could have served such a purpose. We may also recall that one of the floor slabs of the *prodomos* in the Megaron of Mycenae itself, the slab to the right of a person crossing the threshold, rose 0.055 meters above the level of the floor. Did it serve a purpose similar to that of the raised platforms of Pylos?

Of course, definite identification of the purpose which the raised platform served in our room is impossible. We believe that the weight of probability is against its identification as a base for a throne. I would rather favor its use as a hearth. Its position against the wall may have been imposed by the erection of a single column in the middle of the room. The difference in the level of its floor mentioned by Tsountas and by Wace will suggest that it was laid in at least two different times. Blegen's work at Pylos shows that the plastering of floors was carried around the objects set on them and that thus the imprints of such objects, like the flutings of a column, are to be seen even today. The plaster of our area does not show the imprints of the legs of a throne or the rubbing which they would

[9] Iliad, IX, 472: "beneath the portico of the well-fenced court . . . in the *prodomos*, before the door of my chamber."

normally have made on the plastered surface. Besides, a hearth against a wall was found by Tsountas in the compartment we shall call the Room of the Curtain Frescoes (Fig. 14-к) in the Palace itself.[10] A hearth seems to be indicated in the Square Room. If a throne was not placed on the platform, we cannot very well identify the room with its central single column as a throne room. Could we suggest some other use for it?

Both Tsountas and Professor Wace have pointed out that to the northwest of the Square Room only a small area of the Palace remained, held up by the western retaining wall. Unfortunately, whatever stood on that area has been completely destroyed, leaving no traces behind. We may suppose that another very small room stood next to the Square Room, with which it had one wall in common; this seems to be indicated by the well-constructed corner which survived beyond the northwestern corner of the Square Room. Beyond the small room, an area was perhaps left through which the Forecourt was connected with the western passageway. We may now note that Tsountas found a drain built of tiles immediately below the floor of the Square Room. The entire length of that drain has not been investigated, but its direction indicates that possibly it started in the room we are postulating, that it proceeded under the floor of the Square Room, and through its east wall to the Main Court to terminate in the main drain beyond the south wall of the Court. If we bear in mind the possible origin of the tile drain, we could assume that the room we are proposing was a bathroom while the Square Room adjacent to it could have served as a bedroom and for general use; that the two formed a unit, an apartment, reserved for visitors and guests. A single glance at the plan will show how well separated from the rest of the Palace this unit was and yet how near the Court and the Megaron which are usually taken to form the section of the Palace open to the public. The two rooms, with the Forecourt in front of them, formed an imposing unit which was reached directly by the visitors. It could also easily be reached through the West Passage of the Palace. At the same time, by means of the wide doorway at the end of its east wall the unit could be completely isolated from the Megaron. It is interesting to remark that in 1955 Professor Blegen uncovered a bathroom conveniently

[10] *Praktika* 1886, p. 70 and pl. 4.

placed off the court of the Megaron in the Palace of Pylos and in a comparatively similar position to our suggested example.

We may now recall that in Homeric poetry guests are never given a room in the domestic quarters, nor are they allowed to sleep in the main room of the Megaron, but are always accommodated in its porch, in the *aethousa*. The beds of Telemachos, the son of Odysseus, and Peisistratos, the son of Nestor, were placed ὑπ᾽ αἰθούσῃ (in the porch), during their visit to Menelaos, and the two young men slept in that part of the Megaron which was further defined as being ἐν προδόμῳ δόμου.[11] Odysseus slept in the *aethousa* of the palace of Alcinoos,[12] and Telemachos slept in the *aethousa* of the palace of Nestor which is called ἐρίδουπος (echoing).[13] In the *Iliad* Priam and his herald were allowed to sleep ὑπ᾽ αἰθούσῃ which was further identified as ἐν προδόμῳ δόμου.[14]

The Square Room with its adjacent bath and its wide, open doorway would take the place of the *aethousa*. It was still near the Court; as a matter of fact it opens into the Forecourt, as the *aethousa* opens into the Court. It has privacy, and at the same time it is removed from the main section of the Palace. The only objection to such an identification is that the arrangement looks very modern. But do we, men of the twentieth century, alone own the exclusive rights to functional architectural designing? We may end our discussion of the Square Room by repeating that in all probability it was reserved for the visitors and guests of the Palace, that it was the Ξενών or hostel, and so it stands as a material evidence of the hospitality for which the people of the mythical age were so noted.

The Hostel and its Forecourt, the Court and its Megaron, were conceived and designed as one unit. This becomes evident from the study of the plan and of the remains (Fig. 14). The unit stood on an artificially made terrace, the filling of which consisted of loose stones, which was retained by the south line of the Cyclopean wall. The Grand Staircase does not fit into the unit; it is placed obliquely to it, and apparently it was added at a later time, perhaps to replace an older stairway.

Below the Forecourt, excavations revealed a basement room which was destroyed by fire and then filled in to form part of the terrace

[11] *Odyssey*, 4, 297-302: "in the fore-hall of the main room of the Palace."
[12] *Odyssey*, 7, 336.   [13] *Odyssey*, 3, 399.
[14] *Iliad*, XXIV, 644, 673.

on which stood the Forecourt and its Square Room. This basement, known as the Pillar Room, therefore belongs to a phase of the Palace older than that represented by the remains of the Forecourt and of the Square Room.

Two door openings, as we have seen, led from the Forecourt to the Main Court of the southwestern wing (Fig. 14-G). Compared to the courts of the Minoan palaces or even to that of the Palace of Tiryns, it is a small but well-proportioned area, measuring 11.50 meters from east to west and not more than 15 meters from north to south. Its eastern side is taken up by the façade of the Megaron. On the west it is limited by the east wall of the Forecourt and of the Square Room. Its north limiting wall is well preserved and it requires special description. Part of it was hidden under the foundations of the southwestern corner of the Hellenistic temple (Fig. 14), but now, after the removal of that corner, it stands to its entire length. Its western half is the best preserved, standing to a height of 2.50 meters and in six tiers. The wall is built of rubble, but is faced with poros blocks laid in the Mycenaean ashlar fashion, the lowest course of which shows signs of survival from a fire. Between the two lower courses was originally laid a horizontal wooden beam, an indication of the well-known wooden tie system employed by the Mycenaeans. The entire surface of the wall was covered with painted stucco. Behind this north wall of the Court there is another, faced with plaster and apparently belonging to a structure earlier than that represented by the Court. The west wall also apparently had an ashlar facing covered with stucco, of which only one course shows for a distance of 6 meters.

Scanty foundations of the south wall of the Court have survived, which cannot prove whether or not at that side we had a high wall or a mere balustrade. The former would have blocked the magnificent view of the Argive plain which unfolds below that corner of the Citadel. Professor Wace advocated the existence of such a wall: "It seems indeed strange," he wrote, "that an architect building on this magnificent site should have deliberately built a wall across the south side of the court and so shut off the wonderful view of the Argive plain. . . . The lords of Mycenae were probably more concerned for their comfort, which would depend on privacy and safety, than with the scenery. In any case they would have enjoyed exactly the same views, perhaps to better advantage, from the loggias and flat roof of the upper storey."[15] Such a wall, however, would have cut off not only the view but also the light and the sun and would have ruined as such the southern exposure of the Court. As for privacy and defense, the wing standing on such an inaccessible point of the hill could hardly need the southern wall for protection or secrecy. It is, I believe, more reasonable to reconstruct a balustrade on the existing foundations of the south wall, which would limit the Court in that direction, would provide safety to its occupants, and allow them likewise to enjoy the magnificent view. The lack of any remains of an upper roofed story of the Grand Stairway, indicating the nonexistence of such a structure, would also suggest an open vista at this area. The impossibility of enjoying that view from the Megaron, whose walls would presumably be solid, would also indicate an arrangement with a low wall or balustrade. Why, otherwise, would the Mycenaeans have gone to so much trouble to create an artificial terrace at this particular area, if they could not enjoy the benefit of such a site? Professor Wace rightly observed that, when the Court and the apartments around it were designed, the site was adapted to the plan and that plan evidently took cognizance of the view.

The floor of the Court was paved with a thick layer of Mycenaean lime cement which in the last stage of the use of the Palace was covered with a coat of painted stucco. Linear patterns drawn in squares, marked out by double impressed lines, and filled with alternating colors, yellow, blue, red, apparently covered the floor. Because of this and the painted stucco of the walls, Rodenwaldt suggested that the Court was roofed.[16] The area of the Court, however, is so large that even if its south wall was not a mere balustrade but a high wall, it would still have required interior supports if it were roofed. No traces of such supports have been found and this may indicate that the Court was open to the sky.

At the east side of the Court we have the Megaron of the Palace (Figs. 14, H, I, J and 17-20), the most typical mainland unit of its architecture. A good part of its south section as well as of the Court stood on the artificially constructed terrace; for its northern end, the rock had been cut and leveled off. When the Cyclopean retaining wall collapsed, the south side of the Megaron was destroyed and its

---

[15] *BSA*, 25 (1921-1923), p. 189. Cf. also *Mycenae*, p. 75.
[16] *Jahrbuch*, 1919, p. 95.

remains rolled down the slope.[17] Yet its plan is clear (Fig. 14, H, I, J).
Like the typical mainland megara, it is a long and comparatively
narrow roofed structure measuring some 23 meters in length and
11.50 meters in width (inner dimensions). It is oriented roughly from
west to east with its entrance facing west and toward the Main Court.
Two cross walls divide the long structure into three divisions. The
westernmost division, its entrance (Fig. 14-H), is in the form of an
open portico with two columns between the ends of the side walls,
or antae. It measures 3.80 meters in depth and 11.50 in width. The
column bases are still *in situ* and measure 0.57 meters in diameter
(Fig. 19). Large gypsum slabs, usually assumed to have been imported from Crete,[18] were used to pave the floor and the walls were
covered with painted plaster. A small sample of it has been preserved
at the bottom of the northeast corner of its walls. It is part of the
well-known Mycenaean "rosette and triglyph" pattern and seems
to have formed a dado going around the lower part of the walls. A
threshold block at the north side of the portico indicates that a
passage existed there. By its southern column the remnants of a table
of offering were found and below the floor foundations which seem
to have supported the structure. At a small distance from it to the
south, fragments of the gypsum floor slabs are preserved and they
exhibit clear traces of two depressions, perhaps what survived of
shallow basins used for libations.[19] The portico, an essential and
imposing feature of the Megaron, we may call by its Homeric name
of *aethousa*.

A large doorway connected the *aethousa* with the second division
of the Megaron, the *prodomos* (Fig. 14-I). Details of the doorway
are clear, since its threshold is still to be seen *in situ*. It is made up of a
single block of conglomerate (almond-stone) cut to size by means
of a saw, measuring 2.50 meters in length and 1.14 meters in width
(Fig. 20). The actual width (opening) of the door, however, was
much smaller and only 1.90 meters. On the south side of the
threshold, to the right as we enter, the pivot hole is partially pre-

[17] Professor Marinatos has recently pointed out the need for a reexamination of
that slope and has made a small beginning. Cf. *Volume in Memoriam G. P.
Oekonomos*, pp. 9-11.
[18] Professor Marinatos has pointed out the fact that gypsum is obtainable in
Cephalonia too, *op.cit.*, p. 17. Cf. *Mycenae*, p. 76.
[19] To Dr. Papademetriou I am indebted for this information and for the permission
to mention it here. His discussion of the remains will appear shortly.

served (0.15 meters in diameter and 0.35 meters in depth) and in it Tsountas found fragments of bronze with which was shod the end of the pole around which the door revolved. Along its inner side, the threshold possesses a ledge against which the door would rest. The *prodomos* is deeper than the *aethousa* and measures some 4.40 meters in depth. With the exception of the south wall, its sides stand to a considerable height, and they demonstrate not only the way the walls were constructed but also the way in which they were covered with plaster, the outer surface of which was originally decorated with frescoes. Both plaster and the rubble masonry are so badly damaged by the fire which destroyed the Palace that nothing can be made out of the frescoes. The floor presents a border, 1 to 1.15 meters in width, of gypsum slabs laid along the walls with its central area covered by painted stucco. Dark red lines divide it into almost square panels, about 1.25 meters on the side, decorated with motives reminiscent of those on the columns of the Treasury of Atreus, i.e., zigzag patterns painted in blue, red, and yellow. The floor slab in front of the south door jamb from the *prodomos* to the *domos* rose 0.055 meters above the floor level, thus forming a raised platform which can be compared to those found in the Palace of Pylos. The southern wall of the *prodomos* apparently rolled down the precipitous side of the gorge.

A large door opening led from the *prodomos* to the main room of the Megaron (Fig. 14-J). Its threshold, again of conglomerate stone, measuring 2.05 meters in length and 0.89 meters in width, is still *in situ*, although badly damaged by fire. However, the opening was made smaller, *c.* 1.80 meters, by the wooden door frame whose existence is indicated by the holes for its attachment at either end of the threshold block. The lack of pivot holes would indicate that the opening was not blocked by a door; perhaps it was simply closed by a curtain, as seems to be the case at Tiryns and at Pylos.

The main room of the Megaron is an imposing one. It is often called the Megaron, but since the term is also given to the entire unit with its three subdivisions, I believe that the inner room should be designated by another term. I propose to call it the *domos*. It is the main room of the Megaron in which the hearth is to be found and where were held the important activities of the family, especially in its relations with the outer world. Unfortunately, its south wall, most of its eastern wall, and a good portion of the floor adjacent to them, as well as its southeastern corner, have gone down the precipitous slope. Still, we may appreciate its magnificence and size, and for that we have the example not only of the megaron at Tiryns but also of the Palace of Nestor uncovered at Pylos.[20] Apparently this inner and main room measured 12.92 meters in length and 11.50 meters in width. Its floor was paved in a manner identical to that followed for the paving of the *prodomos*; a band of gypsum slabs, 1.15 meters in width, was placed along the walls, and the rest within that border was covered with painted stucco. Again, the stuccoed floor was divided, by means of painted double lines, into square panels ranging in dimensions from 1.25 to 1.40 by 1.25 meters. The patterns which originally decorated these panels have not survived. At least four coats of lime-cement can be distinguished, indicating the custom of renovating the floor from time to time.

The surviving walls of the room are of rubble masonry and originally were covered with plaster decorated in fresco. Though badly damaged by fire, fragments of its frescoes have survived. Tsountas recognized in them horsemen and soldiers, and later Rodenwaldt was able to reconstruct parts of the composition showing warriors with horses and chariots with their squires as well as women in front of a palace standing on rocky ground. The whole is built in the typical Mycenaean fashion, with timber tie-beams and wall-areas between them covered with plaster. Another section seems to display a battle scene. Perhaps the entire composition depicted a battle fought in front of a fortified citadel from the walls of which women followed its course, a composition reminiscent of the battles before the walls of Troy.[21]

The main feature of this inner room was its great circular hearth standing in the center and surrounded by four columns. About one third of the hearth survives today; the rest, along with the floor supporting it, has long since slid down the precipitous slope of the ravine (Fig. 22). It stood only 0.15 meters above the paved floor and was built with a ring of poros stone enclosing a center of clay; both were covered with plaster. At least ten layers of plaster can be distinguished, and it seems that most if not all of them were covered with painted patterns. The most common of these was a

---

[20] *AJA*, 57 (1953), pp. 59-64; 58 (1954), pp. 27-32; 59 (1955), pp. 31-37.
[21] Tsountas, *Ephemeris*, 1887, pls. 11, 12; Rodenwaldt G., *Der Fries des Megarons von Mykenai* (1921); Lamb, *BSA*, 25 (1921-1923), pp. 249ff.; Wace, *Mycenae*, p. 77.

"plume" or "flame" pattern painted on the sides in deep red, while a spiral motive in some instances covered the rim on top. The diameter of the hearth can be closely estimated to have been 3.70 meters. Signs of fire, indicating its use, can be seen clearly on its surface and sides.[22] Four columns stood around the hearth, and their position can be accurately determined because two of the bases and the slab on which was placed the third base are still to be seen *in situ*. By the northwestern base Tsountas found fragments of bronze plates bearing nails, and it seems reasonable to suppose that the columns, which were made of wood, were covered, at least in their lower sections, with bronze plate and ornaments. The arrangement of hearth and columns corresponds to that in Tiryns and in Pylos, and the palaces in those districts will perhaps indicate the details of the southern section of the room.

The south section of the *domos* is located to the right of a person entering the room from the *prodomos*. In the case of the Palace of Tiryns, a person entering the *domos* would find on his right the throne of the ruler of that citadel. Again, in the *domos* of the Palace at Pylos, the location of a throne was found in the middle of the wall to the right of a person entering. It seems to us apparent that a similar position for a throne should be restored in the middle of the south wall of the *domos* of the Palace at Mycenae. The evidence from Pylos is of special importance, since the megaron of that palace seems in many respects to duplicate that of Mycenae: a single doorway leads from its *aethousa* to the *prodomos* and the dimensions of its divisions seem to be near those of the Palace of Mycenae; again, the megaron at Pylos opens onto a comparatively small inner court. It was in the room with the hearth and the throne that strangers would be received and entertained in typical Homeric fashion. We may recall how in the room with the hearth Alcinoos received Odysseus, and in the room with the hearth Menelaos and Helen entertained Telemachos. The *domos*, with its frescoes, hearth, and lofty columns, would be the right place for such receptions.

No tangible evidence has survived which might help us to reconstruct the superstructure of the Megaron with reasonable certainty. Professor Wace believes that the Megaron was in two stories. He bases his belief in the assumed dimensions of the columns and the

---

[22] For the latest complete description of the hearth, see Wace, *BSA*, 25 (1921-1923), pp. 241-244; *Mycenae*, p. 77.

necessity of reaching the level of the Southern Corridor, but the columns which might have solved our problem were burned when the Palace was destroyed. Only their bases survive. The bases of the *aethousa* measure 0.57 meters, while those of the *domos* are 0.56 meters in diameter. If we applied the proportions known to have existed in Crete, we should have to conclude that the columns measured at the most 3 meters, and that height was not sufficient to raise the Megaron above the level of the South Corridor. Consequently, a second story becomes a necessity, and so it was restored in the plans of Piet de Yong. However, we have no indication that the builders of the Megaron used Cretan proportions. Undoubtedly their work was strongly influenced by the Minoan structural system. It is agreed for instance that the Minoan wooden column with its characteristic downward tapering was employed; even gypsum slabs seem to have been imported, perhaps from Crete, and used in the paving of the Megaron. But the Megaron itself as a structure characterizes the architecture of the mainland and in its construction mainland features may have been retained, especially in the realm of proportions. We may note that the average span in Cretan structures ranges from 2 meters to 2.50 meters; the clear spans we have in the *domos* amount to approximately 3.60, 4.55, and 3.78 meters from front to rear and 3.40, 3.93, and 3.06 meters from side to side. Apparently for their spans the Mycenaean builders used proportions other than those current in Minoan Crete. May we also suppose that for the height of their columns too they used different proportions?

It has been noted that the diameter at the bottom of the column in the façade of the Tomb of Clytemnestra is only 0.39 meters while its height is 6 meters; in other words, the height of that column is 15 times the diameter of the bottom of its shaft, while the height of the columns of the Treasury of Atreus is 12 times the diameter of its shaft. When we recall that in Crete columns seem to be five times their diameter at the base, we would necessarily conclude that in the mainland different proportions were in use. The objection, however, could be raised that these columns were employed decoratively and not structurally. This objection was successfully countered by Holland, who pointed out that in the Tomb of Clytemnestra the height of the columns is 1⅔ times the length of the span they served; in the Treasury of Atreus it is 1¼ times the span. Applying the same proportions to the columns of the *domos*, whose span is known, he figured out that the height of its columns should be at least 4.50 meters. Again, he pointed out that "in all the tholoi the height of the door opening is equal to twice its width at the bottom." If the same proportion was held in the construction of the doors of the Megaron, then the calculated height of the columns would again amount to 4.45 meters.[23] With columns of such height, the need of introducing a second story is eliminated. We believe that the Megaron of the Palace, a typical mainland unit, would follow the mainland type and the mainland proportions, and consequently be one story in height. In the Palace of Pylos evidence was obtained to indicate that some kind of mezzanine floor went around the interior of the *domos*,[24] but unfortunately we cannot be sure of the existence of a similar arrangement at Mycenae.

The question of lighting the *domos* and disposing of the smoke of the hearth poses another difficult problem. Was there an opening in the roof corresponding to the area occupied by the hearth? That opening indeed would have been a large one and would have caused trouble in winter weather. And yet the need for letting in light and letting out smoke was pressing. The conception that the "hearth should be regarded as a large immovable altar or table of offering rather than as a hearth for purely domestic uses"[25] certainly is contrary to whatever literary evidence we have.[26] More evidence is now available from the Palace of Nestor at Pylos. In the *domos*, near one of its columns, a table of offering was uncovered, used of course as the family altar and proving that the hearth was used for domestic purposes.[27] In Mycenae, in spite of the older excavations which had cleared the *domos* almost completely, Professor Wace discovered in the neighborhood of the hearth a fragment of an altar,[28] proving that there too a portable altar existed by the side of the hearth. So the

[23] Holland, L. B., "Architectural Commentary," *BSA*, 25 (1921-1923), pp. 278-281.

[24] Blegen, C. W., *A.J.A.*, 57 (1953), p. 60.

[25] *BSA*, 25 (1921-1923), p. 241.

[26] *Odyssey*, XIX, 388-389; XXI, 176-185.

[27] *AJA*, 57 (1953), p. 61.

[28] *BSA*, 25 (1921-1923), p. 242, n. 3. I do not think it possible to attribute the fragment to an inner layer of the hearth, because then its survival is unexplainable. We must recall that the tenth layer was the final layer, contemporary with the floor on which the fragment was found. Again, in the course of the restoration of the Megaron and in its *aethousa*, as we have seen, a stone slab was found, face down, which once supported or was a table of offerings. The slab is now in the Museum of Nauplia, and its foundations prove that the hearth was not used just for religious practices.

need for an outlet for the smoke of the hearth still remains. Tsountas, Dörpfeld (for the Palace at Tiryns), and Holland, among others, postulate an opening in the roof which would also have admitted light to the *domos*. The latter, too, must have been an important factor: the *domos* separated from the court by the *prodomos* and the *aethousa* would have depended on doorways not exceeding 1.80 meters in width for its light and air, if a lantern or windows did not exist. The possibility of a window on its southern wall has with reason been excluded by Professor Wace; there remains only the lantern. If such did not exist, then conditions in the domos, which is supposed to have been the most impressive room in the Palace, must have been terrible indeed, what with the lack of light and air and the smoke of the hearth! Recently, evidence for the existence of an opening in the roof of the *domos* was obtained in the Palace at Pylos. Over the hearth area of that palace were found fragments of a large terracotta pipe-like article, indicating clearly that an opening was left in the roof which was further reduced and covered by that article.

One more problem remains to be mentioned here, among the many which are still to be solved, namely, the type of roof used for the Megaron. No evidence whatever has been preserved, and opinions of experts differ. Some believe that the roofs of the megara were sloping, others that they were flat.[29] It seems that the evidence in favor of a flat roof is the more convincing, and I believe that a flat roof should be placed over the Megaron of Mycenae. Its position on the hillside and the adjacent compartments to its north, would have made a sloping roof a very difficult if not impossible undertaking when we consider the materials employed for roof construction and the fact that not a single terracotta tile was found among the ruins of the Palace. A flat roof would accord with the usual Mycenaean practice.

We may now try to visualize the impressive Megaron of Mycenae with its lofty roof and picturesque position above the wall and battlements of the south side of the Citadel. It dominated the west wing, although in a single story, with its tall, slender wooden columns, its walls filled with frescoes, its floors gaily painted, its hearth ablaze with a lively fire, the smoke of which, rising to the blue sky through the lantern in its flat roof, could be seen from afar, from the plain of Argos and from the Lower City. Even its ruins are impressive

[29] *Mycenaean Age*, pp. 53-54; *AJA*, 41 (1942), pp. 99ff. and 370ff.; 49 (1945), pp. 35ff.

today, although to the average visitor they seem puzzling and often unintelligible. To save them from further deterioration and destruction and to make them more intelligible to the visitor, the Greek Service for the Restoration and Preservation of Ancient Monuments undertook in the summer of 1954 to strengthen the remains and to restore in some measure the original ground plan of the Megaron. A heavy retaining wall was built along the southern line of the Megaron which makes possible the restoration of the entire width of its *domos* and the reconstruction of its south wall. The position of all four columns has been indicated on the floor, and the great hearth will be restored to its entire extent, although the original segment will be differentiated from the modern part. Thus the visitor will be able to see clearly at least the plan of this splendid unit of the Palace, the unit where visitors were received and entertained, the unit in which the feud of the Pelopids may have reached its culmination in a series of bloody deeds ending in the flames which consumed the Palace.

We have noted above that at the north side of the *aethousa* a threshold block (1.85 by 0.65 meters) marks the beginning of a passage. Two small pivot holes indicate that the passage was closed by a double door. Remains of burned wood prove that a wooden stairway led from the door to a small landing which marked the end of the South Corridor to the east. So, to the west of the landing we have the corridor; to the north, a retaining wall which supports a terrace of a higher level. To the east we have a series of rooms, the most interesting of which is the one immediately to the east of the landing (Fig. 14-K). It is a rather long and narrow compartment measuring 6 meters in length and 3½ meters in width. A hearth was found against its north wall. Stone benches, covered with white stucco, were arranged along its west and east sides, while painted frescoes apparently covered the surface of all its walls. The subject of these frescoes is puzzling and unusual, for it seems that, instead of the usual figured compositions, curtains or hangings of tapestry are represented. From these we call this compartment "The Room of the Curtain Frescoes." Its use remains uncertain.

To the east of the Room with the Curtain Frescoes a staircase (Fig. 14, L-M), which has been restored, led up to the domestic section. Of the rooms which once existed in that area only scanty remains of walls survive. One of these rooms is of particular interest.

Only its northwest corner is preserved, but it proves that the room had a stepped floor covered with red stucco (Fig. 14-w). A drain on its east and north sides suggests the possibility of its use as a bath. This identification is enthusiastically accepted by the modern Mycenaeans, who see in the red of the stucco the proof that the little room is no other than the bath in which Agamemnon was murdered! However, the plaster which covers its benches and floor will prove untenable this identification.

The Domestic Quarters could thus be reached through the stairway found on the north side of the *aethousa*, the Main Court, and the Grand Staircase. At the northwest corner of the Main Court we have an opening, with a threshold *in situ*, which gave access to West Corridor o, 1.50 meters in width and 8 meters in length, with stuccoed floor (Fig. 14-o). To the right as one enters the West Corridor from the Court, two steps of stone, originally covered with stucco, lead to a landing from which a wooden stairway led westward and to an upper level or story. By means of the West Corridor o, the Main Court communicated with the West Passage (Fig. 14-R) and through it with the northwest entrance to the Palace.

A heavy retaining wall supports the terrace on which the West Passage was located. That wall (Fig. 14-PP) has been cleared for a considerable distance and apparently formed the western limit of the Palace area. Its construction is characteristically Mycenaean, and its frequent setbacks give it an appearance of strength and stability. It seems clear that it is not contemporaneous in its entire length, but that it represents two building periods. Its north end terminates at a paved area, 5.40 by 3.40 meters (Fig. 14-Q), to which led the northeastern branch of the road from the Lion Gate. This paved area is, of course, an outer court, placed in front of another entrance to the Palace, namely the northwest entrance. Unfortunately, that entrance is badly ruined, but Professor Wace was able to determine here the existence of a Propylon with a single column in its outer portico and with two columns in its inner.[30] The use of a single column between antae in a portico, so characteristic of Minoan construction, is proved to have been used in the mainland also by the propylon of the Palace at Pylos.[31] In that propylon a single column was placed on the axis of both its inner and outer porticoes. The monumental character of

[30] *BSA*, 25 (1921-1923), pp. 210-213.
[31] *AJA*, 59 (1955), pl. 23, 1, 2, and 24 and p. 32.

the northwest Propylon of Mycenae is indicated by the fragments of its limestone frieze carved with the triglyph and rosette pattern so characteristic of Mycenaean times.

The West Passage, RR (Fig. 14), begins at this Propylon and, in a rising but gentle grade, continues to the south above and along the retaining wall with the setbacks which supports its terrace. To the east, the passage is limited by the retaining wall supporting the higher terrace of the Palace. It is possible that on this east side an entrance to the North Corridor once existed; nothing, however, survives of such an entrance today. But from the passage access was obtained to the South Corridor by means of a small open space and a portal, known as the Western Portal (Fig. 14-U), whose huge threshold block (3.17 meters long and 1.10 meters wide) is still *in situ*. Beyond the Western Portal to the south the area is so destroyed that no conclusions are possible. But it seems reasonable to assume that some access to the West Corridor, o, was provided; it further seems possible to assume that the passage ended at the northwestern end of the Forecourt D above the Grand Stairway. Thus the West Passage was an important element in the plan of the Palace and provided an easy, although lengthy, access to the Domestic Quarters through the South Corridor, to the Main Court and the Megaron through the West Corridor, and to the Square Room (hostel?) through its Forecourt.

There remain to be discussed the scanty remnants of a room on the uppermost terrace of the Palace which was identified as the Shrine. It lies on the north side of the North Corridor and a good deal of it is under the foundations of the later Greek temple (Fig. 14-v). In the room Professor Wace found two movable "altars or hearths or tables of offerings of painted stucco on a clay backing." On the basis of these he called the room a Shrine.[32] We feel that the evidence does not justify the name. Fragments of altars were found in other parts of the Palace by Tsountas, and Professor Wace found a fragment beside the hearth of the Megaron and another in the Central Lobby of the Grand Staircase;[33] all these parts could not have been shrines. Furthermore, in the same room was found pottery similar to that discovered in other rooms of the Palace, "two spindle whorls, of the ordinary Mycenaean (Late Helladic III) type, two terracotta spindle whorls of a conical shape, a small tri-

[32] *BSA*, 25 (1921-1923), pp. 223-229.   [33] *Ibid.*, p. 154.

angular piece of stone possibly from some inlay, two or three scraps of gold foil, a small carnelian bead, an amygdaloid bead of glass paste, another glass paste bead shaped like a grain of wheat, part of a small plaque of glass paste, a lead disc, a rolled bronze band, an obsidian and a flint arrow head." Of course the original contents of the room did not remain until the time of the excavation, but what survived does not seem to characterize the room as a shrine. The spindle whorls and the arrow heads seem especially out of place. They seem to indicate that the room was another magazine or storeroom, and certainly such was the room immediately to the west of it. In his general discussion of a Mycenaean palace, Professor Wace states: "the palace was divided by long corridors and off them on the ground floor were storerooms."[34] Certainly off the South and North Corridors of the Palace of Mycenae all the identifiable rooms seem to be storerooms. A Shrine would indeed be out of place among them. The coarse plaster from its walls would also strengthen the suggestion of its use as a storeroom; a magazine in which the altars or tables of offerings were stored in a manner similar to that disclosed at Nirou Chani by the excavations of Xanthoudides.[35]

In the 1939 excavations Professor Wace discovered a lovely ivory group representing "two women squatting with a boy standing by the knees of one of them," in the fill of two rooms lying against and below the great north terrace wall of the Greek temple.[36] In the group the discoverer recognized Demeter, Persephone, and the boy Iakchos, and suggested that they might have belonged to the so-called Shrine, from whence they had rolled to the place where they were discovered. At the same time the existence of this group was used to strengthen the theory that the room was a shrine. Before we can use it as evidence, however, we first have to prove that the group actually came from that room and then that it represents divinities. Both requirements are impossible to prove. Professor Nilsson has already pointed out that the boy could not be Iakchos and that there is nothing in the group to indicate that the figures are divinities.[37] On the other hand, these figures seem to be of the same age, and there is nothing to indicate that the one is older, and therefore Demeter, and the other younger, and therefore Persephone.

[34] *Mycenae*, p. 104. [35] *Ephemeris*, 1922, pp. 15-16.
[36] *JHS*, 59 (1939), p. 210; Mycenae, pp. 83-84, figs. 101-102.
[37] *Minoan-Mycenaean Religion*, 2nd ed., p. xxiv, in spite of Picard, *Religions prehélleniques*, pp. 244-245.

A group which can serve as a parallel to the ivory of the Palace, but in terracotta, was found by Tsountas in tomb No. 79 of Mycenae.[38] The terracotta group is composed of two female figurines of the well-known Φ type, attached to each other at the side and bearing on their connected shoulder a seated child. Another parallel is now available and that also was found in the grave of a child. It was discovered by Dr. J. Papademetriou and D. Theochares in the spring of 1954 in the cemetery of Voula. Again a child is seated on the connected shoulder of two Φ-shaped terracotta figurines attached to each other at the side like Siamese twins. The meaning of the Mycenaean terracotta female figurines, which characterize the last two centuries of the Late Helladic period, is not entirely established, especially the meaning of those found in graves. Some scholars believe that they served the needs of their masters like the *ushebtis* of the Egyptians; others that they represent slaves, wives, and concubines; others that they were the symbols which could insure the comfort of the deceased in the lower world.[39] I believe that figurines of type Φ are "divine nurses" placed in graves of children. Certainly they cannot be identified with Demeter and Persephone. One might suggest that the ivory group also served the same purpose as the terracotta double figurines, and it was prepared to be deposited in a grave, a purpose which the destruction of the Palace made impossible. Thus the presence of the ivory group cannot prove that the small room on the top of the hill was a shrine. That a shrine was contained in the Palace is quite possible, almost certain, but unfortunately we cannot know where it was located, for it was destroyed without leaving any trace.

The orientation of the Hellenistic temple, from north to south instead of in the conventional east-west direction, is used in defense of the identification. But there is a great lapse of time here, and we do not know what the orientation of the Archaic temple was, because from that temple only a piece or so of a cornice and some fragments of sculpture have survived. We also have to remember that the Palace was destroyed at the end of the Bronze Age; that its site apparently was not occupied in Proto-Geometric times; that the earliest remains of the historic period belong to the Geometric period.

[38] A drawing of this figurine was published by Professor Marinatos in *AA*, 1933, p. 303, fig. 15. Cf. Mylonas, in *Geras*, pp. 46-49.
[39] See *infra*, pp. 78-82, for a fuller discussion of the problem.

The Mycenaean shrine, on the other hand, was not an individual building whose orientation was known and remembered, but a unit whose remains would not be distinguishable in the piles of burned debris. Its orientation, therefore, could hardly have been remembered even by the sons of the survivors, especially since no fixed orientation seems to have been observed in Minoan-Mycenaean shrines. We have to find another reason to account for the orientation of the Hellenistic temple. Perhaps the fact that the rock rises from west to east, a rise which would have necessitated the cutting away of hard rock to mark an area large enough for the temple, forced its builders to orient it from north to south, thus laying its entire length upon easily handled debris that offered, for the Hellenistic inhabitants of a small village, a sufficiently strong base for its construction. In that way a lot of work would have been eliminated, of course at the expense of stability and durability; but perhaps these qualities were of secondary importance in the minds of simple and rather poor villagers.

The area immediately around the Palace has not been fully investigated. Only a small section to the southwest of the Square Room by the west retaining wall, known as the pithos area from some storage jars found there and belonging to the Hellenistic period (Fig. 14-T), was explored by Tsountas. Among other things in the fill, Tsountas found a copper ingot, in the shape of an ox hide, *a talent*, the only remnant of the treasures kept in the Palace, and fragments of frescoes. Many of the fragments seem to be burned and apparently were thrown away in a period of reconstruction. On some we find representations of women carrying small cylindrical vases, on others geometric patterns in which the spiral predominates, and on still others decorative plant motives such as lotus patterns and the like.

The remains of the Palace which can be seen today and which we have briefly described belong to its last period of occupancy, to the closing century of the Mycenaean Age. However, the life history of the Palace goes beyond that, and its many phases have been carefully and convincingly worked out by Professor Wace.[40] The curiously oblique orientation of the Grand Staircase certainly proves that it was a later addition to the large unit of Forecourt, Square Room, Court, and Megaron. That unit, known as the southwest wing, occupied a wide terrace and its careful axial design indicates that

[40] For the history of the Palace construction, see Wace, *Mycenae*, pp. 86-90.

it belongs together. But that too is proved, by the abandonment of the Pillar Room, to have succeeded an earlier structure; furthermore, the reused blocks of the great drain, the lower ashlar course of the north wall of the Court, and the fragments of the discarded frescoes, would indicate that it had undergone a restoration and reconstruction some time after its erection. Apparently the reconstruction was necessitated after fire had considerably damaged the south wing. This wing is known to rest on an artificial terrace, filled in with loose stones and apparently retained by the Cyclopean wall of the *enceinte*. Consequently it and the unit it supports must have been built after the construction of the Cyclopean wall, which belongs to what we have termed the first building period. It was then, during the period of ambitious construction, that the Palace was redesigned, that "the site was adapted to a well-thought-out plan," that the "bold terracing and leveling" noticeable on the south slopes of the Citadel occurred. And so in the ruins of the southwest wing visible today we can detect three phases of construction. To the first belonged the Pillar Room and the original Court and Megaron.[41] It was brought to an end by a great fire which caused the filling in and abandonment of the Pillar Room. The second is the phase of reconstruction and restoration of the southwest wing on its original lines following the great fire. To this phase also belong the construction of the northwestern entrance and the building of the road which led to it from the Lion Gate. To the third belongs the Grand Staircase.

The date of the three phases cannot be definitely established. But under the floor of the Pillar Room were found sherds belonging to the Late Helladic III A period, proving that its construction took place after that period had begun. Late Helladic III A is usually made to cover the years from 1425 to 1300 B.C.[42] Since the construction of the Pillar Room occurred after the period was well on its way, we may feel sure in assigning it to the middle of the fourteenth

---

[41] Mackeprang considers the Pillar Room older than the Court-Megaron unit, because "part of the west wall of the court rests upon the east wall of the Pillar Basement and the Court is an inseparable part of the Megaron," *AJA*, 42 (1938), pp. 555ff. However, that wall was restored in sections after the fire, and the part based on the wall of the Pillar Room may have been such a restoration and consequently of no chronological significance for the original relation of Pillar Room to Court. See also Wace, *Mycenae*, p. 133, n. 5.

[42] For the sherds under the floor of the Pillar Room, cf. *BSA*, 25 (1921-1923), pl. xxxi, and *AJA*, 42 (1938), p. 555. For the date, cf. Furumark, A., *Chronology*, pp. 113-115; Wace, *BSA*, 48 (1953), p. 15, n. 22; and *supra*, pp. 13 and 34.

century, to *c.* 1350 B.C. To that date we can assign the first construction of the southwest wing and the building of the Cyclopean wall which acted as its retaining wall. Just when that original wing was destroyed by fire will remain uncertain. One wonders whether or not that destruction could be associated with the burning of the houses of the oil merchant, of the sphinxes, and of the shields beyond the Acropolis walls which occurred in Late Helladic III B times; and whether or not the rebuilding of the wing, which marks the second phase, the laying out of the road which led from the Lion Gate to the northwestern entrance, and the construction of that entrance occurred at the time when the Lion Gate was constructed. Perhaps the Grand Staircase was erected when the northeastern extension of the *enceinte* was added.

The ruins of walls and the floor levels, however, indicate that before 1350 B.C. a palace stood on top of the hill, erected on its natural terraces and especially on its south slope. These remains Professor Wace traces back to the beginning of the Late Helladic I period, when at least a first palace was erected to serve the needs of the rulers buried in the royal shaft graves explored by Schliemann. Successive kings added to it and modified it until the days of the building of the Cyclopean walls of the first period, when it was redesigned and the southwest wing, the most distinctive part of the Palace, was added to it.

We have suggested that Perseus was the builder of the Cyclopean walls of the first period; to him and to his architects we should like to attribute the redesigning of the Palace and the construction of the original southwest wing. Whether that is so or not is impossible to prove, but it is certain that the Pelopids lived in the Palace whose remains we have, and that the Megaron is the one within which Agamemnon grew to become the leader of the Achaeans and where he returned to find an untimely death after the destruction of Troy. The Megaron and its Court, which the visitor can see and inspect, is indeed an important part of the πολύφθορον δῶμα Πελοπιδῶν, "of the Palace of the Pelopids, deep stained with murder." The maze of ruins, brought back to life again by the spade of the excavator, and by the efforts of the Greek Service to restore them to a semblance of their past splendor, would perhaps bring to his mind the poet's exhortation: ἄναγε δόμοι πολὺν ἄγαν χρόνον χαμαιπετεῖς ἔκεισθ᾽ ἀεί.[43]

---

[43] Sophocles, *Electra*, 8-10. Aeschylos, *Choephoroi*, 963-964: "Arise ye halls! Too long a while have ye lain prostrate on the ground."

Within the fortified area of the Citadel apparently lived a few families, perhaps related to the ruling dynasty, or perhaps the families of the military leaders and officers. A number of houses have already been cleared in the Citadel and perhaps more are awaiting excavation. Of these the most important was found at a short distance to the southeast of the Palace, on a terrace supported by the Cyclopean wall at the point of the south tower (Fig. 7-L). It was excavated by Tsountas and was further explored, cleared, and designed by Professor Wace.[44] It is now known as the House of Columns, from the numerous columns which once stood in its court. A long corridor leads from the doorway to this court, which was open to the sky and around which are arranged the rooms and compartments of the house. Beyond its north side we have the Megaron, divided into three sections, a stairway leading to an upper story, and an inner room. Rooms and a basement with four magazines flank the court on its west side, while more basement rooms may be seen beyond its south side. In the east basement room, across corridor Y, a number of stirrup vases were found, on the shoulder of one of which is painted an inscription in Linear Script B. The vase and the inscription are similar to those found at Tiryns, Eleusis, Thebes, and Orchomenos.[45] On the south side, the house rose to three stories, counting the basement as one. Corridors and one large room flank the court on the east side. The house is large and impressive, a dwelling for some influential family. Professor Wace has pointed out how this house parallels the house of Odysseus as closely as one could expect.

Five more houses or structures have been explored on the west and lowest section of the Citadel (Fig. 7, M-O).[46] The first was built right against the Cyclopean wall and between it and the northwest section of the Grave Circle, immediately to the south of the Lion Gate (Fig. 7-M). It is known as the Granary because of the carbonized barley, wheat, and vetches found stored in vessels in its basement. Two basement rooms and two long adjacent and parallel corridors are the characteristic features of this building, which perhaps stood three stories in height (if we count the basement as one). The Granary

[44] For a complete description and discussion of this house and especially its relation to the Homeric House, see Wace, *Mycenae*, pp. 91-97 and fig. 33.

[45] For inscribed vases, see *Archaeology*, 1 (1948), p. 217; *Palace of Minos*, IV, pp. 739-746; Caratelli, "Le iscrizioni preelleniche di Haghia Triada in Creta e della Grecia peninsulare," *Mon. Ant.*, 40 (1945), pp. 603-610, and pls. XXX-L.

[46] For a discussion of these houses, see Wace, *Mycenae*, pp. 54-58, 64-68, and figs. 3 and 25; *BSA*, 25 (1921-1923), pp. 38-96.

was apparently erected after the construction of the Cyclopean wall and the rearrangement of the Grave Circle, in Late Helladic III B times; it was reconstructed and its corridors extended perhaps in Late Helladic III c times; and finally it was destroyed by fire at the end of the Late Helladic III c period. Among its ruins was found a type of pottery produced in the closing years of the Mycenaean era, known as the Granary style.

To the south of the Grave Circle the remains of four houses have been cleared. Three of them were excavated in 1876 by Schliemann, who recognized in their ruins the Palace of Atreus (Fig. 7, N and O). Later explorations of the area by Tsountas and Professor Wace proved that they belonged to houses of the closing period of the Mycenaean era. These are now known as the Ramp House, the House of the Warrior Vase, the South House, and the House of Tsountas. They have been designed to fit the area they occupy, but in the main they exhibit similar features: a court, a megaron-like main apartment, adjacent rooms, and especially basement rooms. The most important is that known as the House of Tsountas (Fig. 7-O), built on an area immediately to the northeast of the so-called "polygonal tower." The court, the megaron, with a square fireplace in the middle of its *domos*, side rooms, and basement magazines, above which once stood other rooms, are clearly defined. Its walls seem to have been coated with fine plaster painted with fresco. To such a fresco must belong a fragment with the well-known three figures with asses' heads bearing a pole.[47]

Each of these houses has contributed to our knowledge through the discovery of elements other than its architectural remains. Among the ruins of the Ramp House, for example, Drosenos found a treasure of gold objects which may belong to a shaft grave. Also among its ruins were found frescoes with representations of sports, bull grappling, and acrobatic displays. The House of the Warrior Vase, as the name implies, has yielded the well-known Crater of Warriors and also proof of the use of wooden thresholds corresponding to the δρύϊνος (oaken) and μέλινος οὐδός (ashen threshold) of Homer. All the houses illustrate the structural system of the Mycenaeans: a wall construction of rubble masonry and wooden framework; timbers set horizontally and vertically so as to form quadrangular panels, by means of which a superstructure of mud-brick was supported and tied

---

[47] *Mycenaean Age*, fig. 156.

to the rubble part of the wall. This system of timber-framing was used even in the construction of the palaces and in parts where ashlar masonry was employed.

The houses were looted and destroyed by fire toward the end of Late Helladic III c, the end of the Mycenaean period, and around 1100 B.C. Thus they shared the fate of the Palace on top of the hill and stand as witnesses of the great destruction which befell the Citadel sometime toward the end of the twelfth century—a destruction which brought to an end the supremacy and cultural activity of Mycenae.

IV

HOUSES AND GRAVES BEYOND THE CITADEL

THE RULERS of Mycenae, their relatives, and perhaps their friends, had their dwellings in the Citadel. The people at large lived beyond the walls and, as we have seen, in small groups surrounded by the graves of their ancestors. Although a great number of tombs were systematically cleared even in the early phase of the exploration of Mycenae, only recently has attention been concentrated on the houses of the living. But as yet, not a single complete house has been brought to light beyond the walls of the Citadel.

The first remains of a house outside the Citadel were discovered and cleared in 1923 by Professor Wace on the north slope of the ridge of the Lion Tomb, outside even the Hellenistic wall of the Lower City. They are made up of a heavy wall built in the Cyclopean style (and therefore known as the "Cyclopean Terrace Wall") and parts of two rooms which it supports. The nature of the building has not been determined, although its ruins were further investigated in 1951.[1] It seems that it dates from the Late Helladic III B period and that it was no longer inhabited in Late Helladic III c times, since on the top of its fill, burials of those times were disclosed. To the southwest of the first wall, a second terrace wall was found and at its western end a "ruined storeroom which seems to have been wantonly destroyed." In it were discovered at least eight pithoi, 1.70 meters tall, and some fifty stirrup vases. Among them was found in 1952 a superb rhyton, measuring 0.55 meters in height and decorated with an octopus pattern brilliantly painted in red-brown color picked out with white. There is no doubt in the minds of the excavators that the storeroom belonged to the house of a wine merchant.[2]

To the east of the House of the Wine Merchant, Dr. John Papademetriou and F. Petsas, in their exploratory campaign of 1950, revealed the foundations of at least four different storerooms. In one

[1] *BSA*, 25 (1921-1923), pp. 403-407, and 48 (1953), pp. 15-16; *JHS*, 72 (1952), pp. 97ff.
[2] *BSA*, 48 (1953), pp. 16-17.

of them, more than five hundred unused vases of the Late Helladic III B period were found, neatly packed. As yet the house or houses to which these rooms belong have not been cleared, but from the evidence obtained here and elsewhere it is clear that the Mycenaean houses had magazines, often in their basement, where vases were stored. Some 20 meters to the south of these storerooms and on the surface of the field was found a clay tablet bearing an inscription in the well-known Minoan-Mycenaean Linear Script B. It is the first tablet to be found at Mycenae, although objects bearing signs were known since the days of Tsountas' excavations.[3]

As yet the history of the area in which these house-remains were found is not clear, but it seems that all of them were destroyed by fire in Late Helladic III B times.

To the south of the Tomb of Clytemnestra and close to the east side of the modern road which leads from the village to the Citadel, Professor Wace and his associates brought to light the remains of three adjacent houses. The middle structure has been cleared completely and because of its contents it has been called "The House of the Oil Merchant."[4] Only its basement has survived and it consists of one long corridor, running from north to south, and some seven rooms or compartments opening to the east of it (Fig. 21). At the north end of the corridor some thirty stirrup jars of Late Helladic III B times were found. Most of them still had stoppers in their spouts, with the original seals over them. Apparently they once contained oil, with which their clay is impregnated, and were deliberately smashed so that the oil they contained would add fuel to the flames which destroyed the house.

The northernmost room, No. 1, proved very interesting. Around its wall were found, set in small bases and in alcoves with low clay side-walls, eleven large storage jars or pithoi, apparently used for storing oil (Fig. 21-1). Under one of them an arrangement for heating was provided, another proof that oil was stored in the pithoi. Behind another and in the northeastern corner of the room was found an inscribed clay tablet broken in three pieces. It seemed "analogous," writes Professor Wace, "to an old piece of paper torn up and thrown in a corner." Thirty-seven additional tablets were found in Room 2;

[3] For a brief report of this exploration, cf. *PAE*, 1950, pp. 203-233. *Mycenaean Age*, pp. 268-269, for objects bearing signs.
[4] *JHS*, 71 (1951), pp. 255ff. and figs. 1, 2; *BSA*, 48 (1953), pp. 9-15.

apparently they had fallen from the floor above (Fig. 23). They are also covered with signs in the Minoan-Mycenaean Linear Script B, and most of these seem to be records of accounts. Room 4 was found filled with vases of the Late Helladic III B style. In the corridor as well as in some of the rooms, fragments of frescoes were found, apparently fallen from the rooms above, proving the importance of the house.

To the north of the House of the Oil Merchant two rooms of a second house have been excavated thus far (end of the 1953 campaign). They have yielded a unique collection of carved ivories of exquisite workmanship and detail. Among these are ivory plaques bearing the carved figures of lions and a great number of model figure-of-eight Mycenaean shields, from which the house has been named the "House of the Shields." One represents the helmeted head of a Mycenaean warrior. Some of the ivories were probably used as inlays for furniture, in a manner described fully in the Homeric poems. A series of fine stone vases were also found in the rooms, as well as part of an Egyptian alabaster vase of the XVIIIth Dynasty.

To the south of the House of the Oil Merchant, only fragmentary remains of another structure were found, known as the "House of the Sphinxes" from a carved ivory plaque bearing two sphinxes facing each other and heraldically placed with their forepaws resting on the capital of a fluted column. Again, a quantity of carved ivory was found among which are models of Mycenaean columns and some four plaques with sphinxes. We ought perhaps to emphasize the fact that "no comparable collection of ivories has been found for at least sixty years."[5] A tablet in the Linear Script B and seven seal impressions, all from the same signet, were also found in this house. On the front of each impression we have the representation of a man standing between two wild goats. On the back of the impressions are inscribed a few signs of Linear Script B, again illustrating the use of the script for common purposes.

All three houses were destroyed by fire in Late Helladic III B times. It is unfortunate that, due to their location on the sloping hillside, only their basements have been preserved. Still, their remains have contributed considerably to our knowledge of the Mycenaean house and of Mycenae's culture. First of all, they corroborate the evidence obtained in the Citadel that basement rooms were a common

[5] *JHS*, 74 (1954), pp. 170-171 and pl. x.

feature of the Mycenaean house, a characteristic mentioned several times in the *Odyssey*. Then, the existence of large and—as their contents prove—prosperous houses beyond the walls of the Citadel seems to indicate that in the thirteenth century Mycenae enjoyed peace and prosperity. The burning of the houses in the Lower City seems to correspond to that of the Palace, evidenced by the remains of the Megaron and Court unit. Could that burning be attributed to the civil strife reflected in the legendary feud of Atreus and Thyestes which marks the transition of power from the Perseid to the Pelopid dynasty? Or, could the burning be attributed to a hostile invasion?

In trying to answer these questions, we must bear in mind that Crete as a powerful state had passed out of existence about 1400 B.C.; that no other power existed in continental Greece capable of inflicting such blows on the Mycenae of the thirteenth century; that the Palace was rebuilt right after it was burned; and that Mycenae continued to be prosperous and powerful in the years which followed. These facts seem to exclude a destruction by a foreign power. The probability that the fire was caused by an upheaval, by an outbreak of civil strife which resulted from the struggle for power, is more likely. The Mycenaean legends have preserved the story of the feud of Atreus and Thyestes over the assumption of authority.[6] The date of the destruction of these houses and of the Palace by fire, perhaps *c.* 1250 B.C., will agree well with the beginning of the Pelopid dynasty: one generation before the coming of Agamemnon, who took part in the sack of Troy.

Another important result of Professor Wace's exploration of the houses is the discovery of inscribed tablets in the house of commoners.[7] No tablets have been reported from the Palace area, although an inscribed stirrup jar was found in a basement room of the House of Columns. However, a good deal of that area was telescoped in later years and its evidence was perhaps completely destroyed then. From the Palace at Pylos we learn that special archives rooms were used for the keeping of the tablets in the mainland as they were in Crete. Very few specimens were discovered outside the archives rooms even in Pylos. There can be no doubt that such an archives room existed in the Palace of Mycenae, perhaps among the storerooms off the

---

[6] Wace, *JHS*, 74 (1954), p. 171; *ILN*, December 1950, pp. 1941ff.

[7] For these tablets, see Bennett, E., and Wace, "The Mycenae Tablets," *PAPS*, 97 (1953), pp. 422-470. For those of Pylos, see Bennett, *The Pylos Tablets* and *Minoan Linear B Index*.

North Corridor, and that the room and its contents were destroyed by later operations. The tablets from the House of the Olive Merchant are mostly records of business transactions. They are comparable to those found by Professor Blegen in Pylos, and they prove that the script was used not only by and for the rulers but also by common people for regular business transactions. They prove the literacy of the people of Mycenae and thus put an end to certain theories about illiteracy in the later Mycenaean world. The σήματα λυγρά, the baneful tokens, of the famous passage in the *Iliad* were so called because they were θυμοφθόρα (life-destroying) and not because they seemed mysterious to an illiterate people.[8]

The pioneer work of the late Alice Kober and of Professor J. Sundwall, the discoveries of Professor Blegen at Pylos, the studies of Bennett and of Ktistopoulos, and finally the work of Ventris, have shed considerable light on the tablets of the mainland of Greece and the Linear Script B and have opened up the road for its final and complete decipherment.[9] Scholarship will be especially indebted to Ventris, whose achievement can be considered one of the greatest in that field. There seems to be no doubt that the script employed in those tablets, Script B, developed from the Minoan Script A; that Script B was introduced from the mainland to Knossos, the only Cretan site where it has been found thus far—perhaps introduced by the conquering Achaeans who controlled Knossos in Late Minoan II times (a probability advanced by many scholars but not proved as yet); that the language used is the Greek language of the historic period, while that of Script A seems to be pre-Hellenic. A good many readings suggested by Ventris and interpreted by Ventris-Chadwick seem to be correct,[10] including those of Professor Blegen's extraordinary Pylos tablet recording an inventory of vases;[11] others are still to be made and interpreted satisfactorily; but the fact seems to have been established that Greek was written and consequently spoken at Mycenae during the Late Helladic III period.

[8] *Iliad*, VI, 168-170; Harland, J. P., *AJA*, 38 (1934), p. 84; Nilsson, M., *Homer and Mycenae*, pp. 78-79.

[9] For a complete bibliography, see Dow, S., "Minoan Writing," *AJA*, 58 (1954), pp. 77-129.

[10] "Evidence for Greek Dialect in the Mycenaean Archives," *JHS*, 73 (1953), pp. 84-103.

[11] Blegen, "An Inscribed Tablet from Pylos," *Volume in Memoriam G. P. Oekonomos*, pp. 59-62.

The graves built during the period characterized by the construction of the Cyclopean walls and that of the first great Palace on top of the Citadel are well known and rather numerous. They are distinguished into two types: chamber tombs and tholos or beehive tombs.[12] The former were apparently used for and by the people, the latter by royalty.

The chamber tombs are underground, cave-like graves cut horizontally into the slope of a hillside, either in the rock or in earth below a crust of rock. They are composed of two parts: a chamber and a *dromos*, the horizontal approach to the former. The *dromos* is open to the sky and is usually cut at right angles to the chamber and the slope. Its floor inclines either gradually or sharply, depending on its length, so as to allow enough depth to make possible the carving of the chamber completely in the rock. Sometimes the required depth is attained by means of steps. In our period, in Late Helladic III times, the *dromos* is usually long (Tomb 505 of Mycenae has a *dromos* 35 meters in length) and its sides incline toward each other so that the opening above is very much narrower than the width of the floor. The *dromos* leads to a rectangular doorway, with a horizontal lintel and sides inclining inward, thus making the opening at the top narrower than that at the bottom. No thresholds or arrangement for a door are known, but occasionally the face of the doorway was covered with plaster and decorated in color with rosettes or other geometric patterns. The chamber, hewn in the living rock, presents a variety of shapes ranging from oval to round to rectangular, and of varied dimensions. The largest chamber at Mycenae measures 5.50 by 6.50 meters and has a height of 6.50 to 7.00 meters.[13] The roofs of the chambers are also varied and their shape depends in the main on the quality of the rock in which they were hewn. Most of the Mycenaean roofs are "slightly hipped."[14] In some examples side chambers are to be found; in others, niches are cut in the walls.

[12] For descriptions and discussions of these tombs, see especially: Tsountas-Manatt, *Mycenaean Age*, pp. 115-158; Tsountas, *Ephemeris*, 1888, pp. 119-180; Wace, *BSA*, 25 (1921-1923), pp. 283-402; *Chamber Tombs at Mycenae*, especially pp. 121-146; Wace, *Mycenae*, pp. 13-19, 26-46, 119-131. Blegen, *Prosymna*, especially pp. 228-263; Persson, *The Royal Tombs at Dendra Near Midea, New Tombs at Dendra*, and *Asine*, pp. 356-359.

[13] Wace, *Chamber Tombs*, p. 12. Tomb No. 505 of Mycenae. It is almost equal to the tomb found by Tsountas on the west side of the Makri Lithari.

[14] Three of the Dendra chamber tombs exhibit a "saddle roof" and the same is true of tomb I:2 of Asine: Persson, *The Royal Tombs of Dendra*, pp. 75 and 98; *New Tombs at Dendra*, p. 158; *Asine*, pp. 163 and 358.

Again, on the floor of some, both in the *dromos* and in the chamber, pits or cists were dug; in others a bench is to be found in the chamber, built or carved out of the rock.

The chamber tombs were family graves and were used over and over again in the course of the centuries. It is a well-established fact that only inhumation was practiced during Mycenaean times, and it seems that the dead were placed in a more or less extended position on the floor of the chamber without regard to orientation. Sometimes the head was raised on a support. We have no evidence from Mycenae that coffins were employed for the burial. Gifts and possessions, known as *kterismata*, were carefully arranged around the body. Vases were the most common gifts; ornaments and personal possessions were also common; sometimes even tools were placed by the body. It seems that after the burial a toast was drunk in honor of the interred, and the goblet used for the purpose was smashed against the doorway of the chamber.[15] Fragments of these shattered cups found in a number of graves attest to the custom. Then the door was completely blocked by a stone wall, and the *dromos* was filled with earth, recalling the χεύειν χυτὴν γαῖαν, piling of earth, typical of Homeric burials. A funeral meal seems to have been the concluding act of the burial rites, and a marker, or σῆμα, was placed over the grave for identification purposes. When a second death in the family occurred and the grave was to be used again, the earth from the *dromos* as well as the wall blocking the doorway was removed and the body and its funeral offerings were laid on the floor at the side of the earlier burial. The door was blocked again, a toast was offered, the funeral meal was eaten, and the *dromos* was filled with earth. This ceremony was repeated over the years and as the need arose. When the floor was filled with bodies, the remains of those buried before and their offerings were pushed aside and against the walls of the chamber, or were placed in side chambers and niches, or in the cists cut in the floor of the chamber or of the *dromos*. Sometimes bones and broken offerings were thrown out of the chamber and into the *dromos*, in order to make room for later burials in the chamber. This operation was characterized by lack of respect for the bones of ancestors. Furthermore, on the occasion of this cleaning up, the older offerings were broken, and apparently objects of value, such as

[15] *Prosymna*, p. 238; *Chamber Tombs*, p. 131; Marinatos, in Keramopoullos' *Geras*, p. 65.

jewelry and weapons of metal, were stolen by the very relatives of the deceased.

This behavior, in contrast to the reverence and care exhibited for the bodies at the time of burial, sheds a good deal of light on the beliefs of the Mycenaeans regarding an existence after death. It can be explained only if we assume that they believed that the spirit of man, what Homer called the "psyche," was sentient and remained around the grave as long as the flesh was in existence. During this time the corpse had to be treated with respect; it had to be provided with supplies; it had to be given favorite objects which belonged to it in life. The moment the flesh was dissolved and the body was transformed into a pile of bones, the spirit was believed to be released from this world, to have descended into its final abode never to return to the world of the living. It was no longer interested in the affairs of the living, nor could it influence their future. And so the bones could with impunity be swept aside or even thrown out of the grave. The fact that the offerings were stolen and broken after a while proves that they were not meant for the lower world, that they were meant for the trip to that world. The end of that journey was indicated by the complete decay of the flesh. The fact that ornaments of precious metal and even weapons of bronze were taken by the descendants seems to indicate that personal objects were laid in the grave with the body, not to serve it in the lower world, but because of fear of exciting the anger and revenge of the dead by withholding objects in which he had pleasure in life—anger which could be a potential carrier of disaster during the period when the dead were still sentient and abode in the grave, during the time, in other words, when the flesh was still intact.[16]

We must also note that the funeral offerings were not renewed from time to time, nor were additional gifts placed in the graves; in its last abode the spirit had no need of gifts. This, along with the lack of respect shown for the remains of ancestors, proves definitely that no cult of the dead existed in Mycenaean times as is usually assumed. Such a cult is incompatible with the attitude of the living toward the bones of the dead. At any rate, no evidence indicating such a cult has been unearthed thus far.[17]

[16] For an account of the rites and beliefs, cf. Mylonas, "Homeric and Mycenaean Burial Customs," *AJA*, 52 (1948), pp. 56-81.

[17] Cf. Mylonas, "The Cult of the Dead in Helladic Times," *Studies Presented to David Moore Robinson*, I, pp. 64-105.

Signs of fire, remnants of charcoal and ashes found in chamber tombs, are now proved to be the results of fumigation and purification of the chamber necessitated by its long use and the repeated burials over centuries. Niches found in chambers and in *dromoi*, which have been cited as indicating the existence of a cult of the dead, are proved to have been used for burials and especially for the burial of children. The evidence available to date seems to prove that a cult of the dead was practiced around Mycenaean chamber tombs, but not in Mycenaean times. It seems that such a cult was started in Late Geometric times and was continued into the Classical era.

No evidence for embalming was obtained in the chamber tombs, and it seems certain that this art was not practiced by the Mycenaeans. The number of buttons of terracotta or of steatite found in the graves proves that the bodies were laid fully clothed on the floor and occasionally on wooden biers. Among the funeral offerings we must note the vases, of excellent quality, most of them painted with brilliant colors and interesting designs. The spiral was the favorite motive throughout the period, but plant and marine motives were also common. They were at first rendered in a realistic manner, but with the passing of years they became more and more stylized until they became mere decorative patterns. Their study, started by Furtwängler and Löschke, has been greatly advanced, especially through the efforts of Professors Wace, Blegen, and Furumark.[18]

Small terracotta figurines are included among the funeral offerings from chamber tombs.[19] The meaning of these figurines has not been established as yet, and at times various interpretations have been advanced. They appear abruptly about 1300 B.C. and are characteristic of the closing centuries of the Mycenaean era. Some of them represent long-horned animals; there are a few chariots; some are in the form of three-legged chairs; but the majority represent female figures. The last mentioned have been divided into various types, the most important of which are types Φ and Ψ, as they have been called by Professor Furumark (Fig. 27, a, b). Both types possess a cylindrical

---

[18] Besides the works of Wace and Blegen cited above, see Furumark, A., *The Mycenaean Pottery*, 1941, and *The Chronology of Mycenaean Pottery*, 1941.

[19] Tsountas, *Ephemeris*, 1888, pp. 168-169; Blegen, *Zygouries*, pp. 203-206, and *Prosymna*, pp. 355-360. Wace, *Chamber Tombs at Mycenae*, pp. 215-217. Furumark, *The Chronology of Mycenaean Pottery*, pp. 86-89. Picard, "Oushabti égéens," *Rev. des ét. anc.*, 32 (1930), pp. 97ff.

lower part, but type Φ presents an oval, flat torso, lacking hands; a pinched-in face; and a flat, triangular head. Occasionally figurines of this type are modeled with a "stephane," or wreath, on the head. Their sex is clearly indicated by well-modeled breasts placed on the flat torso. Figurines of type Ψ possess an equally flat torso with less prominent but still well-defined breasts, but the shoulders are drawn out sharply to form wing-like projections giving the torso a half moon or sickle shape. They also have pinched-in faces with prominent noses and triangular, flat heads which as a rule are covered with a stephane. From the rear edge of the stephane originates a narrow and flat plastic band, dotted horizontally with color, which hangs vertically behind the neck, often reaching to the waist. Both types are decorated by parallel stripes painted in brilliant black to brown color, indicating garments. Figurines of the Φ and Ψ types have also been found in what we may assume to be sanctuaries or shrines of the period.

Closely allied to the two types described above are figurines known as *kourotrophoi*, i.e., figurines distinguished by the form of a baby which is thrust against the breast and held there by atrophied hands, or precariously stuck against the stripes below the breasts (Fig. 27, d). A variation of the *kourotrophos* type are "multiple figurines," two examples of which are thus far known, both coming from graves. Two figurines of type Φ are attached to each other at the side, like Siamese twins, and bear a child on their common shoulder.

A good number of figurines are known not only from this site, but also from other Mycenaean sites in the mainland of Greece. They were seldom used in Crete, and there they certainly were an intrusive element. Unfortunately, the conditions under which most of them were found are not recorded. Some were discovered in the piles of bones swept aside and against the walls of chamber tombs, and therefore their original position will remain unknown. Others were found in disturbed context; of others still, we have no information whatsoever. And yet the conditions under which they were found will, I believe, help us considerably to determine their meaning and function. Long ago Kandanes remarked that a good many of the figurines found in the Nauplia district came from graves of children.[20] Recently Professor Blegen observed that the majority of the figurines he found in Prosymna were of the same origin.[21] All the figurines we found *in situ* in the Mycenaean graves of Eleusis were offerings given to

[20] Ἀθήναιον, H (1880), p. 520.   [21] *Prosymna*, p. 256.

children,[22] and Dr. Papademetriou found figurines in children's graves at the cemeteries of Voula and Varkiza.[23] We cannot be sure, of course, that such figurines were not placed in the graves of adults, but we can be sure that they characterize child burials. We must bear this fact in mind, as well as the beliefs of that time about death and the trip to the lower world, when we try to determine the meaning of these figurines. We must also bear in mind an observation made by Tsountas in the early days of the exploration of Mycenaean tombs. Then he observed that such figurines were not found in all the graves, but in comparatively few, and that the graves in which they were found were the poorer ones.

On the evidence yielded by the graves at Prosymna, Professor Blegen has suggested that some at least of the terracotta figurines were toys for children, while others could have been representations of nurses. This suggestion was rejected by Persson, who compares them to the *ushebtis* of Egypt and attributes to them a similar function.[24] Professor Nilsson, accepting Persson's interpretation, suggested that figurines of the Φ and Ψ types when found in shrines should be interpreted as votaries and representations of divinities, respectively, but when found in graves as filling a function comparable to the Egyptian *ushebtis*. Noting especially that they were found in poorer graves, he maintains that "anyone who was unable to procure jewelry and costly things, thought to make up for the want by these cheap figures which, however, it was imagined would procure a luxurious after life for the man who had not known much but work and necessity in this life."[25] We cannot accept this interpretation. If these inexpensive figurines were capable of securing comfort and ease in the lower world, then we should expect to find them in every grave. Human beings, rich or poor, have always been anxious to secure a future of comfort and ease and to pile up assurances for the days to come. That no religious or other scruples prevented the rich from using the figurines is indicated by the fact that such figurines were found in some rich graves. The fact that they are found in only a few graves nullifies Nilsson's interpretation. The fact that they are found in graves of children will account for their discovery in poorer graves.

[22] Mylonas, *Volume in Memoriam G. P. Oekonomos*, pp. 35-44.
[23] To Dr. Papademetriou I am indebted for permission to mention this fact.
[24] *The Royal Tombs at Dendra*, p. 89; *New Tombs at Dendra*, p. 33.
[25] *Minoan-Mycenaean Religion*, 2nd ed., pp. 307-308.

It is evident that children's graves would be less well-equipped with offerings and gifts than those of the adults, and the explanation is at hand: the graves in which figurines were found are poorer because they are children's graves, or children perhaps in some numbers were among those buried.

Their comparison to the *ushebtis* is also unacceptable. If they performed a similar function, then we would expect to find that the ideas of the Mycenaeans of what happens after death would parallel those of the Egyptians. That certainly was not the case. The fact that such figurines along with the other funeral offerings were swept away after the decomposition of the flesh indicates that they were not for the lower world but only for the trip to the lower world. The fact that they were found in children's graves excludes the supposition that they were concubines and slaves meant to serve their masters in that capacity in the lower world. They could not be symbolic representations of mothers who were still living. And then it remains unexplained why the same types were used to represent votaries and a divinity on the one hand (figurines found in sanctuaries and shrines) and on the other concubines and slaves (figurines found in graves).

The only interpretation possible is to suggest that in both occasions they filled a similar function. Figurines of type Ψ were representations of a female divinity. The type, as Professor Marinatos pointed out some years back, evolved from the Minoan Goddess with raised hands and represents a divinity in the attitude of blessing.[26] Figurines of type Φ are representations of divine nurses. The "multiple figurines" and the *kourotrophoi* will certainly back this identification. We may assume that the *kourotrophoi* were placed in graves of infants.

We believe that the evidence from Crete will further strengthen our interpretation. Of the many figurines found in the houses and shrines of that island, the idols known as "bell-shaped" have been considered by Professor Nilsson as "cult objects" and representations of divinities.[27] And yet two bell-shaped figurines were found in the Late Minoan III graves (No. III and No. VII) of the Mavro Spelio cemetery. One of these could be considered as a *kourotrophos* since the female form represented holds an infant in her arms. Professor Nilsson explains their presence as "a sign of the Mycenaean influ-

[26] *Ephemeris*, 1927-1928, p. 20. For the gesture see Dussaud, R., *Rev. de l'hist. de relig.*, 51 (1905), pp. 43ff. For the figurines, cf. Mylonas, *Yearbook of the School of Philosophy, The University of Athens*, 1954-1955, pp. 139-152.
[27] *Minoan-Mycenaean Religion*, 2nd ed., p. 309.

ence," and states further that "the common Mycenaean idols being very rare in Crete, the Cretan type was used instead."[28] But the Cretan type represented a divinity; how then could the Cretans use it instead of the Mycenaean if the latter stood for mortal slaves, concubines, and the like? The substitution, we believe, indicates the divine or semi-divine character of the Mycenaean female figurines, for otherwise it would never have taken place.

The belief which motivated the placing of these figurines in children's graves is easily determined. Death has always been considered a mystery by people, and the efforts of man's mind from the beginning of time were concentrated in developing ideas which would provide a measure of assurance and comfort. The Mycenaeans too developed such beliefs, which we have outlined briefly, and seem to have felt confident that the adult who was well equipped with supplies, weapons, and the possessions he liked in actual life could negotiate comfortably the trip to the lower world. The fate of small children must have seemed hopeless indeed. All their years they had depended for guidance and for their very life on their parents, and all of a sudden they were left alone to face a long and terrifying trip to the unknown. Placing them under the protection of the Goddess of Blessing and under the care of divine nurses would appear natural and also essential, an act which would ease the worry of parents who felt helpless in being of service to their little ones. In this idea, perhaps, has its beginning the tradition current in historic times according to which a number of gods and heroes were brought up by semi-divine nurses.

Figurines representing chariots could well have been toys, while female animals could also have provided the milk supply needed for the trip. Thus I believe we can suggest a consistent meaning for these figurines, vouched for by the facts known to date. Another question regarding these figurines, however, will have to remain unanswered—that of their origin. We have noted above that they appear suddenly around 1300 B.C., fully developed and in common use. What were their antecedents? They could not have developed from Minoan prototypes, since such figurines are not to be found in Crete. The Cycladic figurines, used in the islands of the Cyclades in the Early

[28] *Ibid.*, p. 300. See Forsdyke, "The Mavro Spelio Cemetery at Knossos," *BSA*, 28 (1926-1927), pp. 254ff., for a discussion of the graves. For a dissenting opinion that funerary figurines are rare in Crete, cf. Picard, Ch., *Religion préhellenique*, pp. 204ff.

Bronze Age, and apparently with a similar function, could have served as prototypes, but as far as we know a chronological gap of many centuries separates the two groups. We can only hope that further research and excavation will provide an answer to this question.

In a limited number of graves remains of animals were found among the funeral offerings and the human remains. Bones of dogs were found by Persson in Tomb 1 of Asine and the royal tomb of Dendra, by Professor Keramopoullos in the *dromos* of Tomb 6 at Thebes, and by Professor Wace in Tombs 505 and 533 in the Kalkani cemetery; dog's teeth were among the finds from the Vaphio Tomb, and the skeleton of a horse was found in one of the graves of Nauplia.[29] Perhaps these few instances indicate that occasionally a favorite dog or horse was killed so as to accompany his master on the trip to the lower world. Evidence for the immolation of human beings is more flimsy. Six skeletons found by Tsountas in the fill above the door of Chamber Tomb 15 in the Lower City of Mycenae, a skeleton found by Professor Blegen above the door of Tomb VII at Prosymna, and a skeleton found by Professor Wace in Tomb 505 of the Kalkani cemetery, may be considered as examples of such immolations.[30] But even in these cases we cannot be sure. A few years before his death Tsountas told me that he might have been influenced in his interpretation by the belief in human sacrifices fostered by Schliemann's excavations of the Grave Circle of Mycenae. At best we can only suppose that in very rare cases and for particular reasons a favorite slave or a captured enemy was killed over the grave of the master. But the practice seems to be foreign to Mycenaean custom.

The information available for the chamber tombs of Mycenae and for the burial customs of the Mycenaeans of the period during which the Cyclopean walls were constructed and the first Palace was erected is certainly extensive, although by no means complete. It is interesting to observe that this Mycenaean evidence agrees with that obtained in other contemporary sites, proving that a striking uniformity of funereal architecture and customs existed in the mainland of Greece in Late Helladic III times, in such sections as have been explored.

The second type of grave in use at Mycenae during the period under consideration is the tholos or beehive tomb. In the main this

[29] *Royal Tombs at Dendra*, p. 18; Frödin-Persson, *Asine*, p. 358; *Chamber Tombs at Mycenae*, p. 116; *Deltion*, III (1917), p. 137; *Mycenaean Age*, p. 152.
[30] *Ephemeris*, 1888, p. 130; *Prosymna*, p. 235; *Chamber Tombs at Mycenae*, p. 145.

type is similar to the chamber tomb and has the same number of parts. It is mostly hewn in the living rock of a hillside and is composed of a *dromos*, a passage cut perpendicularly to the slope, a *stomion*, or deep doorway, and a round chamber. This round chamber, the tholos, was hewn from the top, like a huge well, and its roof was covered by means of a corbel vault, i.e., by tiers of ashlar masonry laid in rings and in such a way that each tier projected slightly beyond the edge of the one below it. Thus the distance to be covered was gradually reduced until a small opening was left at the apex, which was closed by a single slab, the underside of which was usually hollowed to give the impression that the vault came to a point. Behind the rings of stone, loose earth and rubble were piled to weigh them down and then the area between the walls of the shaft and the loose earth and stones was filled with thick layers of water-resisting yellowish clay known today as *plesia*. The projections of the masonry in the interior of the round chamber were cut away and the surface smoothed. The resulting vault is conical in shape and in section looks like a traditional beehive, hence the name. Holland has proved that the lintel of the doorway lies at about the level of the hillside and that consequently the stone vault projected above that surface.[31] That projection was covered over with earth forming a mound, making the round chamber an underground structure. A σῆμα, or stele, or an identifying stone, must have been placed over it.[32]

The tholos thus differs from the chamber tomb in that it has a round chamber which is roofed over artificially. The walls of its *dromos* are also lined with masonry in our period (Figs. 28 and 29). They may also differ in their use, for the general assumption is that they were built for the use of one royal personage, and not for a family over many generations. At Mycenae not a single tholos tomb was found intact, although nine beehive tombs were brought to light, and until an intact tholos tomb is found we shall be unable to know the way in which they were used. As a matter of fact, out of the forty tholos tombs known to exist in the Mycenaean area, only one,

[31] *BSA*, 25 (1921-1923), pp. 397ff. Cf. *Ephemeris*, 1889, pp. 136-137; *Dendra*, p. 20; Valmin, N., "Tholos Tombs and Tumuli," *Corolla Archaeologica*, 1932, pp. 216ff.

[32] For markers over graves, see *Prosymna*, p. 237; *Chamber Tombs at Mycenae*, p. 128; *Dendra*, p. 113; Mylonas, *AJA*, 52 (1948), p. 71. Apparently the custom was started in Middle Helladic times. Now we have stelai-markers from Eleusis and Lerna, dating from those times. For the latter see Caskey, J., in *Hesperia*, 23 (1954), p. 14 and pl. 3, c.

the tholos tomb of Dendra, seems to have escaped plundering. In that tomb three skeletons were found laid in two cists, while gifts were placed in a third as well as with the bodies.[33] The question, however, can be legitimately posed: is one example out of forty sufficient to establish the use of the tholoi? It will indeed be strange if descendants, however regal, avoided the use of an ancestral grave at a time when the people, including the wealthy, seem to have made use of the family chamber tombs and when so little importance was laid on a life in the lower world. I believe that the tholoi too were considered as temporary shelters for the trip to the lower world and as such, I believe, they were used over the years for a number of burials by members of the same family.

The most developed and perfect examples of the tholos tomb type were constructed in the period under consideration and are known today as the "Treasury of Atreus" or the "Tomb of Agamemnon" (as the people of the modern village of Mycenae call it) and the Tomb of Clytemnestra.

The Treasury of Atreus is excellently preserved and has been noted since the days of the early travelers. It was finally cleared in 1878 by Stamatakes and since the days of Elgin has been recognized as the most impressive of the tholoi. It differs from the normal type in that it has a side chamber. There is only one other example known with a similar, although much smaller, side chamber, the so-called Treasury of Minyas at Orchomenos. The *dromos* of the Treasury of Atreus measures 36 meters in length and 6 meters in width and possesses walls lined with conglomerate blocks of ashlar masonry fitted carefully in regular horizontal courses (Fig. 24). Some of the blocks employed in the facing are of great size (one of them measures 6 meters long by 1.25 meters high); and a few were taken from an older building. Its east end, or the opening of the *dromos*, was blocked by a wall of well-cut poros blocks of the sandstone variety, some of which are reused stones, while its west end is blocked by the façade of the grave. At that point its lined sides tower some 10 meters above its floor, which is paved with hard whitish earth packed over the rock.

The façade, some 10.50 meters high and 6 meters wide, is well preserved, although its decoration has been removed. It exhibits a doorway of monumental proportions—5.40 meters high and 2.70

[33] Persson, A., *The Royal Tombs at Dendra.*

meters wide at the ground and 2.45 meters at the top. Two receding fasciae carved in the masonry and carried around frame the doorway, which is spanned by an enormous lintel stretching a little beyond the sides of the *dromos*. Above the lintel we have the characteristic relieving triangle, once blocked by a decorated slab, and above this, ending the façade and crowning its upper section, a projecting double row of conglomerate blocks. On either side of the doorway we still have *in situ* two rectangular bases, made up of three superposed and graduated plinths, which originally supported engaged half-columns secured to the façade by means of dowels, for which the dowel holes, seen beyond the door opening, were cut in the masonry. The half-columns formed part of the decoration of the façade, of which we now have only small fragments.

The depth of the doorway, the *stomion*, is imposing and measures 5.40 meters. The double door closing the opening was placed in the middle of the *stomion*, as can be proved by the threshold (some 1.20 meters in width and made up of two conglomerate blocks hemmed in place by a small rectangular piece of poros and a smaller poros wedge) and the corresponding parallel rows of bronze nails on the wall and on each side which helped to keep the door frame in position. The façade lintel covers only a section of the depth of the *stomion*; the balance is filled by an immense block, measuring 8 meters in length by 5 meters in width and 1.20 meters in thickness, and of an estimated weight of 120 tons. In spite of its weight, it is beautifully fitted in its position, and its face in the tholos is worked so as to carry the double curvature of the wall.

The main round room, the tholos, measures 14.60 meters in diameter at its floor level and has a height of 13.39 meters, almost equalling its diameter. It is made up of thirty-three superposed courses of perfectly joined conglomerate blocks. On the face of its wall from the third course upward we find holes and remnants of bronze nails, evidence that its interior once was enlivened by applied decoration, most probably bronze rosettes and even a frieze of bronze plate. Its floor, which is of solid rock, was covered with hard-packed whitish earth. A doorway, 2.50 meters high, 1.50 meters wide, and 2.40 meters deep (Fig. 25), surmounted by its large lintel and relieving triangle, cut on the north side of the tholos, led to a passage-way, 2.30 meters long, and thence to a side chamber about 5.80 meters high and 6 meters square. It is hewn out of the living rock and in all respects is reminiscent of the rock-cut chamber tombs. Its crumbled walls today are bare of any decoration which once might have covered them, but in the center of its floor were found a cutting and two worked blocks which seem to indicate that a pillar originally stood there to support its roof. Small pivot holes on the lintel and the threshold and a corresponding single, vertical row of nails on the door jambs indicate that a door, of a light construction, originally closed the chamber. Dowel holes left on its lintel and two deep holes in the masonry of its triangular opening prove that its relieving triangle was blocked by a slab, perhaps decorated, which has disappeared.

A mere glance at the Treasury of Atreus will be sufficient to prove that it is one of the most impressive monuments of the Mycenaean world. The planning and skill in construction, its proportions and lofty vault, the care with which its rings of stone were fitted and smoothed, the precautions taken to free it from the seepage of rain water, the apparent facility with which huge blocks were carved to fit a round structure and were eased into their positions, indicate the high degree of excellence which the architects of Mycenae had reached in the fourteenth and thirteenth centuries B.C. We wish it were possible for us to visualize the burial ritual held in this magnificent grave, to recover its interior as it was left when the body of the last king was deposited on its floor or in the side chamber, and a solid wall of stones was built across the *stomion*! But the contents of the grave were gone long before the days of Pausanias, and all we have left is the varied pictures our imagination can provide as it is stimulated by the impressive and massive architectural remains.

The date of the Treasury of Atreus has given rise to a great many arguments and theories. The detailed investigations and studies of Professor Wace, however, have definitely proved that the early date for its construction, the seventeenth century B.C., advanced by Sir Arthur Evans and Sir John Myres is untenable.[34] There can be no doubt that the Treasury of Atreus marks the latest development of the construction of the tholos tombs and should be placed much later. The recent exploration of the walls of the *dromos* and of the tholos have proved that they must have been constructed after the beginning

[34] Wace, *Mycenae*, pp. 28-33 and especially pp. 119-131. Sir Arthur Evans, *Palace of Minos*, III, p. 201; IV, p. 244, and *Shaft Graves and Beehive Tombs of Mycenae*; Sir John Myres, *Who Were the Greeks?* pp. 282-284, 381-382, 574. Cf. *Catalogue of Greek and Roman Sculpture in the British Museum*, I, part I, p. 14.

of the Late Helladic III period, to which, and to Late Helladic II times, belong the contents of the deposit through and over which parts of the tomb were built. But exactly when was the tomb built? This is a question which must be answered with reservation. We may recall that under the southern block of the threshold Professor Wace found a few objects of gold, some beads, and fewer sherds. The most interesting of the sherds is typical of the Late Helladic III B period and certainly offers a good chronological upper limit for the construction. The beads too, some of faïence, seem to belong to a type which was still in use in Late Helladic III c times, as can be proved by the finds in the graves of Eleusis. Furthermore, among the sherds found in the various trenches, and especially in the "pockets" spanned by the huge blocks of the *dromos*, were a number of Mycenaean figurines. We have already seen that these figurines are characteristic products of Late Helladic III B times, the same times to which belongs the painted sherd found under the threshold block. Their number, and the frequency with which they occurred in the trenches dug around the Treasury seem to indicate an advanced rather than an early date in the Late Helladic III B period. We may recall now that similar figurines were found under the fortification wall to the south of the Lion Gate and that Professor Wace considers that gate and its walls and the Treasury of Atreus as almost contemporary. The evidence to date seems to justify the conclusion that they are almost contemporary, but it also seems to indicate that both should be placed in advanced Late Helladic III B times and after 1300 B.C.. Until the date is proved otherwise by new evidence, we feel justified to suggest *c.* 1250 B.C., as the date of the construction of the Treasury of Atreus.

Perhaps we could go a step further and accept the view that the same ruler was responsible for both the Lion Gate and the Treasury of Atreus, the former to be a really monumental entrance to his Citadel, the latter a worthy burial place. We have seen that Atreus was perhaps responsible for the construction of the gate; we may now suggest that the tholos tomb known as the Treasury of Atreus was originally the actual grave of that great king. The name under which that structure is known today was not given to it in modern or mediaeval times, at a time when old traditions were dead, as was the case with the tombs of Clytemnestra and Aegisthos, but in antiquity. The tombs of Clytemnestra and Aegisthos were unknown to the Hellenistic inhabitants of the district; the Treasury of Atreus was visible and known to them. Could we possibly believe that the tradition which associated that splendid monument with Atreus was based on the fact that it actually was his grave, that it was constructed by him? Traditional information has been proved correct or almost correct so many times that we are inclined to believe that in this instance, too, it is correct and that in the Treasury of Atreus we have the grave of that great king. The date of its construction, c. 1250 B.C., will in a general way agree with the life span of the traditional founder of the Pelopid dynasty.

Another problem connected with the Treasury is only partially solved. It deals with the decoration of its façade. Only fragments of that decoration have survived, and they are scattered in a number of museums: in Athens, London, Munich, Karlsruhe, and Berlin. These fragments indicate that the façade was covered with slabs of stone of various colors. The fragments in the British Museum are the most important; they were part of Lord Elgin's collection and form the basic elements upon which a restoration has to be based. Until recently the restoration given by Perrot and Chipiez was more or less accepted, although it was considered overloaded with ornament.[35] That restoration now has to be abandoned in the face of evidence discovered recently. In 1939, the ephor of the district, Dr. Marcellos Mitsos, found in the fields adjacent to the Treasury some pieces belonging to the façade. In 1940-1941, Professors Marinatos and Wace located in the cellars of the National Museum of Athens other important fragments and suggested a new arrangement of the decoration of the façade.[36]

The arrangement of the lower section of the façade below the lintel remains as before: two engaged half-columns of green stone, bearing a carved pattern of chevrons placed horizontally across the column with the areas between filled with spirals (Fig. 24). A similar pattern seems to have decorated their bulging echini which were surmounted by double abaci. The upper abacus marks the beginning of the second or upper section of the façade, to be called the tympanon.

[35] Perrot, G., and Chipiez, C., History of Art in Primitive Greece. Mycenaean Art, London, 1894, II, plates opposite pp. 63 and 73. Cf. Hist. de l'Art, VI, pp. 608ff. and pl. V. For an excellent discussion of the fragments in the British Museum, see Catalogue of Sculpture, Vol. I, part I, pp. 14-31.

[36] For Professor Wace's initial arrangement, see Mycenae, fig. 51, and for his amended arrangement, Keramopoullos' Geras, pl. 20, p. 312. For Professor Marinatos' arrangement see Volume in Memoriam G. P. Oekonomos, pl. I, opposite p. 16.

The new evidence has imposed a complete change in the old decorative scheme used for that section. It is now proved that two half-columns of green stone, one on each side, were placed over the abaci, thus carrying the vertical line of the lower half-columns to the top of the façade. The lower part of these engaged columns is undecorated, and perhaps it was covered with bronze sheathing, but the rest of their height is decorated by a continuous band of spirals reaching to the capital (Fig. 26). Judging by the similar arrangement in the façade of the Tomb of Clytemnestra, both Professor Marinatos and Professor Wace place a fragment of porphyry in the British Museum bearing a band of beam ends surmounted by a row of spirals across the bottom of the tympanon and between the abaci serving as bases to the newly found upper half-columns. Above this, they place a band of the Mycenaean elongated rosette and triglyph pattern, fragments of which are preserved in the British Museum and in the National Museum of Athens. The top of this band is level with the line of the base of the relieving triangle which was blocked by a slab of red stone. Fragments of the lower part of that slab are decorated with three superposed rows of spirals which were carried across the width of the façade.

Professor Wace fills the remaining height of the tympanon with alternating plain slabs (three in number) and slabs (three in number) bearing a triple or a double row of spirals. Professor Marinatos believes that the slab of the relieving triangle was completely covered with horizontal rows of spirals, interrupted, about halfway up the triangle, by two wider bands (one of which is decorated with the elongated rosette and triglyph pattern, the other with running spirals) carried across the tympanon. Both form a base above which he places the famed gypsum slabs with the bulls in the British Museum, one on either side of the triangle.[37]

In the main, the two restorations differ in Professor Marinatos' placing of the Elgin slabs with the bulls on the tympanon and in Professor Wace's non-continuous decoration of the engaged columns. The evidence seems to indicate that the decoration on the body of the engaged columns was continuous and that the slabs with the bulls were not attached to the façade. Their smooth lower edges perhaps indicate that they were originally standing on a shelf and the two rows of dowel holes which are to be seen across the tympanon and about

[37] Perrot, misinterpreting the Elgin slabs, placed lions in those positions.

the middle of its height[38] will not permit the placing in its upper part of both a double or triple decorative band and the slabs with the bulls. In Figure 26 we have combined Professor Wace's and Professor Marinatos' restorations and have included the suggestions made by the former in his article in the *Geras*.

All restorations are advanced as tentative and subject to further study, which may prove necessary in view of additional evidence brought to light in the last two years, which might or might not bear on the subject.[39] In 1952-1953, in the course of the opening up of the car road which leads to the south end of the *dromos* of the Treasury, a number of fragments of colored stone were accidentally brought to light. In the summer of 1953, Dr. Papademetriou further explored the area in which the fragments were found and discovered additional pieces, some of which bear carved decoration. The study of these pieces is forthcoming. Meanwhile, it is not certain whether these fragments belong to the decorated façade of the Treasury and might therefore impose a further modification of the schemes proposed, or more probably to the decoration of the side chamber. The proximity to the Treasury of the area in which they were found seems to indicate that they once belonged to that structure, but one cannot be entirely sure. What is certain, however, is that the old scheme of Perrot now has to be abandoned and that we must visualize the façade as possessing two attached half-columns on either side of its tympanon and above the well-known half-columns of the lower section.

Slightly later in date, *c.* 1225 B.C., is the so-called Tomb of Clytemnestra, a monument which, along with the Treasury of Atreus, marks the highest development in tholos tomb construction. It lies only about 120 meters to the west of the Lion Gate and near an older tholos tomb known as the Tomb of Aegisthos. Unlike the Treasury of Atreus, the Tomb of Clytemnestra was buried and well

[38] The dowel holes are marked in the original drawing by Thiersch, *Ath. Mitt.*, 4 (1879), pl. XIII, upon which all restorations are based.

[39] Professor Marinatos' latest investigations around the Treasury have proved that gypsum slabs had been worked in the neighborhood of that monument and that therefore the Elgin slabs could belong to it. Rejecting Sir Arthur Evans' suggestion that they decorated the *dromos*, he places on the façade the fragments in the British Museum. Professor Wace, who originally thought that the slabs might have belonged to the Tomb of Clytemnestra, now suggests (*Geras*, p. 314) that perhaps they are part of the decoration of the side chamber of the Treasury. However, the walls of that chamber are so crumbled that it is impossible to know whether they were originally faced with a decoration. For Sir Arthur's position, see *Palace of Minos*, III, pp. 192ff.

hidden and apparently was unknown to the historical age of Mycenae, because across its *dromos* a theater was constructed in Hellenistic times; a few of the seats of that theater are still preserved *in situ* (Fig. 28). It seems that the locality of the tomb was detected during the closing years of the Turkish occupation and that between 1807 and 1812 Veli, the pasha of Nauplia, destroyed the top of its vault and through it cleared the tholos of its contents, but he left the *dromos* intact. The *dromos* was investigated by Mme. Schliemann in 1876, so the tomb for a while was known as Mme. Schliemann's Treasury; it was completely cleared by Tsountas in 1897.[40] Since the days of its investigation, the monument fell into disrepair and the seepage of water almost completely ruined it. Its restoration became imperative and at the suggestion of Dr. John Papademetriou it was started by the Greek Service for the Restoration and Preservation of Ancient Monuments in the spring of 1951 and was completed in the fall of 1951. With its vault restored and the sides of the *dromos* relined, the monument rivals in impressiveness the Treasury of Atreus.[41]

The Tomb of Clytemnestra is oriented north and south, and its *dromos* is some 37 meters long and nearly 6 meters wide (Fig. 29).[42] Its sides are lined with conglomerate blocks laid in horizontal courses, though the blocks of the lining are much smaller than those employed for a similar purpose in the Treasury of Atreus. The southern end of the *dromos*, its opening, is blocked by a low wall built of poros stone. Its northern end is well bonded with the façade of the tomb. This façade again shows a double division, the lower section pierced by the doorway and the upper section or the *tympanon* with its relieving triangle.

The opening of the doorway is somewhat higher than that of the Treasury of Atreus, measuring 5.48 meters in height and 2.48 meters in width, and narrows slightly upward. Again, it is framed by a double receding fascia. On either side of the doorway originally stood half-columns made of gypsum attached to the wall. Their semicircular bases of polished conglomerate are still *in situ* (Fig. 30). The

[40] *Mycenaean Age*, pp. 122-124.

[41] I am grateful to Professor Orlandos and Dr. Stikas for their permission to mention their work and for the photographs of Figs. 32 and 33 and the drawing of Fig. 36. The story of the early work around the *dromos* of the tomb is told by Papademetriou in *Ephemeris*, 1948-1949, "Chronika," pp. 43-48.

[42] For a description see Wace, *BSA*, 25 (1921-1923), pp. 357-376, pl. 58; *Mycenae*, pp. 35-38.

bases as well as the semi-columns were fluted; thirteen flutings are clearly to be seen on both. Part of one of the columns is still preserved; it tapers slightly downwards, like the semi-columns of the Treasury. Above the echinus of the half-columns we again have a double abacus and across the base of the tympanon, from abacus to abacus, we have a band of bluish limestone decorated with the well-known beam ends or raised discs motive (Fig. 31). A small part of this band is still in its original position. Over it perhaps ran two bands of greenish stone, the one decorated with spirals, the other with elongated rosettes and triglyphs, in a manner similar to that found in the Treasury of Atreus. Fragments of red slabs in the National Museum of Athens would indicate that the relieving triangle and the rest of the tympanon were covered with thin slabs of colored stone with perhaps some carved decoration. On either side of the relieving triangle and above the upper abacus of the fluted half-columns are projecting pilasters (Fig. 31) corresponding to the upper half-columns of the Treasury of Atreus. Whether or not similar half-columns were placed in front of these pilasters cannot be determined from the photographs. Professor Marinatos states that on one of the abaci, which would have formed the base on which the half-column would stand, he clearly saw the marks of its lowest periphery.[43] And so he places superposed half-columns on the tympanon. Professor Wace believes that the pilasters were used instead of half-columns.[44] The tympanon again is crowned by projecting blocks which form a cornice, in a manner similar to that employed in the Treasury of Atreus. It is unfortunate that we cannot know more about the decoration of the façade of this impressive tomb.

The *stomion* is some 5.40 meters deep and is spanned by three blocks of stone, the outer two being the lintels of the façade and of the tholos itself. In the central block, and at a distance of 3.50 meters from the façade, pivot holes, which prove the existence of a door at that point, can still be seen, and below them on the floor the threshold made up of two large conglomerate blocks which apparently were covered with a bronze or wooden casing. On the side walls holes are clear, for the nails which helped secure the wooden jambs of the door. For the round chamber and its vault I am indebted to Dr. E. Stikas, who was kind enough to give me the following information. At the

[43] Marinatos, *Volume in Memoriam of George P. Oekonomos*, p. 12.
[44] In Keramopoullos' *Geras*, p. 312.

time of the restoration the vault was standing to a height of 8.55 meters. Around the grave was found a little over one-fifth of the total amount of stone which was used for the reconstruction of its fallen upper part, actually 37 running meters out of 170. These, however, because of their characteristic curvatures exhibited in their face, were instrumental in determining the shape of the upper part of the vault (Figs. 32, 33, and 34). When they were placed in their original position, they proved that the curvature of the vault from floor to top was not a continuous one, as is usually drawn, but that toward the top it exhibits a change in curve, as indicated in Fig. 36. Dr. Stikas states that he noticed a similar change in the curvature of the vault of the Treasury of Atreus. The vault as restored is 12.96 meters high and it covers a circular room 13.52 meters in diameter. The blocks employed for the construction of the vault are comparatively small (their depth is greater than their frontage) but the height of the lintel (0.65 meters), is continued around the vault by thirteen blocks, thus forming a wider band in the masonry, relieving the uniformity of the courses and providing a firm base for the vault. In the floor of the north sector of the tholos an oval pit was dug at the time of its construction, apparently to catch the water seeping through the hillside. An underground drain, cut in the rock and passing under the threshold and the *dromos*, carried the water beyond the poros wall blocking the entrance to the *dromos*.

It is again unfortunate that the tomb was emptied of its contents before the days of scientific investigation. In addition to a quantity of sherds, some fragments of two pithoi bearing a medallion decoration and made of dark gray stone, found by Mme. Schliemann in 1876 and Professor Keramopoullos in 1913, have survived. Three interesting finds were made in the course of the investigation and study which are worth mentioning. At the time of its excavation a wall of poros stones, standing to a height of nearly five feet, was still blocking the doorway, proving that the custom of blocking the doorway after the last burial was followed in the tholos tombs as well. In the *dromos*, at a point 5.50 meters from the façade, Tsountas, in 1892, discovered and explored an intact pit grave 2.75 meters long by 1.20 meters wide and 0.46 meters deep, apparently belonging to a woman. Two richly carved ivory handles of bronze mirrors, ornaments in gold leaf, and beads of various materials were found in the grave. In the summer of 1954, while Dr. Papademetriou and I were investigating the new Grave Circle of Mycenae, we removed the fill to the south of that circle; it proved to have been the dump of a previous excavation. Its position seems to indicate that in all probability it was made up of the earth removed either by Mme. Schliemann or by Tsountas from the *dromos* of the Tomb of Clytemnestra. Among other objects found in this earth were two carved gems, one of which bears the figure of an animal, and the other a design not only interesting because of the excellence of its workmanship but also important because of the subject represented.

The second gem, of clear chalcedony, is lentoid in shape and measures 0.026 by 0.025 meters. The work is done in intaglio in a crisp and precise manner typical of Minoan-Mycenaean gem carving (Fig. 35). On an exergue, formed by repeated half-moon shapes, we have the representation of a female figure with arms bent and raised in the familiar Minoan attitude of blessing, riding sidewise on a mythical animal with the muscular body of a lion and the hairy neck and head of an animal which looks like that of a wild horse. The female figure with elaborately arranged hair is dressed in the Minoan fashion, with a tight girdle around her tiny waist, a tight bodice with the prominent breasts exposed, and a voluminous, apparently flounced skirt. There can be no doubt that a divinity is represented riding on a mythical, hybrid animal. The composition reminds one of the terracotta figurine in the collection of Mme. Stathatou, published by Doro Levi, and even more so of the compositions on a sealing from Aghia Triada and on the well-known glass plaques from Dendra found by Persson.[45]

The third discovery was recently made by Professor Wace. In the course of his excavations in 1952-1954, he uncovered south of the Perseia Fountain an ashlar poros wall which is now believed to have formed "the supporting wall which held up the base of the mound of earth piled over the dome" of the tomb. It has been figured that the original mound, supported on the east by the poros wall, must have had a radius of 25 meters, a figure which agrees with the evidence obtained for the mound which originally covered the Treasury of Atreus. Apparently a good deal of that mound was destroyed by Veli Pasha and Lord Sligo, who are among the best-known despoilers

[45] Levi, Doro, in *Studies Presented to David M. Robinson*, I, pp. 114ff., pl. 117, fig. 2; *Annuario*, VIII-IX, p. 137, figs. 148-149; *AJA*, 49 (1945), pp. 270ff.; Persson, A., *Royal Tombs at Dendra*, pp. 88ff. For the gem see Orlandos, A., Tὸ ἔργον τῆς Ἀρχαιολογικῆς Ἑταιρείας κατὰ τὸ 1954, fig. 47.

of Mycenae. Professor Wace further maintains that there is good reason to suppose that this mound, not far from the Lion Gate, was pointed out to Pausanias as the "Tomb of Atreus."[46]

To our period belongs a third tholos tomb at Mycenae known to scholars as the Tomb of the Genii, but to the modern inhabitants of the site as the Tomb of Orestes. It was discovered and explored by Tsountas in 1896 and is preserved in almost perfect condition.[47] It is located among a good number of chamber tombs and is smaller and simpler in construction than the two we have discussed. Its *dromos*, running from west to east, is only 16.60 meters in length and 2.60 meters in width. The diameter of its preserved tholos at the floor is only 8.40 meters and the height of the vault about 8 meters. On its floor were found three grave pits, originally roofed with slabs of limestone and conglomerate; they as well as the tholos were found empty. Among the scattered fragments left by the despoilers, Tsountas found some small plaques of glass paste decorated with genii standing with beaked ewers before columns and pillars, apparently ready to pour libations.

Chamber tombs continued to be made and used until the end of the Mycenaean age. The tholos tomb of Clytemnestra built after the Treasury of Atreus and consequently dating from the end of the thirteenth century B.C. seems to be the last erected at Mycenae, as far as we now know. However, six other tholos tombs are known from the site, in addition to the three we have discussed, making a total of nine. The six are earlier than the period of the construction of the Cyclopean walls of the Citadel and seem to prove that the beginnings of tholos tomb construction go back to the end of Late Helladic I times at least. A regular development of their construction is already indicated, a development which reached its highest point of perfection in the Treasury of Atreus and the Tomb of Clytemnestra. We are indebted to Professor Wace for the thorough study of the tholos tombs and their classification in three groups, each of which exhibits distinguishing characteristics in this progressive development.[48]

To the first group, and in chronological order, belong the tombs

[46] *JHS*, 74 (1954), p. 170.

[47] It is fully described by Wace, *BSA*, 25 (1921-1923), pp. 376-387, pl. 60; *Mycenae*, pp. 43-44.

[48] *Mycenae*, pp. 16-19. Our dating differs from that adopted by Wace and perhaps the problem of the development and dates of the tholos tomb should be reexamined.

known as the Cyclopean, the Epano Phournos, and the Tomb of Aegisthos, dating according to Wace from about 1510 to 1460 B.C., from the end of the Late Helladic I period to almost the middle of Late Helladic II period. The lack of a relieving triangle, the building of the tholos in rubble masonry, and the unlined *dromos* walls are among the chief characteristics of the group.

To the second group belong the Panaghia Tomb, the Kato Phournos, and the Lion Tomb. The appearance of the relieving triangle, the practice of dressing the stones employed in the construction of the vault, the lengthening of the *dromos* and the lining of its sides with rubble masonry, the facing of the façade with poros blocks (in two out of the three examples) form the characteristic features of this group. Professor Wace dates this group from about 1460 to 1400 B.C. I believe, however, that both the upper and the lower chronological limits should be altered; the lower chronological limit of this group should be placed around 1300 B.C. to allow for the many innovations and developments which characterize it and to bring it in proper chronological relation to the third group, whose chronology is more or less known.

To the third group, dating from shortly after 1300 to 1200 B.C., belong the tombs characterized by ashlar masonry in conglomerate which we have discussed: the Tomb of the Genii, the Treasury of Atreus, and the Tomb of Clytemnestra. It should be noted that some scholars under the leadership of Sir Arthur Evans have maintained that the chronological sequence presented should be reversed: that the Treasury of Atreus and the Tomb of Clytemnestra must be placed at the beginning of the series, the tholos tombs with the more primitive features at the end as marking a gradual degeneration of the type.[49] These assumptions have been disproved by Professor Wace, whose classification is based upon well-established facts.

We may now note that the latest tholos tomb at Mycenae known to us is that of Clytemnestra, dating from about 1225 B.C., and ask the questions: Was the construction of tholos tombs abandoned after that date? Where were the kings of Mycenae of the twelfth century buried? The definite answers to these questions are impossible to give

---

[49] For the general theory of Sir Arthur Evans regarding the tholos tombs, the shaft graves, and their interrelations, see his *The Shaft Graves and Bee-Hive Tombs of Mycenae*, 1929. The old Phrygian-Carian theory (cf. *Mycenaean Age*, pp. 245-249) is no longer accepted. Cf. *British Museum Catalogue of Sculpture*, I, part I, p. 14.

because we cannot exclude the possibility of discovering still other tholos tombs at Mycenae in the future. The dramatic appearance of the new Circle of Mycenae in an area so well known is a clear warning against rash statements excluding future possibilities. When the date of the last tholos tomb was placed around 1300 B.C., the answers to our questions were more difficult since they involved two centuries. However, if we accept the dates proposed for the Treasury of Atreus and for the Tomb of Clytemnestra, the period to be accounted for becomes much smaller and permits us to suggest that in the last century of the Mycenaean era, a century characterized by foreign wars (the Trojan expedition) and internal strife (the feud over the death of Agamemnon) the ruling family of Mycenae used the royal graves, the tholos tombs, of its ancestors for the burial of its dead.[50]

Neither the chamber nor the tholos tombs could have developed from the types used at Mycenae toward the end of the Middle Helladic period. The characteristic graves of that period were the cist graves, apparently for the common people, and the shaft graves, for the rulers, and neither could have served as a prototype.

Professor Wace has suggested that perhaps the chamber tombs were developed from Early Helladic rock shelters similar to those excavated at Zygouries,[51] as the chamber tombs of Crete seem to have developed from comparable rock shelters. Thus a mainland prototype was suggested. However, the Zygouries examples find few parallels thus far in the funereal architecture of the Early Helladic period, and then the entire Middle Helladic period, of which the cist grave is characteristic, intervenes between them and the chamber tombs of the Mycenaean era. Sir Arthur Evans has naturally postulated a Minoan prototype, pointing out that in the cemetery of Mavro Spelio as early as the Middle Minoan II era the custom was current of deepening natural caves for burial use.[52] These, according to Pendlebury, "foreshadow" the construction of the later chamber tombs.[53] The earliest examples of the regular chamber tombs of Mavro Spelio, however, belong to the Late Minoan period[54] and according to Sir Arthur Evans find their real prototypes in graves of the Middle Kingdom in Egypt. To Egyptian influence Persson attributes the

[50] Professor Marinatos is of the same opinion, cf. *Geras*, p. 85, n. 4.
[51] *Chamber Tombs at Mycenae*, p. 125.
[52] *Palace of Minos*, II, pp. 555-557.
[53] *The Archaeology of Crete*, p. 133.
[54] Cf. Forsdyke's account in *BSA*, 28 (1926-1927), pp. 243ff.

beginning of the chamber tomb construction in the mainland of Greece, and in Egyptian rock-cut graves he finds the closest parallels.[55] There can be no doubt that toward the end of the Middle Helladic period connections between Mycenae and Egypt were very close, and that Egyptian practices influenced the burial customs of the Mycenaeans. Professors Wace and Blegen have recently shown that "more than eight times as many mainland (Helladic) as Cretan (Minoan) vases are known from Egypt" dating from the Late Bronze I and II periods, from the sixteenth and the fifteenth centuries B.C.;[56] and the increasing number of funeral offerings placed in graves, the one example of embalming from Shaft Grave V, the death masks, the ostrich eggs, the Nilotic scenes on a Mycenaean dagger, and the like, indicate strong Egyptian influence. The suggestion is now made, and on good ground, that the gold found in the royal shaft graves of Mycenae was brought from Egypt.[57] In view of the evidence available to date, we may feel safe in accepting Persson's suggestion that the chamber tombs of Mycenae are derived from the Egyptian rock-hewn graves of the Middle Kingdom.

The problem involving the tholos tombs is not so easily disposed of. The Minoan derivation of this type, which enjoyed a brief popularity, is rapidly losing ground. Some scholars tried to see a similarity between the tholos tombs of Mycenae and the round ossuaries of Mesara of the Early to Middle Minoan Period.[58] But Professor Marinatos has definitely proved that the ossuaries were not tholoi and that consequently they could not have served as prototypes for the Mycenaean specimens. At best they could be conceived of as foreshadowing only the Mycenaean Grave Circles. The tholos tomb found near Knossos, and hailed as the prototype of the mainland tholoi, is proved to date from around 1500 B.C., later than the earlier example of the first group of Mycenae. The other two tholoi from Crete—the tholos of Aghioi Theodoroi and that of Knossos—certainly belong to Late Minoan II-III times. On the other hand, the circular well-houses of Arkhanes, usually dated from

[55] *The New Tombs at Dendra*, pp. 165-175.

[56] *Klio*, 1939, p. 147. Cf. also Pendlebury, *Aegyptiaca*.

[57] Persson, *New Tombs at Dendra*, pp. 146, 195; Marinatos, S., *Studies Presented to David M. Robinson*, I, p. 127; also *BSA*, 46 (1951), pp. 102-116; Mylonas, "The Cult of the Dead, pp. 100-102.

[58] See especially the *Palace of Minos*, II, pp. 39-43. Sir Arthur also suggested that the tholos came to Greece from the Asiatic side, *Palace of Minos*, III, p. 261. Marinatos, *Deltion*, 12 (1929), p. 141, n. 1.

around 1580 B.C., could not very well have served as prototypes in spite of their early date, since Professor Blegen has now proved that one of the tholoi of Messenia, explored by Kourouniotes, dates from the last phase of the Middle Helladic period and consequently ante-dates the wells. Besides, as Sir Arthur Evans has conceded, the first three courses of the well-house have a "distinct outward slope" and there is no real evidence indicating that the upper courses, now missing, inclined inward.[59] There seems to be no doubt that the tholoi of the mainland were not influenced by the funereal architecture of Crete. Nor do they seem to have been influenced by the graves of Spain, as has been suggested recently. In all probability the tholos tomb was created independently by the people of the mainland and constitutes one of the characteristic developments of their architecture.

The latest discoveries at Mycenae may allow us to suggest a probable derivation. We have seen that toward the end of the Middle Helladic period the common cist grave of that period was replaced by the chamber tomb, by a new type which had no antecedents in Greece, but apparently was derived from Egypt. The chamber tombs, however, were used by and for the people. The need for a special type of sepulcher for the ruling families must have been felt as soon as the chamber tomb was put into use. That need was satisfied by the creation of the tholos tomb, which is also a rock-hewn sepulcher but of a different form. That form could not have been derived from Egypt, where we do not find tholoi, nor from Minoan Crete. I believe that it was developed locally with the Grave Circle as a prototype.

The chamber of the tholos tomb, meant for important persons, was made in the specific form of the Grave Circles, within which their equally important ancestors were buried before them. The Grave Circles were open to the sky, and one could imagine that the sky over them formed a majestic vault. Similarly, the corbel vaults of the tholoi added impressiveness and a monumental quality to the sepulcher worthy of the dignity and power of the ruling family. Certainly, the low, irregular roofs usually found in the chamber tombs could not have served that purpose. The round chamber hewn in the rock, in imitation of Egyptian practices, and shaped in the form of

[59] For the tholos near Knossos, cf. *JHS*, 59 (1939), pp. 203-204; *AJA*, 43 (1939), pp. 128-129, figs. 5-7; *ILN*, March 2, 1940, p. 284; Persson, *New Tombs at Dendra*, p. 167; Wace, *Mycenae*, p. 119. On the well at Arkhanes, cf. Sir Arthur Evans, *Palace of Minos*, II, p. 65, pl. XIV. For the Messinian tomb, cf. Blegen, "An Early Tholos Tomb in Western Messenia," *Hesperia*, 23 (1954), pp. 158-162.

the Grave Circles—to be differentiated from the graves of the common people—was covered over with a corbel vault over which earth was poured to form a mound following the custom of pouring earth over the shaft graves. Corbelling does not seem to be an element foreign to the structural system of the Helladic world. Tsountas, in his early excavations of the cemetery of Syros, discovered what may be termed circular graves roofed over by a primitive corbel vault made of unworked stones.[60] At the cemetery of Aghios Kosmas, we found a few roughly circular graves similarly roofed on the corbel principle.[61] Of course, these examples date from the Early Helladic period, but they are not so far removed from Mycenaean times, since the graves of Aghios Kosmas should be placed at the very end of the period, while there is every reason to believe that the latest graves from Syros may be placed in the early years of the Middle Helladic era; and then it is reasonable to assume that corbelling as a structural device continued after that. It is interesting, furthermore, to note that the primitive vaults of Syros and of Aghios Kosmas were built of small irregular stones and that the early tholos tombs of Mycenae exhibit vaults built similarly of rubble masonry.

In the three early examples of tholos tombs at Mycenae—the Cyclopean, the Epano Phournos, and the Tomb of Aegisthos—we find no shafts or pits cut in the floor reminiscent of the shafts within the Grave Circles. Will the absence of such shafts prove prejudicial to our suggestion? I do not think so. The large round room was constructed to take the place of the shafts, and with the door of the tholos walled up and the *dromos* filled in, the placing of the body on the floor was considered adequate. After all, the common people of Mycenae in the Middle Helladic period, and in the days when the ruling class laid their dead in shaft graves, buried their dead in cists made of slabs or in shallow pits cut in the rock; but when they adopted the rock chambers they merely laid their dead on the floor and not in cists as they used to. Of course, pits are found in Mycenae, and in chamber tombs, but the earliest seem to belong to Late Helladic II times, to a time when we have pits in the tholos tombs as well.[62] Well-made shafts are known from the tholos tomb of Kato

[60] *Ephemeris*, 1899, p. 80, figs. 5 and 10. Cf. the tomb of Krasi also, Marinatos, *Deltion*, 12 (1929), p. 102ff.

[61] Mylonas, "Excavations at Haghios Kosmas," *AJA*, 38 (1934), p. 269; *Ephemeris*, 1952 (1955), pp. 117-134.

[62] *Chamber Tombs at Mycenae*, pp. 52, 54, 68, 110, and 114.

Phournos and the Lion Tomb (to limit ourselves to Mycenae) both belonging to the second group of tholoi, and from the Tomb of the Genii. Many of the shafts in the chamber tombs were used as charnel pits where the bones were thrown or packed; some, for the burial of an individual of peculiar distinction. It seems that in the tholoi, pits were used for the burial of such an individual and some for the storing of the funeral offerings. Both were thus disposed so as to avoid future disturbances and even casual spoliation when the tholos was made ready to receive other and later occupants. It should, of course, be emphasized once more that none of the tholoi at Mycenae were found undisturbed; all were completely cleared in the past; that only the tholos tomb of Dendra survived in its original state, and that definite conclusions based on one case are impossible.

We may finally remark that some of the Late Mycenaean III graves of the cemetery of Eleusis, which from their construction appear to have belonged to important people, possess a circle of large stones enclosing the area of the sepulcher.[63] It is tempting to see in these circles the degeneration of the tholos tomb, and the relapse, after many centuries, to the circle from which the tholos was derived.

The suggestion that the tholos and chamber tombs and their contents mark a departure and a change from earlier burial habits, indicating a change of dynasty or an infiltration of people, does not seem to be valid. To avoid repetition, we shall consider the suggestion after we have studied the shaft graves of Mycenae, and their position in the evolution of burial customs in the mainland of Greece.

[63] *PAE*, 1952, p. 66.

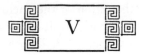

V

GRAVE CIRCLE A AND ITS
SHAFT GRAVES

THE YEAR 1876 was, as we have seen, a memorable one in the history of archaeological research, because in that year Heinrich Schliemann discovered and explored Grave Circle A of Mycenae. Believing firmly in the historicity of the passage in Pausanias, he attributed the five shaft graves he explored to Agamemnon and his associates, who were murdered with him on his return from Troy. Later excavations proved that the graves had nothing to do with the legendary king, but this did not detract from the great importance of Schliemann's discovery, for his work at Mycenae opened up a new field of research and brought mythical Greece within the orbit of early history. The story of the discovery and the fabulous contents of the graves have been told and described in a number of monographs by the most distinguished students of antiquity, beginning with Schliemann himself.[1] It will therefore be necessary to mention only the outstanding basic facts regarding them and to elaborate only certain controversial points.

Circle A is located to the south of the Lion Gate. Its area is surrounded by a parapet made largely of slabs of shelly sandstone set vertically and placed in a double row at a distance of 1.35 meters from each other (Fig. 37). This interval between rows was filled with earth and small stones and was roofed over by slabs of the same shelly sandstone under which were placed wooden beams resting in almost rectangular sockets (Fig. 38). The purpose of the beams was perhaps to keep the vertical slabs in position rather than to support the horizontal roof slabs. Thus was formed a solid circular wall, 0.92 to 1.52 meters high and 1.35 meters thick, enclosing an area 27.50 meters in diameter. In that enclosed area and alongside the east side a narrow pavement of slabs was disclosed forming a margin at the foot of the

---

[1] We have already referred to these publications; they as well as others are found in the Bibliography at the end of our study. In the preparation of this chapter, we have naturally depended on these studies and especially on Karo's monumental publication, *Die Schachtgräber von Mykenai*, with its excellent plates. The finds from these graves are exhibited in the National Museum at Athens.

parapet wall. In the north section of the enclosure, at a short distance from the Lion Gate, we have a well-constructed entranceway 2.50 meters in width and 3.63 meters in length, with long rectangular enclosures of upright parallel slabs standing for the door jambs and on either side of the threshold, which was made of three large blocks of shelly sandstone. No door closed the opening (Figs. 37 and 38).

The slabs employed for the construction of the eastern section of the parapet average 1.05 meters in height and were laid in the rock which has been worked to receive them, while those of the western section are taller, measuring 1.69 meters in height, and are set on a supporting wall which, because of the abrupt falling off of the rocky ground, attains a maximum height of some 5.50 meters. This supporting wall also served to retain the artificial terrace enclosed by the parapet and seems to be formed of two sections. The distinction was made by Tsountas when he uncovered the wall to its rock bedding in 1891. He then found out that the wall "is vertical to a height of 5 feet and thence slopes inward,"[2] exhibiting a batter of about 75 degrees. According to Professor Wace, "the vertical part was probably intended to be covered by soil on its outside. On the other hand that above it was intended to stand free," hence the batter.[3] In view of the evidence yielded by the new Grave Circle, Tsountas' interpretation that the vertical part "is probably a remnant of the older foundation wall on which the present one was afterwards built" seems to be nearer the truth. The batter of the later wall may have been conceived as necessary since it served as a retaining wall as well for the later terrace of the Grave Circle. The height of the older wall which, according to Tsountas, reaches only "five feet," and according to Professor Wace, "never more than a meter high," corresponds well with the preserved height of the enclosing wall of the new Circle, and even with the height of the parapet of Grave Circle A still standing within the Citadel. Its construction, in stones and not in slabs, again agrees with that exhibited by the enclosing wall of the new Circle. Like the latter, the lower vertical wall does not seem to have acted as a retaining wall, but merely as an enclosing wall, and to have followed the formation of the sloping ground. It is interesting to note that the vertical wall exhibits only one row of stones. That

[2] *Mycenaean Age*, p. 111.
[3] *BSA*, 25 (1921-1923), p. 107. Professor Wace's recent investigation of the walls yielded no new evidence. Cf. *BSA*, 49 (1954), pp. 244-247.

is the type of construction employed for the encircling wall of Grave Circle B with stones used only to form the outer and inner faces and the interval between filled with smaller stones, pebbles, and earth, a type of construction which is repeated in a more elaborate form in the double wall of vertical slabs of Grave Circle A. It seems that in the low vertical wall we have the remnants of the original circle which enclosed the shaft graves found by Schliemann, a wall which, I believe, was not built at a later date to enclose a given number of graves, but which was built to enclose an area within which shaft graves were to be cut as need arose.

The shaft graves of Mycenae have no architectural character and can be defined as rectangular oblong trenches or shafts cut vertically and deeply in the earth and the rock under it. The smallest measures 3.00 by 3.50 meters, the largest 4.50 by 6.40 meters, while their depth varies from 1 to 3 or 4 meters. Their sides to a given height above their floor, ranging from 0.75 to 1.50 meters, are lined with rubble walls, which reduce the size of the grave at its bottom and which were apparently built in connection with the construction of the roof. That construction was not understood either by Schliemann or Stamatakes, but was suggested by Dörpfeld on the basis of oral information. It is now proved correct by the new evidence obtained in Circle B. According to Dörpfeld, a number of beams were placed from rubble wall to rubble wall, to support stone slabs which formed the roof.[4] A number of shelly sandstone blocks found by Schliemann over some graves were regarded as roof slabs; however, these are too heavy to have been used in that capacity, and we should rather believe that small and thin slabs of slate were employed for that purpose, similar to those found in the newly excavated shaft graves of Circle B. The roof therefore stood at a small elevation from the floor of the grave and thus the bodies were placed in an empty area and were not covered with earth. The comparative disturbance of the skeletons and of their funeral offerings noticed by Schliemann and attributed to a hasty and careless burial was apparently caused by the collapse of the roof when the wooden beams had decayed. Over the roof, earth was poured to fill the shaft and over the earth on the top, as a rule, stelai or other grave markers were placed.

The floors of the graves were covered with pebbles and on them the bodies were placed, sometimes in a contracted attitude. Around

[4] Cf. Schuchardt, *Schliemann's Excavations*, p. 160.

them their funeral offerings were arrayed. No real evidence indicating cremation was obtained and, in spite of Schliemann's statements and Dörpfeld's ingenious explanations, the bodies were certainly inhumed and not "burned" or "toasted."[5] In one instance, in Grave V, a body seems to have been preserved by embalming. In the six shaft graves the remains of nineteen persons were found, of which twelve seem to have been men, four women, and two children. With the exception of Grave II, in which one skeleton was found, the shafts contained from two to five bodies.[6] Grave III contained the skeletons of three women and two children, but those of two women were found in Grave IV along with the skeletons of three men, and consequently we cannot conclude that women were buried separately. From the evidence obtained, it is clear that no definite orientation for the bodies was observed and that none was required. In Grave VI the bones of the earlier occupant of the grave were brushed aside to make room for the final burial.[7]

A brief note should be added regarding the rich funeral offerings found in the graves. Comparatively few vases were reported among these, but a goodly number of bronze swords and daggers. Of the former, most interesting are the swords with engraved decoration on their blades; of the latter, the daggers, from Graves IV and V, on whose bronze blades inlaid designs in various precious metals were revealed. Some of these weapons may have been wrapped in linen or may even have had a scabbard of linen decked with gold buttons, since Schliemann often mentions the discovery of linen shreds found with swords. The handles of the swords were apparently made of perishable material and consequently did not survive, but in one instance the gold sheathing of a handle was discovered; it comes from Grave IV and exhibits a cylindrical gold hilt of cut work ending in

---

[5] Dörpfeld, W., "Verbrennung und Bestattung der Toten im alten Griechenland," *Mélanges Nicole*, 1905, p. 95ff., and "Verbrennung und Beerdigung der Toten im alten Griechenland." *Comptes rendus du Congres internat. d'archéologie*, 1905, pp. 161ff.

[6] The numbers of skeletons found in the shaft graves are as follows: Grave I (Schliemann's Grave 2), three; Grave II (Schliemann's 5), one; Grave III (Schliemann's 3), five—three women and two children; Grave IV (Schliemann's 4), five—three men and two women; Grave V (Schliemann's 1), three; and Grave VI, explored by Stamatakes, two.

[7] In view of the evidence obtained in the new shaft graves, one wonders whether the bones of the previously buried were not disclosed brushed against the sides in some of the other graves also. Such bones usually are so decayed that their existence might not have impressed Schliemann.

dragons' heads below the top of the blade.[8] Originally this was thought to have been the top of a scepter, but its use as cover for a hilt is now established. Spearheads, arrow points, and broad and long blades, which must have served as knives, were among the objects found by the skeletons of men. No remnants of shields or other pieces of armor were discovered, although breastplates made of gold foil are among the finds and the so-called *Gamaschenhälter*, which are taken to indicate the existence of leather leggings.[9] Also from Grave I, we have flakes of boar tusks which apparently covered the surface of a helmet similar to that of Meriones described in the *Iliad* (x, 261-265) and illustrated by a number of ivory carvings.[10] Gold masks were laid in graves of men; a total of five were found in Graves IV and V; and, according to Schliemann, over the faces of the deceased.[11] Thinner and summarily rendered masks covered the faces of the two children in Grave III, whose bodies were also wrapped in gold foil. Women apparently were not given masks, but elaborate diadems and bands decorated their heads. A variety of hairpins kept the bands in position, while other pins, some of which exhibit heads in rock crystal, originally thought by Schliemann to have been scepters, kept their clothes in proper position. Of the pins which might have been worn as jewelry we may mention the silver pin with the gold pendant from Grave III, which Professor Marinatos explains as "an elaborate symbol, which expresses the wish for happiness and long years for kingdoms and kings."[12]

To women in the main belong discs of gold-leaf bearing on their

[8] Karo, *op.cit.*, pl. 87, no. 294. For the swords, see pls. 73, 81, etc. Karo, 201, distinguishes these swords as of two types. Type A has a long blade and rounded shoulder and a short tang. Type B has a shorter but broader blade, slightly horned shoulders, and a long tang with flanged sides for the handle. Examples of type A are identical to the swords found by Professor Marinatos at Arkalochori (*Palace of Minos*, IV, 2; Suppl. pl. 68; *Geras*, p. 57, n. 1) and apparently illustrate a Minoan type. We have no examples similar to those of type B from Crete, and perhaps that type developed in the mainland. Both types, however, were used for thrusting and not slashing.

[9] Cf. Karo, *op.cit.*, p. 221. Lorimer, H. L., *Homer and the Monuments*, pp. 253-254. Since the writing of her book, a greave made of bronze was found by N. Ghialoures in a Late Helladic grave in the neighborhood of Olympia. I am indebted to the discoverer for this information.

[10] *Chamber Tombs at Mycenae*, pp. 212-214 and fig. 518; *Mycenae*, p. 60; *Schachtgräber*, pp. 218-219. At Dendra, Persson found examples in glass paste, *The Royal Tombs at Dendra*, p. 36, pl. 25, 1.

[11] For the masks, see *Schachtgräber*, pls. 49, 51, and 52 and pp. 76, 121, and 180, and especially Fischer's study, pp. 320ff. For the child's mask see *ibid.*, pl. 53.

[12] "Numerous Years of Joyful Life from Mycenae," *BSA*, 46 (1951), pp. 102-116.

face elaborate designs in repoussé work, since some 700 pieces were found in Grave III where women and children were buried. Thirty-seven discs and twenty-one fragments come from Grave V, which was used for the burial of three men. Some of these discs, only 0.06 meters in diameter, bear holes for attachment; others bear traces of some sticky material by means of which they were glued on the article they decorated. Originally it was believed that they were applied to the garments of women or to the shrouds in which they were enveloped, a practice indicated even by Biblical references: "Ye daughters of Israel, weep over Saul, who clothed you in scarlet, who put ornaments of gold upon your apparel," exhorts the writer of II Samuel I: 24. Later, Staes, in an interesting study, tried to prove that these discs, as well as the masks and some of the diadems, were used to decorate wooden coffins in which the bodies were laid.[13] He further pointed out that a good many bronze nails were found in the graves and that in the cross-shaped rosettes we have a central nail, which in one example measures 0.05 meters. Staes' theory was revived and vigorously supported lately by Persson.[14] Karo's examination of the evidence, however, has proved conclusively that no wooden coffins were employed in the shaft graves explored by Schliemann.[15] That conclusion is now strengthened by the results obtained in the excavation of Circle B; a total of twenty-four graves were excavated in that Circle, of which at least fourteen are typical shafts. Traces of coffins were not found in those graves although special attention was given to the possibility of their existence. Furthermore, Schliemann observed that some of these discs were found under the skeletons, an impossible position if the discs decorated a coffin. And then, if the masks as well as the discs were used to adorn coffins, we ought to find them both, wherever the masks were revealed. Yet, in Grave IV, where three masks were found, no discs or cross-rosettes with nails were revealed. It seems reasonable to conclude that the gold discs were applied to garments, as a rule to women's apparel, and occasionally to men's clothing. That gold ornaments were attached to men's clothing is proved by the last burial in Grave Nu of the new Circle. Under the jaw of the skeleton a gold band was found, which evidently decorated the upper end of the garment in which that person was buried. Around the

[13] *Ephemeris*, 1907, pp. 31-60.
[14] *New Tombs at Dendra*, pp. 113ff. See also Meurer, M., *Jahrbuch*, 1912, pp. 208ff.
[15] *Schachtgräber*, pp. 38ff.

wrists of the man's skeleton of Grave Iota, gold bands were found which originally were sewn to the garment worn by that man. And in Grave Omicron, among the funeral offerings belonging to the woman buried last in that grave, is a cross-rosette of gold-sheet with a central nailhead reminiscent of the crosses from the shaft graves within the Citadel. No traces of a wooden coffin were found in that grave. We believe that the evidence is now definite, that all these objects of gold foil were used as applied decoration for the clothes in which the bodies were deposited in the graves.

Gold and silver cups were laid by the side of both men and women. Of these the most attractive is the gold cup with the doves reminiscent of Nestor's "beauteous cup" (*Iliad*, xi, 632-635) and the silver goblet with inlaid plant motives in gold. With the cups should be mentioned three rhytons from Grave IV: the gold mask of a lion head, the silver rhyton trimmed in gold in the form of a bull's head, and the fragment of the funnel-shaped silver rhyton with the siege scene.[16] Gold rings with carved bezels, beads of agate, sardonyx, amethyst, amber, gold foil cut in the shape of a triple shrine or a garmented lady, earrings and a bracelet, gold plates decorated in repoussé which once covered wooden boxes, a great number of buttons in gold, and gold bands of various sizes, are among the rich funeral offerings of the graves. In addition, we have a number of vessels of almost pure copper (98½ per cent copper), while the swords are of bronze (86 per cent copper and 13 per cent tin). Indeed, no richer graves have been explored in Greece, and Schliemann's finds will perhaps remain the outstanding single discovery in Greek archaeological research.

Above the shaft graves, Schliemann found a number of stelai at different levels. On the upper strata he found seventeen, eleven of which were sculptured. The relation of these stelai to the graves over which they were placed remains uncertain. According to Schuchardt, the plain stelai were placed over the graves of women, while the sculptured ones were used for men. Heurtley believes that the plain stelai were erected at the time of the leveling of the terrace of the Circle to take the place of sculptured stelai which had been destroyed.[17] The discovery of unsculptured stelai over the shaft graves

[16] *Ibid.*, pls. 118-122. For the gold cups, see pls. 109 to 113. For the so-called Nestor's cup, see Marinatos, "Der Nestorbecher, aus dem IV. Schachtgrab von Mykenae," *Festschrift Schweitzer*, pp. 11-18.

[17] Schuchardt, *op.cit.*, pp. 168-169. Heurtley, *BSA*, 25 (1921-1923), p. 143. The

of the new Circle B, where no leveling or replacing of stelai occurred, seems to make the suggestion untenable. The unsculptured stelai from Circle B were found over Graves Gamma and Omicron; in the former the skeleton of a woman was found with three others belonging to men; in the latter, remains of women alone were revealed. The new discoveries seem to strengthen Schuchardt's theory, which, however, still cannot be proved completely. Some of the unsculptured stelai could have been covered with painted stucco in a manner similar to what we find on a later stele discovered by Tsountas in one of the chamber tombs he excavated.[18] The stucco and color could have disappeared during their long years of exposure. But this too is an hypothesis which cannot be proved.

Heurtley divides the sculptured stelai stylistically into three classes.[19] To the first, and presumably earliest, belong some fragments of poros on which the design is rendered by deep incisions. To the second belong most of the stelai, made of slabs of shelly sandstone, and bearing a design cut out of the background in a technique reminiscent of wood carving. To the third belongs stele No. 1429, found over Grave V, the most advanced technically and with the strongest Minoan influence. In all the three types the work seems primitive and much inferior to that noticed on gems and objects decorated in repoussé, and because of that it has been suggested that the sculptured stelai as well were covered with stucco and color. There is no evidence that will prove the truth of this suggestion.

It is generally assumed that the subjects portrayed on these sculptured stelai are scenes of war or hunting. I believe that I have proved that they are representations of chariot races, perhaps held in honor of the dead.[20] The charioteers are not equipped with the appropriate weapons for either war or the chase. We have representation of the latter on the bezel of a gold ring from Grave IV, and there a charioteer and a hunter mount the chariot.[21] In connection with the representation of the chariot scene on stele No. 1428, found over Grave V, we may now add an explanation of the position of the sword which has puzzled scholars for a long time. Schuchardt observed long ago that "the sword is not buckled on the man's waist, but hangs by

---

possibility that the plain stelai were painted cannot be dismissed lightly. The stelai are now kept in the National Museum at Athens.

[18] *Ephemeris*, 1896, pp. 1-22, pl. 1.   [19] *BSA*, 25 (1921-1923), pp. 138-144.
[20] "The Figured Mycenaean Stelai," *AJA*, 55 (1951), pp. 134-147.
[21] Karo, *op.cit.*, pl. 24, 240. Mylonas, *op.cit.*, fig. 1c.

the side of the chariot box. But in that case the box is much higher than what we should expect" from other representations.[22] When we recall that the Homeric custom was to suspend the sword from the shoulder (*Iliad*, XI, 29ff. etc.), we shall not find it impossible to see on the stele a warrior whose sword is strapped to the shoulder.

With the exception of the stele over Grave III, which was "fastened with horizontal slabs," all standing stelai were merely placed in the earth and apparently their sculptured face was turned towards the west. Since no definite rule of orientation was observed in the laying of the dead, this position of the stelai is generally accepted to have been imposed by the original approach and entrance to the circle, by the road which originally led to the Citadel and bypassed the area.

In addition to the stelai found at different levels, Schliemann brought to light a circular well-like construction which is usually known as the "altar" of the shaft graves. The occurrence of this structure has been taken to prove that a cult was practiced in honor of the buried kings and in the Circle itself. In my study on the "Cult of the Dead in Helladic Times,"[23] I did not scrutinize as carefully as I should have the general belief in the existence of such a cult within the Circle but tried to offer a plausible explanation. I argued that the Mycenaeans could have believed that a few chosen individuals were fated not to end the same way as the common man, but were allowed to have an interest in and to influence the life of the living even after their bodies had decomposed. It was natural, perhaps, to assume that an exceptional prince, with a life filled with benevolent acts or mighty deeds, a prince who in actual life was so different from and so much above the average man, should be treated differently after death, that he should be allowed to come to the help of the people to whose service he had devoted his life. Such a belief, perhaps, is reflected in a few instances in the Homeric poems. The Dioskouroi were favored with a special arrangement, and Menelaos was not fated to end his existence in Hades, but was to be transported to the Elysian Fields. And again I supposed that the cult could have been introduced in imitation of Egyptian practices.

However, a careful reexamination of the available evidence and a study of the formation of the ground of the Circle led me to conclude that the so-called circular altar had nothing to do with a

[22] *Schliemann's Excavations*, p. 169.
[23] *Studies Presented to David M. Robinson*, I, pp. 96, 99-100.

cult of the dead. It was found over the fourth shaft grave, and consequently it is connected with that grave and not with all of them. Professor Keramopoullos' suggestion that originally it was placed over the rocky top of the small cave he explored is conjectural and does not correspond with Schliemann's records.[24] My suggestion that the altar, like some of the stelai, was reassembled on top of the soil of the circular area, is unsubstantiated by the known facts. It is definitely stated that Schliemann found the structure at a depth of 26 feet from the surface. Three feet below it he found the floor of the grave, and this at a depth of 33 feet below the surface. When we recall that the height of the altar was 4 feet, we realize that there is no discrepancy in Schliemann's measurements: $(26+4+3=33)$. He has also recorded that the debris reached a height of 9 to 10 feet above the top of the parapet enclosing the circular area. The height of the parapet ranges from 3 to 5 feet, and consequently the floor of the enclosed area at the level of its threshold must be placed at a depth of at the most 14 to 15 feet below the surface before excavation. But the top of the altar was found 26 feet below the surface and consequently at least 11 feet below the floor of the enclosed area, which certainly proves that the altar was covered below a deep layer of earth at the time when the parapet was constructed, that consequently it could not have been used for cult purposes when the Grave Circle took the shape known to us. It seems more probable that it served the burial ritual. Professor Marinatos has recently drawn attention to the clay pipes through which offerings were poured into the Sumerian royal graves before the area was completely covered over, and compares them to the altar over Grave IV.[25] We may point out the "bothros" found by Soteriades in the Middle Helladic mound of Drachmani[26] as a Greek parallel to the practice.

The condition of the small cave between Graves IV and I, explored by Professor Keramopoullos, could not prove the existence of such a cult, at least not when the area was enclosed by the parapet wall. The excavator states that it was mostly filled with earth in which sherds of all periods, from the Middle to the end of the Late Helladic period, were mixed and that it was not filled by Schliemann during his

[24] *Ephemeris*, 1918, pp. 56-57.
[25] *Geras*, p. 65, n. 1. Woolley, Sir L., *Ur und die Sintflut*, pp. 46-47. Dr. Papademetriou does not believe that the structure found over Grave IV is an altar; his study on it will appear shortly.
[26] *Ephemeris*, 1908, pp. 93-94.

excavation, but that it contained an ancient fill. The cave could have been filled up only at the time of the artificial leveling of the area; this in turn would indicate that it was filled up and under a deep layer of earth when the parapet wall restricting the area was constructed, and consequently it could not have been used as a center of a cult in Late Helladic III times. Thus the reexamination of the available data definitely shows that we have no evidence proving the existence of a cult for the dead in Grave Circle A. Tsountas, in his initial study of Mycenaean culture, excluded the possibility of a cult and expressed the view that a mound was erected over the entire area supported at the base by the parapet wall.[27] His view of the existence of a mound has been proved untenable; there can be no doubt that the circular area could be entered through the open entranceway; but his exclusion of a cult is certainly correct.

No stratified fill was disclosed over the shaft graves, but pottery of all periods, from the Middle Helladic to the closing era of the Late Helladic period, dark, red, and loose earth, animal bones and some human, stones and slabs, were found indiscriminately piled over the shafts. The animal bones are certainly the remnants of funeral meals held after each interment. The human bones, which gave rise to the theory of the practice of human sacrifices, apparently belonged to other disturbed graves. The mixture of pottery, earth, and stones is no longer a mystery, but can be easily explained, and in fact helps to decipher the history of the circular area. That history is closely allied to the date of the parapet which encloses the area and with the function of the east section of the Circle.

The eastern half of the circular area now appears free of graves. Professor Marinatos has suggested that this free section had a "religious destination: for the carrying out of the cult for the dead"; that even "a small shrine, not unlike perhaps the shrines pictured in gold foil from Graves III and IV" stood there.[28] Professor Wace, on the other hand, believes that the eastern area was leveled off at the time of the rearrangement of the Circle, that originally shallow graves cut in the rock might have been there. Above and on the rocky ledge to the side of Grave III Schliemann found a grave containing three skeletons, and Stamatakes cleared at least four additional graves cut in the rock and in the eastern section.[29] In the New Circle B, smaller

---

[27] *Mycenaean Age*, pp. 106-108.   [28] *Geras*, pp. 82-83.
[29] *Mycenaean Age*, p. 97, Stamatakes' report to the Greek Archaeological Society, December 4, 1877.

graves cut in the rock or even in the earth were found among the shaft graves, proving that some cists, insignificant from the point of view of construction and offerings, were included in the circular area. In view of the lack of evidence indicating the existence of a cult of the dead in Mycenaean times, we find it difficult to accept the suggested shrine and would rather follow the belief that the present appearance of the eastern section is due to the leveling done at the time of the rearrangement of the circular area.

Professor Wace, after careful investigation and study of the remains, has concluded that the double ring parapet is not contemporary with the shaft graves. When the Lion Gate and the Cyclopean wall to the south of it were constructed, the area of the shaft graves was rearranged and was enclosed by the ring wall. Then the eastern section was cleared and leveled off and the earth from it and other material brought from the outside were used to fill the western half and bring it to almost the same level as that of the eastern; the retaining west wall was constructed, a good number of stelai were raised to the new level, and the entrance to the enclosure was placed on the north section, toward the Lion Gate. This rearrangement and artificial leveling would explain the juxtaposition of sherds belonging to different periods.[30] These conclusions have found wide acceptance. Recently, however, they have been questioned by Professor Marinatos, who maintains that the parapet made up of the double row of vertical slabs is contemporary with the shaft graves.[31] The mixed stratification, or the lack of it, he attributes to the digging of the ground imposed by successive burials, to the disturbances caused by the later construction of the Cyclopean wall and of the Granary between it and the circular area, and to the transference of the entranceway from the western to the northern section of the Circle after the erection of the Lion Gate. He further points out that under the northern threshold slab of Grave Circle A, Early and Middle Helladic (but only one Late Helladic) sherds were found; that the material of the slabs employed for the erection of the double ring is the same as that used for the stelai; that material is nowhere else used and does not seem to be local. "It would be very difficult to imagine," Professor Marinatos states, "that the king who two and a half centuries later

---

[30] *BSA*, 25 (1921-1923), pp. 103-126.

[31] Professor Marinatos first announced his conclusion in a lecture before the Greek Archaeological Society on April 13, 1951. Cf. *Geras*, pp. 78-79.

surrounded Mycenae with walls made special archaeological re-searches to find (and use for the parapet) the same material used for the stelai, the shelly sandstone which had fallen into disuse long ago."

The argument based on the material is now strengthened by the fragments of stelai found in the new Circle B, which are of the same shelly sandstone or of poros. It is true that, with the exception of a few steps of the Grand Staircase of the Palace, nowhere else in Mycenae, in the construction of the Palace or of the tombs, does that material seem to have been used; and it is equally true that the provenance of that stone is unknown. It is supposed to be derived from the area of Cleonae, and Professor Marinatos writes that the stone is reported "to exist in the area between the Isthmos and Corinth but deep below the surface and is found only during the cutting for wells." One wonders whether stone would have been carted from such great distances in the closing years of the Middle Helladic period. Is it not possible to suppose that in Mycenae too and in strata deep below the soil shelly sandstone is to be found? that accidental discoveries some centuries apart will account for its use in the Circle and in different periods? Otherwise, how can we explain the shelly sandstone used in the construction of the steps of the Grand Staircase?

We are on easier ground when we consider the argument of the pottery found below the northern block of the threshold and that from the eastern section of the enclosed area. If we assume that the area was telescoped before the construction of the parapet, we can easily account for these sherds. In such an operation the upper layers are always removed; this would be especially true in the instance of the enclosed area, where even the rocky surface of the eastern half of the circle seems to have been cut away. The sherds below the threshold block are easily explained. It is generally accepted that the north entrance, with its doorposts and threshold, was constructed at the time of the building of the Lion Gate. Before the threshold blocks could be laid, the ground below them had to be prepared and leveled. During that operation the topmost fill, containing later sherds, could have been removed. On the other hand, Late Helladic III pottery was found in and around the retaining west wall of the Circle, proving, according to Professor Wace, that the retaining wall should be regarded "only slightly later in date than the building of the Lion Gate." Also, Late Helladic III sherds were found in the fill between the vertical slabs of the eastern sector and below the preserved roof slabs.[32] The evidence of the pottery seems to indicate a late date for Grave Circle A, and its enclosing parapet.

It has been suggested that the construction of the Cyclopean wall and of the Granary, and the transference to the north of the entrance, may account for the discovery of sherds of all periods in the fill of the Circle. That suggestion seems to us improbable, for even if it could explain the lack of stratification in the entire area, a task which seems to us impossible, it would still have to account for the late sherds found by Professor Keramopoullos in the hollow or cave between Shaft Graves I and IV, and for the two terracotta figurines found by Schliemann in Grave I. Both the Grave and the hollow are in the middle of the Circle and are removed from the area of operations. In Graves V and VI, which were exposed to the building activity, no intrusive Late Helladic elements seem to have been found. Of course, Schliemann believed that the middle body in Grave V had been robbed, an act which could be considered as an intrusion made at the time of the building operations. But that conclusion perhaps was prompted by the lack of rich ornaments which he could associate with that body. For if a theft had occurred it had to take place either after the roof of the grave had caved in and all the bodies were covered with earth or before the caving in of the roof, when all three bodies would have been exposed to view. In the former case it would be difficult to see how the despoiler could have dug the earth covering one body only and could have reached its funeral offerings without completely ruining the skeletal remains—a process so delicate even for an experienced archaeologist. In the latter case it will remain unexplained why the adjacent bodies, whose rich offerings would be visible, were left intact. It is indeed possible to assume that the despoiling occurred in the course of the burial of the last person interred, but in that case its significance to our problem is nil. I think that the consideration of the available evidence would indicate that if the second body was despoiled the event must have occurred before the grave was finally closed, and not at a later period, during the building activities of Late Helladic III times.

The construction of the parapet will give us reason to pause, especially if we compare it to that of the wall of the new Circle B. The latter is built of large stones irregularly placed in a system

[32] Wace, BSA, 25 (1921-1923), pp. 109-110.

which could be termed "primitive Cyclopean." The double slab roofed construction seems to us very advanced for the closing years of the Middle Helladic period. The elaborate entranceway with its rectangular sideposts, recalling the deep doorways of the tholos tombs, can hardly be considered as the work of Middle Helladic builders. Of course, that construction was built when the entranceway was transferred in Late Helladic III times from the west section of the Circle; but then the question would arise: what was the form of the original entranceway? If we assume it to have been similar to the later construction on the north side, then again the objection that it is too advanced structurally will become pertinent. If we figure out that the original entranceway was a mere opening between simply terminated side walls, then we have to account for the extra slabs of shelly sandstone used for the construction of the later entranceway and its threshold. In that case we have to face the objection based on the material used both for the stelai and the parapet. If additional slabs of shelly sandstone could be found in later years for the entrance, one would think that they could be found and used for the entire Circle.

There is another detail which points toward a later date for the parapet. We have noticed that originally wooden beams were placed between the vertical slabs of the double ring and immediately below the roofing slabs. The ends of these beams rested in almost rectangular sockets cut on top of the vertical slabs. We find a similar dowel hole on top of the gypsum slab with the legs of a bull (in the British Museum), which seems to belong to the Treasury of Atreus.[33] The slab with the bull therefore belongs to about 1250 B.C. Is it possible to believe that the same type of dowel hole was employed both in the Late Helladic I and in the Late Helladic III periods, that its use lasted from at least 1580 to 1250 B.C., for over three centuries?

Because of all the questions raised, I believe that we shall be nearer the truth if we accept Professor Wace's conclusions that the double ring wall of slabs is not contemporary with the shaft graves; that at the time of the construction of the west section of the Cyclopean wall and of the Lion Gate the area of the shaft graves was rearranged; that the level of its surface was then raised; that some of the stelai were reerected on that level; and that the double ring parapet was constructed to enclose the area set aside as the cemetery of the early

[33] Evans, Sir Arthur, *Palace of Minos*, III, p. 201 and fig. 138.

kings of Mycenae. However, these conclusions have to be modified in one small detail. The double ring of slabs does not seem to have been the first wall which was built around the area of the shaft graves. As we have seen, an original circular wall enclosed their area, similar to that found beyond the walls. To that original circle belongs the vertical wall disclosed on its west side. On that original was constructed the later retaining west wall on which the vertical slabs were set. Where such retaining was not necessary, the original wall was removed and replaced by the double row of slabs. The existence of a circular wall contemporary with the shaft graves, and as a matter of fact somewhat older, is indicated, I believe, by the way in which the later parapet encloses the area without infringing upon any of the shaft graves. Of course, it goes over the north side of Grave VI, but it does not cross its interior. It will be hard to explain how this enclosing of graves deeply buried in the soil, whose sides and area were not exactly defined, could be accomplished so neatly unless we postulate an earlier original circular wall which enclosed them, a wall which could be seen at one time and which wherever needed was employed as a foundation for the later retaining base of the parapet.

Finally, we shall consider the date of the rearranging of the Circle area, and whether or not the area was considered a *heroon*. The date of the rearrangement, of course, is closely allied with the date of the west section of the Cyclopean wall and of the Lion Gate. It is evident that the Cyclopean wall at that point develops a curve concentric to the Circle which ties the two together (Fig. 7). But we have seen that the date of this construction remains in doubt. Professor Wace places the construction of the Cyclopean wall and of the Lion Gate from about 1350 to 1330 B.C. To the same general date he assigns the final establishment of the Grave Circle. Other scholars suggest a later date.[34] Evidence from the Circle itself is very scanty. The sherds obtained from its area are very limited in number. In the discussion of the date of the Circle, however, we must give most careful consideration to the finds made by the earlier explorers, by Schliemann and by Professor Keramopoullos. We have seen that the latter explored a hollow, or cave as he calls it, under the rocky formation between Graves I and IV, disclosed when torrential rains in 1913

[34] *Mycenae*, pp. 133, 62; Daniel, *AJA*, 44 (1940), pp. 556ff.; 52 (1948), pp. 107ff.; Mackeprang, *AJA*, 42 (1938), pp. 555ff. For our views on the matter, *supra*, pp. 32-34.

caused the collapse of the edges of the rock; and that it was filled sometime in the past but not by Schliemann and his workers. Since a mound of earth was over it when Schliemann was exploring the Circle, and since no sherds of the historic period were found in it, it is evident that the hollow was filled when the area was leveled and the stelai were rearranged—in other words, that it was filled when the Grave Circle as we know it now was being constructed. It is evident that once the level of the Grave Circle was established, sherds could not have crept below it and into the hollow. Therefore, the contents of that hollow or cave should date the construction of the Circle. In discussing the sherds found, Professor Keramopoullos writes that he found them mixed (φύρδην μείγδην is his expression) "in the entire depth of the cave; some of them belong to the early Mycenaean times, to which belong the older of the Mycenaean graves, others to the exit of the Mycenaean period; the last, I repeat, were scattered (κατεσπαρμένα) in all the layers of the cave even in the deepest."[35] This observation proves, as we have seen above, that the leveling operations occurred at the time of the construction of the Grave Circle. The latest of these sherds are of real interest to us, and they are illustrated in figures 4 and 5 of Keramopoullos' study. Among the plain ware found is a single-handled kylix which is close to Furumark's figure 17 (p. 274), dated to Late Helladic III B. The concentric arcs of Keramopoullos' sherd in figure 4, 4 can be compared to that of Furumark's figure 58 (p. 345), dated to Late Helladic III B. The sherd with the stemmed spiral, Keramopoullos' figure 5, 2, should also be placed in Late Helladic III B, since on it we have a single stemmed spiral which is a "motive in the proper sense of the word."[36] The sherd with the bivalve shell, Keramopoullos' figure 5, 3, could also be Late Helladic III B, while those with the whorl-shell decoration could be placed in Late Helladic III A. It seems as if the sherds illustrated by Professor Keramopoullos will place the filling of the cave in Late Helladic III B times, and perhaps late rather than early.

Turning now to Schliemann's finds, we may note that in the fill over the graves he found a good deal of pottery which, however, is neither available now for study nor was it fully described by its discoverer. But in addition to pottery Schliemann mentions the finding

[35] *Ephemeris*, 1918, p. 53.
[36] Furumark, *Mycenaean Pottery*, p. 367. The other references are to this work.

of typical terracotta Mycenaean figurines whose chronological upper limit is generally placed around 1300. Also, as we have seen, he obtained two figurines in Grave I, and he has given us a drawing of these.[37] Both belong to the Ψ type; the one seems to have a solid cylindrical stem, while the other has a hollow and broader stem. Furumark places the Ψ type in Late Helladic III B times and suggests that the specimens with the hollow foot are later than those with the solid.[38] But how were these late objects found in Grave I?

A glance at the plan of the Circle will show that Grave I is almost at the center of the enclosed area, well removed both from the entrance and from the western retaining wall (Fig. 7). Operations in those areas could not have affected its contents. How, then, did the figurines find their way into its interior? Professor Karo, in his description of the figurines, states that they were found in the fill of the grave.[39] Apparently that statement is due to an effort to explain objects now known to belong to Late Helladic III B times found in a grave the contents of which should belong to Late Helladic I times. Schliemann, however, is definite in his record that they were found in the grave and with the other offerings. As a matter of fact, he compared them with other figurines found in the fill over the Grave Circle and stated that the fill over this grave was composed of "unmixed natural earth, which had been brought from another place."[40] It is clear that had he found them in the fill, he would not have included them among the offerings. Their presence in the grave should be explained in some other way.

Professor Keramopoullos noticed that the "north side of the cave— between Graves I and IV—had an irregular small opening, some 0.50 meters in diameter, which perhaps was made when Grave I was dug and which was closed by mud brick." He has kindly informed me that at the time of his excavations the brick closed only the lower half of the opening and it is reasonable to assume that part of it toward its top was left open even at the time of the construction of Grave I, or at any rate in Mycenaean times. Through that opening the figurines must have found their way to the grave at the time of

[37] Schuchardt, *Schliemann's Excavations*, figs. 159-160, pp. 185-186; Karo, *op.cit.*, pl. CL, 204-205.

[38] *Chronology of Mycen. Pottery*, pp. 87-88. Cf. also Wace, *BSA*, 25 (1921-1923), pp. 23-29.

[39] *Schachtgräber*, p. 68; pl. 150, Nos. 204 and 205.

[40] Schliemann, *Mycenae*, pp. 154-155.

the rearrangement of the Circle, of the leveling of the area, and of the filling up of the hollow or cave. Since a hollow space or an irregularly filled space always exists between the side of the walls lining the grave and its fallen roof, such an accidental intrusion is understandable. And it should be noted that Schliemann has recorded the fact that all four sides of the grave were lined with walls "5 ft. high and 1 ft. 8 in. thick."

The date of the figurines will indicate the time of the leveling operations and consequently of the rearrangement of the Circle and of the construction of its parapet of slabs. That date should be placed after 1300 B.C. and about the middle of the thirteenth century. In turn, the date of the Grave Circle, as we have it now, will help date the construction of the Lion Gate and the Cyclopean wall to the south of it, which thus is placed again in the middle of the thirteenth century B.C.

Was the Grave Circle a sacred temenos where a cult of the dead was practiced? As we have seen, there is no evidence whatever to prove the existence of such a cult in the Late Helladic III period when the rearrangement of the Circle and the building of the parapet took place. The "altar" over Grave IV, if it was an altar, even the cave of Professor Keramopoullos, were then deeply buried and could not have been used for such a purpose, and no other evidence was obtained indicating the existence of a cult. The fencing in of the area, and the concentric curve of the west extension of the Cyclopean wall, which was certainly made to avoid crossing the area of the shaft graves, are the data left to us on which we must base a conclusion. Tsountas long ago pointed out that the entranceway to the Grave Circle was an "open passage" and added: "Now it is hardly conceivable that a consecrated place should be left open to all comers, even to dogs, which we know were kept inside the Mycenaean acropolis." Tsountas also pointed out that "before the entrance there are remains of houses . . . [which] rendered access to it well-nigh impossible. Such encroachment on a sacred precinct could hardly have been tolerated."[41] Professor Wace's excavations have proved that the lengthening of the east and west corridors of the Granary almost blocked the entrance, and access to the Circle was made even more difficult by the supporting wall of the roadway from the Lion Gate to the ramp. And yet no structures were built over the Grave

[41] *Mycenaean Age*, pp. 107-108.

Circle although the Granary was squeezed between it and the Cyclopean wall.

The only reasonable explanation of the data seems to be that the area of the shaft graves was respected as the cemetery of the ancient kings, but was not used as a temenos where a cult in honor of these kings was held. It was an important historic landmark, a monument like any other tholos tomb, which had to be respected, but it was not an area for worship. In historic times the area was also respected, but was it a *heroon* or temenos? Again, the answer is difficult. There is one single sherd with the inscription on it τοῦ ἥρωος]εἰμί (I belong to the hero), which may indicate its use, although we cannot exclude the possibility that the sherd rolled to the area from higher levels. The fact remains, however, that no later structures were built over the area, and the suggestion that the stelai were still standing within the circle and could be seen before the destruction of 486 B.C. is acceptable; perhaps they gave rise to the tradition, repeated by Pausanias, that the graves of Agamemnon and his followers, including his charioteer Eurymedon and the children of Cassandra, were within the Citadel.[42] As Professor Wace has pointed out, it is doubtful that the Circle or any part of it was visible in the days of Pausanias, and when the traveler wrote his account of the graves he was repeating the local tradition.

The questions raised by Schliemann's discoveries are numerous, but many of them can now be answered in the light of evidence obtained in the last few years. The enthusiastic excavator was sure that the bodies laid in the shaft graves were cremated on the very floor of the shafts, and pointed to the pebbles covering their floors as proof: they were placed there to help ventilation and thus to fan the flames of the pyre. We now know that covering the floor of a grave with pebbles was an old custom in the mainland of Greece, which appeared in Middle Helladic times and which characterized those times;[43] that the Mycenaeans were thus following an ancestral habit. Schliemann noted that the floor of the graves was covered with clay, and this has given rise to speculation. Now we know that the clay found on the floors originally covered the roofs of the shafts to make them watertight. The contracted position of the skeletons caused

---

[42] Wace, *Mycenae*, p. 8 and Marinatos, *Geras*, pp. 79-80.
[43] For Middle Helladic burial customs see Blegen and Wace, "Middle Helladic Tombs," *Symbolae Osloenses*, 9 (1930), pp. 28-37, and Mylonas, "The Cult of the Dead in Helladic Times," pp. 68-82.

him to assume that they were summarily and hastily buried; we now know that the position was normal and characteristic of Middle Helladic times.

However, there are other features which have puzzled scholars even in our own day. As a rule, the Middle Helladic graves contain but one interment and very few if any offerings; the shaft graves, excepting Grave II, contained more than one skeleton and were filled with gifts. There is an apparent gap between the two groups, but this was filled by the discoveries made in the cemetery of Eleusis in the summers of 1952, 1953, and 1954.[44] In that cemetery and in cist graves of the Middle Helladic period we have more than one person buried and with their bones we find offerings which become more numerous in the closing years of the period. In the graves of Eleusis we have the proof that the custom of brushing aside the bones of an earlier occupant, a feature known from the shaft graves, appeared in the second half of the Middle Helladic period, as well as the erection of stelai and markers over graves. The striking amount and quality of the offerings found in the shaft graves can be attributed to Egyptian influence and to the opulence which followed relations with that area, even to the gifts given by the Egyptians to Mycenaean mercenaries who may have assisted in the expulsion of the Hyksos.[45] But the principle underlying the placing of offerings with the bodies, we find in operation in Middle Helladic times.

The form of the grave, the long shaft with its walls, contrasts sharply with the usual Middle Helladic cists made of slabs. But at Eleusis we can trace the development of the oblong built grave of considerable dimensions from the earlier cists. There, too, we can see how with the increase of the space available in the grave the bodies were gradually laid in a more extended position, and that stage was reached before the end of the Middle Helladic period. There can be little doubt that the shaft graves as a type were normally developed from the earlier cist graves, that, as Professor Wace[46] pointed out some time ago, "they are elaborate or royal versions of ordinary M.H. graves," and that the burial customs revealed by them are a continuation of those held in southern Greece in the second half of the Middle Helladic period. Their size and their contents will only

[44] Mylonas and J. Travlos, *PAE*, 1952, pp. 58-72; 1953, pp. 77-87.
[45] As suggested by Professors Marinatos and Persson, *supra*, p. 99.
[46] *BSA*, 25 (1921-1923), pp. 120-121. *Chamber Tombs at Mycenae*, p. 165.

prove that the shaft graves were the sepulchers of the ruling family of Mycenae. That they are actually sepulchers and not mere depositories used in times of danger to store the contents of tholos tombs located beyond the Citadel, as maintained by Sir Arthur Evans and by Percy Gardner,[47] has been proved by the discovery and exploration of the new shaft graves. That they were not limited to Mycenae is indicated by the shaft grave found in 1954 by Professor J. L. Caskey at Lerna and by the graves of Eleusis.

There can be no doubt that the ruling family whose remains we have in the shaft graves was not that of Agamemnon, for the graves antedate that ruler by three or four centuries. The graves belong to the sixteenth century B.C. and are usually dated from 1580 to 1500 B.C. It seems that Grave VI is the earliest, and almost contemporary with it is Grave II. Then come Graves IV and V, Graves III and I being the latest.[48] We may finally note that the shaft graves of Circle A formed part of an extensive cemetery of the Middle to Late Helladic I period. A good section of that cemetery was left outside the Citadel when the western extension of the Cyclopean walls was erected. Within the Citadel Middle Helladic graves were found beneath the Ramp House (four certain and two possible), and under the South House (one), and Tsountas mentions a number of cuttings under the House of the Warriors which may have been graves. The "golden treasure," found by Drosenos and Stamatakes at the northwest angle of the Ramp House, could have formed part of the contents of a plundered shaft grave, and there can be no doubt about the plundered shaft grave under the Granary.[49]

After this brief discussion of the shaft graves and their contents, we must consider the suggestion advanced early in the study of Mycenaean antiquities that the tholos and chamber tombs and their contents mark a departure and change in burial customs. That they are different types of graves which could not have evolved from the Middle Helladic cists and the shaft graves we have admitted before; we have also tried to indicate their origin. But do they mark a change in burial customs? The suggestion was based on the observation that

[47] *Palace of Minos,* IV, pp. 237ff. and *The Shaft Graves and Bee-Hive Tombs of Mycenae,* 1929. Gardner, *New Chapters in Greek History,* pp. 76, 78. For the grave of Lerna, cf. Caskey, *Hesperia,* 24 (1955), pp. 32-34.

[48] *BSA,* 25 (1921-1923), pp. 119-120.

[49] See *Mycenae,* pp. 51, 61; Schliemann, *Mycenae,* pp. 351-362; *Mycenaean Age,* p. 114.

"the beehive dead are never embalmed, nor do they wear masks, nor are laid on pebble beds"; not a sword was found in some sixty-odd chamber tombs explored by Tsountas, and the wealth of objects found in the shaft graves has no parallel in the explored tholos and chamber tombs.[50] In considering the points raised we have to recall that not a single tholos tomb was found intact in Mycenae, that actually we have but the tholos of Dendra as our only evidence, that in our evaluation we actually compare the contents of the shaft graves, sepulchers of kings, with those of the chamber tombs, sepulchers of commoners. But even so, the suggestion does not seem weighty.

Let us consider in order the points raised. In the shaft graves of Circle A we have the remains of 19 persons; at least 24 skeletons were cleared in the shaft graves of Circle B, making a total of 43 instances of burial. Of these only 1 case yielded evidence of embalming, the skeleton found by Schliemann in Grave V. Certainly 1 instance in 43 cases does not indicate a custom; on the contrary, it proves that embalming was an intrusive element, imported presumably from Egypt, tried but once and then abandoned. To the same conclusion we will be led by the consideration of the masks. We must recall that such masks were unknown in Middle Helladic burial practices but appear suddenly in the shaft graves. Five masks were found in Graves IV and V and 1 in Grave Gamma, a total of 6 known thus far against at least 30 skeletons of men cleared. This proportion again seems to indicate that placing masks over the faces of men was not a prevalent custom, if it was a custom at all. It certainly has no antecedents in Greece, nor did it have a place in the burial traditions of the people;[51] it was an intrusive element, an innovation whose abandonment after its novelty had worn off was rather natural.

The floors of the shaft graves were covered with pebbles, following a long-established custom. The purpose of these pebbles was to provide a means of drainage for water which could seep into the graves. How anxious the people were to avoid seepage is indicated by the clay employed over the roof of the shafts. In a tholos or a chamber tomb the need for providing drainage is practically non-existent since they are well roofed sepulchers; hence the discontinuation of pebbly

---

[50] *Mycenaean Age*, p. 344. We may add that only a few bronze daggers and knives were found by Professor Wace in the graves he excavated: *Chamber Tombs of Mycenae*, pl. VII.

[51] The gold bands of Mochlos: Seager, R. *Explorations in the Island of Mochlos*, Figs. 8, 9, 41 are considered by their discoverer as diadems.

floors was natural. In the tholos tomb of Clytemnestra, where water could seep into the tholos, drainage was provided by means of a catch-pit and drain. The scarcity of weapons and valuables in the chamber tombs can be accounted for by the practice of descendants in removing objects of value or of use from the graves during a later interment, a practice noticed by both Professor Wace and Professor Blegen.[52] Perhaps the gifts placed in the tholos tombs were less numerous and less exotic, but this moderation indicates only that the exuberance experienced possibly under Egyptian influence and sudden wealth naturally receded before the conservatism which characterized the burial customs of the people and before the belief in a future life which required no provisions and ornaments especially made for the grave. For there can be no doubt that a good many of the gold ornaments of the shaft graves, of thin gold foil, were made especially for the graves. But characteristic furnishings such as cups and goblets, which appear constantly, from the time the custom of placing offerings in graves recommenced until the end of the Mycenaean era, continue to be laid with the dead. As a matter of fact, the study of the burial customs as revealed by the shaft graves and by the tholos and chamber tombs will lead to the definite conclusion that no break or change followed the introduction and use of the latter. All are family graves, all are furnished for the trip to the lower world; the same carelessness toward the bones of ancestors characterizes both the period of the shaft graves and that of the tholos and chamber tombs; there is the same custom of interment, the heaping of earth, the marking of the graves, funeral meals and libations. If we take into consideration the possibility of the derivation of the tholos tomb from the Grave Circle, we may well wonder whether the usual differentiation of the shaft grave dynasty and the tholos tomb dynasty is valid. It certainly cannot imply a new element in the population, since no changes occur in the culture and practices of the people. We may certainly assume that the ruling family of Mycenae, whose ancestors were buried in the shaft graves, initiated the tholos tomb under Egyptian influence, just as the common people, under the same influence, abandoned the traditional cist graves and proceeded to bury their dead in chamber tombs. The difference in the form of the burial chamber was due to the desire of distinguishing the royal graves from those of commoners, the same

[52] *Chamber Tombs of Mycenae*, pp. 138, 145; *Prosymna*, p. 247.

desire which a short time before had created the shaft graves out of the cists of the Middle Helladic period.

The problems connected with the shaft graves and their occupants are many and interesting. A number of them have been solved; solutions for others can only be suggested at this time; still others remain unsolved. For years scholars were hopeful that other shaft graves would be discovered and be excavated in our modern ways. That hope was realized in 1952. We may continue to hope that some intact tholos tombs will be next in the order of discovery, and that final conclusions will be possible. Until then we can be sure of one fact: the tholos and chamber tombs do not mark a break or change in Mycenaean practices of the Middle and Late Bronze Ages.

VI

GRAVE CIRCLE B AND THE NEW
SHAFT GRAVES

THE story of the discovery and exploration of Grave Circle B is
another example of the benevolent intervention of Τύχη Ἀγαθὴ in
the affairs of the archaeologist. Human instrumentality was doubtless
of consequence, but homage should be offered to Lady Luck, whose
smiling countenance may illumine the paths of the field worker. The
year of the discovery of Grave Circle B will mark another high
point in the exciting story of Mycenae and her remains, and the
details of its exploration are necessary in this first effort toward a
fuller discussion of the results.[1]

In the spring of 1951 at the request of the ephor of the district,
Dr. John Papademetriou, the Greek Service for the Restoration and
Preservation of Ancient Monuments, under the direction of Professor
Anastasios Orlandos and under the supervision of Dr. E. Stikas,
began the restoration of the Tomb of Clytemnestra. By October 1951
the task was completed and it was then decided to recreate its original
aspect of a mound by covering the stone vault of the tomb with earth.
In the course of that operation, three or four pieces of a poros stele
were found a few meters to the west of the apex of the vault; some
of these pieces were still standing on the original base which supported
it (Fig. 41). Excavations below the area of the stele revealed the
expected sepulcher, which turned out to be a shaft grave similar to
those found by Schliemann within the Citadel. The grave was cleared
and its contents removed by the *epimeletes* of the district, Seraphim
Charitonides. It became clear at the outset that not only the shape of
the grave but also its contents corresponded to the remains in the
Citadel, and this caused a good deal of excitement.

In November 1951 Dr. Papademetriou and I visited the site and
examined the area of the new shaft grave. A little to the south we
detected three stones jutting from the surface; they seemed to be

[1] For a brief announcement of the discoveries, cf. Mylonas, G. E., and J. Papademetriou, *Archaeology*, 5 (1952), pp. 194-200; 8 (1955), 43-50; Papademetriou,
PAE, 1952, pp. 427-472, 1953, and 1954; Marinatos, *Geras*, pp. 54-86.

worked stones, they were *in situ*, and, what was more exciting, they seemed to have been set on a curve. The last observation made us wonder whether they might not form part of a circular wall enclosing the area within which the grave was found. In January 1952 we conducted a preliminary investigation which proved that the stones actually did belong to a circular enclosing wall, a good section of which was then detected to the northwest of the excavated shaft grave. From that section we could roughly figure the diameter of the circle, which almost equalled the diameter of the Grave Circle within the Citadel. Since the shaft grave cleared by Charitonides was not in the center of the indicated new Circle but near its edge, it became evident that within its area more graves were likely to be found.

The importance of the discovery was immediately realized by the Greek Archaeological Society, and its Council decided that the excavation of the Circle should be carried out as expertly as possible. It assigned the funds from the Pharmakopoulos bequest to the project and entrusted the excavation to the ephor of the district, Dr. Papademetriou, and to an advisory committee composed of Professors Antonios Keramopoullos and Spyridon Marinatos of the University of Athens and myself. In the first campaign, in the summer of 1952, all the members of the Committee were active; in the second and third campaigns—the summers of 1953 and 1954—the author collaborated with Dr. Papademetriou in the direction of the excavation. The *epimeletes*, D. Theochares, undertook and made all the architectural and other plans. The personnel also included Seraphim Charitonides (for the first campaign), Katherine Biddle and Nike Mylonas of Vassar College, and Constantine Papademetriou. Dr. J. Lawrence Angel, of the Daniel Baugh Institute of Anatomy, undertook the study of the skeletal material, and V. and N. Tombazis, the photographic part. We were fortunate to have the services of the master technician John Karametros, to whose care and devoted skill we entrusted the cleaning of all the graves, and who deserves high praise for his work. Arghyres Marines served throughout as our expert vase-mender. It will be impossible to include here the names of all the faithful laborers who contributed so much to the success of the project, but those of Constantine Dases and Athanasios Konizeras, of Mycenae, and Teles Tsitsekos, the chief guard of antiquities of the site, cannot be omitted from any description of the exploration of the new Grave Circle.

[129]

The excavation of the new Circle was completed in September 1954. A good deal of the material uncovered is still to be treated in the laboratory and to be studied. Even the preliminary reports of the campaigns have not been published. It becomes evident, therefore, that it is as yet impossible to describe and discuss the work fully; that the present account has to be limited to a general presentation of the excavation, that it is preliminary in form, and that it contains only a few of the impressions and notes of the writer.

At the very beginning of the exploration it became evident that some system of naming the graves had to be devised to differentiate them from the shaft graves discovered by Schliemann. Since Schliemann's discoveries are usually given Latin numerals, we decided to call the new shaft graves by the letters of the Greek alphabet.

The new Grave Circle B is located by the side of the modern road to the Citadel, some 130 meters to the west of the Lion Gate and only 10 meters west of the apex of the vault of Clytemnestra's tholos (Fig. 3). Of its circular wall only a small segment and a few stones remain today. A good deal of the eastern side was destroyed in Late Helladic III times when the Tomb of Clytemnestra was constructed. A glance at the plan will show how the circle of the tholos encroached upon the enclosing circular wall, and how by mere chance the excavators of the former missed Graves Alpha and Rho (Fig. 87). It seems as if a good part of the western section of the Circle was destroyed when the modern road to the Citadel was constructed, but there can be no proof that the Circle on that side was still preserved at the time of the modern construction. The southern half of the Circle, standing on the slope, apparently collapsed at an early period and only a very few of its stones can be detected below the slope to the south. As a matter of fact, its southwestern arc must have been ruined before the historic era had set in, since a Geometric round structure was found built over that section. At the southeast section we have only the three blocks which told the tale of the existence of a circle. They measure only 1.10 meters in length, while the preserved northern arc has a length of some 16 meters. From that length the diameter of the circular area can be figured as close to 28 meters, almost the same as the diameter of Grave Circle A. The preserved north arc was somewhat damaged when the modern water channel of the village was carried across its width; however, it still suffices to offer a good account of its construction (Fig. 40).

The wall is made of large unworked stones roughly hewn and of uneven size and height, set erect by each other, forming the inner and outer faces and laid on a prepared layer of thin and small flat stones which project a bit beyond its base. On top of this first row, smaller stones are piled and all interstices are filled with even smaller stones and clay. The thickness of the wall, between its inner and outer faces, is filled with small stones and earth rather carefully piled. The construction could be termed "primitive Cyclopean." The wall has a thickness of some 1.55 meters and attains a maximum height of 1.20 meters. The northern section seems to be preserved to its original height, its top being level. In many parts its top was found covered by a thin layer of what seemed to be poros dust and chips, a layer which extended into the circular area in the neighborhood of Grave Nu. The pottery found around the wall and in it, purely Middle Helladic Minyan—gray and black—and matt-painted, indicates that the Circle was built in late Middle Helladic times.

Within the circular enclosure, 24 different graves were found, of which only 14 can be considered as real shaft graves. Grave Alpha, cleared by Charitonides, is such a real shaft grave. On top of it and some 0.80 meters below the original surface, fragments of a stele were found with its original base (Fig. 41). The stele is of poros and on the upper section of its front bears an incised representation of a charging bull attacking hunters. The work is primitive, but compares with that on fragments x and xi found by Schliemann in Grave Circle A.[2] Apparently the stele faced west. The measurements of the shaft were originally given as 3.30 meters in length, 2.35 meters in width, and 3 meters in depth, but subsequently the sides of the grave have been cleared to their original face and the length was found to amount to 3.90 meters (from east to west), the width to 2.90 meters.[3] Above its floor its sides are lined with low rubble walls which were used in the support of the roof. The floor was covered with pebbles and on them was found the skeleton of a man, lying on his back in an extended position from east to west, with the head on the east side. The bones of another person were found piled along the north side of the grave. The grave contained rich funeral offerings, among which were three bronze swords, a dagger with engraved

[2] Heurtley, BSA, 25 (1921-1925), pp. 54-86.

[3] As a matter of fact the measurements of graves given here should be considered as tentative. They are what I recorded in the excavation diary at a time when the graves and their walls were being cleared.

spirals on its bronze blade, two silver and two bronze vases, gold bands, a gold bracelet, a gold ornament of the "garter type" (Gamaschenhalter) beautifully decorated in repoussé work (Fig. 42), a pin of rock crystal, and some twenty-five vases of late Middle Helladic times. One of these is a jar bearing a wavy decoration in whitish color on dark ground.[4]

Grave Beta was found and cleared in the first regular campaign, in the summer of 1952. It is a shaft dug in the rock and measures 2.60 meters in length, 2.28 meters in width at the opening, and 2.27 by 1.40 meters at its floor; its depth averaged 2.95 meters. It is oriented approximately from north to south and, to a height of 1 meter from the floor, its sides were lined with the usual walls which supported the timbers for its roof. The walls along the long sides were of rubble, while those along the short sides were made of mud brick. The roof was made of timbers spread from long wall to long wall, covered with a matting of twigs, leaves, and branches and sealed with a thick layer of greenish clay known to the villagers as *plesia* from the site where it can be found even today. The fill over the roof contained few sherds, but a great amount of the crumbled rock which was dug in the making of the shaft and some bones of animals certainly from the funeral meal. Its quality made it apparent that it had not been worked by repeated digging and that the shaft was not used for repeated burials. This observation proved correct when the grave was completely cleared. On its floor covered with pebbles, only one skeleton was found in an extended position, lying from north to south with the head near the north side (Fig. 44). Both hands, the elbows being somewhat bent, were brought toward the pelvic area. The head was slightly turned to the right shoulder, but the position may have resulted from a slight rolling over after the decay of the flesh. Above the head, and along the north side of the grave, five vases were found in the position in which they had been placed, while two additional vases were disclosed in the southwest corner beyond the feet. A plain gold band was found around the left arm, and two thin gold bands were revealed, the one above the other, on the right side of the pelvis. A broad triangular dagger of bronze was uncovered with its broad side over the right elbow and its point toward the hand.

The grave was not very rich. In the course of the exploration of Grave Circle B richer and more interesting sepulchers were unearthed,

---

[4] For a brief report, cf. Papademetriou, *PAE*, 1951, pp. 197-203.

but the excitement caused by this grave will remain unsurpassed. Ever since Schliemann's graphic descriptions of the shaft graves within the Citadel, scholars had been looking forward to the day when they would see the contents of such a grave in their original position. At long last we had such an undisturbed grave: the well-preserved skeleton in its original position, lying on its pebbly floor, with the funeral offerings as they had been left so many centuries ago! The excitement reached a climax when their Majesties King Paul and Queen Frederika of Greece, who have been so closely associated with the cultural activities and efforts of their country, visited the excavations and with their gracious interest and enthusiasm sparked our expectations which, as the work progressed, proved well inspired and founded.

The anthropological study proved that the skeleton belonged to a man, some forty years of age, a man who in life must have measured 1.70 meters in height. Of the vases found against the north side, four were typical stemmed goblets of the closing years of the Middle Helladic period, while the fifth was a jar bearing a matt decoration of bands and on the main zone ivy plants painted as though swaying in a mild wind (Fig. 43a). One of the two vases from the south-western corner is a spouted jar with an interesting geometric decoration in matt black color painted directly on the clay (Fig. 43b).

Grave Gamma is one of the larger and better preserved shaft graves of Circle B and is oriented from northeast to southwest, but for convenience we shall call it from north to south. It measures 3.80 meters in length by 2.80 meters in width and 3.50 meters in depth; these dimensions, however are reduced to 3.20 by 1.80 meters at the floor by the lining walls which are preserved to their original height of c. 0.80 meters. Again, the lining walls are of rubble masonry along the long east and west sides, and of mud brick along the short north and south sides. On these walls rested the wooden beams, now turned into grayish powder, supporting the roof; the central beam must have measured some 0.25 meters in thickness. The roof consisted again of a matting of dry leaves, twigs, and plants, and of a thick layer of waterproof clay *plesia*. The leaf matting was perhaps kept tight and in position by a row of flagstones found on top of the rubble wall which lined the long sides of the grave. In other graves such flagstones were found placed over and on either side of the roof beams, perhaps to protect their ends from direct contact with the earth-fill above.

In Grave Gamma the earth filling the shaft was found to contain the crumbled remains of rock, turned almost to reddish earth and pebbles, soft grayish earth, fragments of clay *plesia* derived from repeated replacements of the roof construction, animal bones, and a great quantity of sherds from which some forty vases were pieced together. Professor Marinatos has suggested that these vases were broken and left at the site after they were used at the funeral meal held over the graves (a meal attested by the animal bones).[5] We have seen how it was customary that goblets which may have been used for a last toast to the dead should be broken against the door jambs of the chamber tombs; and some of the vases found in the fill may well have served that purpose and met with that fate. Others, however, must have once been laid in the grave as funeral offerings and were removed in order to make room for the people who were to be buried next. It must be noted that only nine painted vases were found in Grave Gamma, where four persons were buried; in Grave Beta, which was not so rich and in which only one person was buried, seven vases were discovered, and a total of twenty-five vases were reported from Grave Alpha, which contained but two burials. This may indicate that some of the vases which were originally placed in Grave Gamma were removed to make room for later burials. This view was strengthened by the discovery of a number of vases arranged neatly over the west edge of the roof of Grave Nu; they were no doubt placed there after they were removed from the interior of the grave. It should now be noted that no vases were found in the fill of Grave Beta, which was never reopened after its single burial was completed, although animal bones were found, proving that a funeral meal was held over its roof. In a similar manner, no sherds were reported from the fill of Grave II, in which one body was laid, while Schliemann reports sherds from the fill of Graves III, IV, and V used for the burial of many people.[6] If all the vases found in the fill are to be attributed to the funeral party, then we should find some over graves where even one person was buried and where, as in the case of Grave B, we have evidence for a meal held

---

[5] Marinatos, *Geras*, pp. 63-66.

[6] Schliemann states that the fill over Grave I was "natural" and "unmixed" and was brought "from another place," *Mycenae*, p. 150.

over its roof. On the other hand, if vases were taken out of the graves to make room for subsequent burials and either placed on the roof or merely thrown out, then we ought not to find them in the fill of the graves in which only one person was buried. The lack of remains of pottery in the fill of Graves II and Beta, in which one person was buried, seems to indicate that a good many of the vases found in the fill of graves were taken out to make room for those buried later. The shape of vases will not change this conclusion, since cups and vases holding liquids are found in both the graves and the fill.

At about the height of the rockcut top of Grave Gamma were uncovered a number of stone fragments belonging to a stele and to two bases of stelai. Only one-half of one of the bases was found, while the other base is almost completely preserved. To judge from its sculptured decoration, the latter was originally a stele and was later transformed into a base. The stele found, only a large segment, is of shelly sandstone and is undecorated. Perhaps it stood on the completely preserved base. No fragments of the stele supported by the other base were discovered. From the depth in which the fragments were found and their position, Professor Marinatos, to whom we owe the first careful study of the stelai over Grave Gamma, has concluded that they were piled in the way found when the roof of the grave caved in and the earth over it sank at least 0.50 centimeters from the surface. The hole which resulted was then filled up and one of the stelai was reerected on the new level; the stele on the surface was destroyed or disappeared in later years as was the case with many another surface monument.

The base which originally was a stele presents points of great interest (Fig. 45). It is made of soft poros and measures about 1.05 meters in length and 0.62 meters in width at the bottom and 0.60 meters at the top. Its face is covered with carved decoration in technique similar to that met with in the stelai of Class II from Grave Circle A; in other words, the design is produced by cutting away the background. Consequently, the figures are flat, but they have strong contour lines and a good decorative quality. The area to be decorated, almost the entire surface of the stele, is framed by two fillets and is divided by a raised band in an upper, larger register decorated with connected spirals and a narrower lower register filled with a figure composition. A good deal of this decoration is missing, having been cut away when the stele was transformed into a base, but the compositions are clear.

The spiral motif is well known from stele No. 1428 found over Grave V by Schliemann. The figure decoration has no parallel. Its middle part is missing, but the composition was successfully completed by Professor Marinatos. In the lower part of the composition we have the backs of two lions standing on their hind legs on either side of a central unit now mostly missing. To that unit belong the two rear legs, and the end of the tail of an animal to be seen beside the rear legs of the lion to the left. At the corner and behind the legs of that lion we have the sign of Waz.[7] Above the lions and on either side we have two human forms. The one to the right is standing and is brandishing an object with both hands. It could be a long knife similar to the one held by the standing figure on stele No. 1428 and to those found by Schliemann in Grave IV; but since it is held by both hands it may perhaps be better to see in it a short, stout club. The other man is represented as wounded or dying, but certainly on his back, with legs drawn up and hands bent on either side of the head. Over the fallen man, to fill the space, the sculptor added another of those geometric forms which is usually interpreted as an altar.

The tail and rear legs in front of the lion to the left must belong to a large animal, possibly a bull or cow, which is rearing up on its hind legs, thus filling the space left between the two lions and the two men—a large animal which is being attacked by lions. The design, an animal being attacked by two others, as Professor Marinatos has pointed out, is a common Minoan theme, here treated in a typical Mycenaean fashion and perhaps given a narrative content. We may now note that while the lion to the left is standing vigorously on its hind legs and is bending its neck in a characteristic attitude of attack, the lion to the right seems to be lying on its haunches with its tail on the ground line and head fallen back. It is apparent that while the one lion is attacking briskly, the other is perhaps lying stunned or wounded. If we bring the human forms into the composition and relate them to the animal scene—and there is no reason why we should not—then we will agree with Professor Marinatos that one of the men, having successfully attacked the lion which is lying

[7] For the use of that Egyptian symbol in Greece, see Marinatos in *BSA*, 46 (1951), pp. 106-108.

stunned, is continuing his assault, while the other was less successful and was put *hors de combat* by the wild animals. The story told by the relief is clear: two lions are attacking a herd of cattle. The men in charge try to save their bulls and oxen by attacking the lions. In the course of the action, one of the men is killed or seriously wounded, while the other successfully attacks one of the lions. But the other lion is attacking another of the animals of the herd.[8] Thus on the stele we have a representation dealing with the activities of perhaps one of the first men buried in the grave.

On the floor of the grave, which was covered with pebbles, were found the skeletons of four persons (Fig. 46). Along its west side and extending from north to south the complete skeleton of one person, skeleton No. 1, was found occupying almost one-half of the width of the grave. Its position is striking, with legs apart forming a wide bow and the hands resting on the hips. The head seems to lie on its back. Professor Marinatos, who was present at the clearing of the skeleton, attributes the attitude to a huge figure-of-eight shield which covered the person and which was held by means of hands and feet. However, no evidence of leather or wood was found to strengthen that suggestion, and in the campaign of 1953 at least two more examples of skeletons in this position were found, one of which belonged to a girl who could not have been buried under a shield. Along the right side of skeleton No. 1 were revealed a bronze sword, whose point rested almost on the kneecap, and a bronze dagger with ivory handle.

Along the east side of the grave two skeletons, Nos. 2 and 3, were found, one almost on top of the other. The position of their bones would indicate clearly that they were pushed carefully aside to make room for the burial of the person laid along the west side. Again, from the position of the bones it seems that these two were originally laid in a more or less extended position. Along the right side of the two skeletons were found a number of swords, daggers, small narrow knives, and a spear point of bronze. According to Dr. Angel, the skeleton along the eastern side, No. 3, belonged to a woman. The fourth skeleton was found beyond the feet of the three and across the width of the grave, stretched from east to west with the head to the east. His hands were apparently held together over the pelvic area.

---

[8] Marinatos, *Geras*, p. 74. Cf. the graphic description on the shield for Achilles made by Hephaestos, *Iliad*, XVIII, 572-586: two lions attacking a herd while the shepherds are trying to save it.

The head seemed as if it were turned to its right side and faced north. Beyond it were found three vases, two cups, and a hydria with matt-decoration of concentric circles.

At the time of excavation it was believed that the skeleton was that of a woman, but Dr. Angel's study proved that it belongs to a young man, about 28 years of age, some 1.70 meters in height, with a skull fracture and an extremely clean-cut trephination done just before death. Was death precipitated by the operation? This is the first and oldest instance on record of such an operation in Greek territory, antedating, as a matter of fact, the examples known from Egypt.[9] The position of the skeleton across the grave, in a slanting position, is interesting and one wonders whether it belonged to the person buried last. There can be no doubt that it was not the first person to be buried in the grave; in that case he would have been laid along the length of the sepulcher. He would be either the last or the one before the last. It seems to me that he was placed in that position before they started moving the earlier remains to the side, in which case he is the one to be buried before the last; consequently skeleton No. 1 must belong to the person buried last. If that is the case, one wonders what was placed in the area of the grave occupied by him before his interment. I would suggest that in that area were originally stored the vases belonging to skeletons Nos. 2 and 3—to the persons who apparently were the earlier occupants of the grave. When the person to whom skeleton No. 4 belongs was laid in that section of the grave, the vases stored there were thrown out of the sepulcher. It is curious to note the paucity of gifts found with No. 4— not a single weapon and only three small vases. Could this fact indicate that the young man was an unimportant member of the family, or that he died before he had a chance to amass wealth and fame which would entitle him to more elaborate funereal gear? His case will recall that of the middle skeleton of Grave V, whose lack of funeral offerings, in contrast to the rich furnishings of the other two occupants of the grave, caused Schliemann to assume that he was despoiled in antiquity. Immediately above the head of skeleton No. 1, a large vase was located and to the left of its base was found a mask of electrum, resting almost on its edge; behind it were revealed gray remnants of decayed wood. The position of the mask is puzzling; was

---

[9] I am indebted to Dr. Angel for this information. Another cruder example is now reported from Lerna.

it in its original position or was it removed to that point at a later time, and even placed in a wooden box; and does it belong to skeleton No. 1? Unfortunately I cannot give a personal impression of the matter, because I was not at Mycenae at the time of its discovery. Beyond the area of the mask and along the northern side of the grave were found, neatly packed, more swords, parts of a bronze vase, a gold cup which was crushed but well preserved, two small vases, a large jug with a globular body, and interesting painted decoration of spirals (Fig. 47),[10] and a larger vessel, a monochrome hydria. Under the packed swords were found the remnants of a wooden box, whose sides were apparently covered with silver plate, and a carved amethyst bead. By the base of the jug, and near the assortment of bronze weapons which belong to skeleton No. 2, a well-preserved gold cup was found still standing on its base. The painted jug had been placed over some thin gold bands (Fig. 48), which must have belonged to skeletons Nos. 2 and 3 and which were piled there at the time when the skeletons were pushed to the corner.

We must especially note the engraved gem. It is an amethyst per-forated bead, 0.009 meters in extreme length, on which we have in intaglio the head of a man vividly portrayed (Fig. 49). He is repre-sented bearded, but without moustache, with long hair, reminiscent of the long-haired Achaeans, a rather broad skull, and an almost Grecian nose with both nostrils showing in a manner so beloved to modern artists. The eye in full front is vivid, and the modeling of the high cheekbones extraordinary. The ear, large for the head, is high but effectively placed. Does this portrait represent one of the people buried in the grave? That will be difficult to maintain, but it is possible to suggest that in general it does give the appearance of the Mycenaean rulers. Perhaps it will be instructive to compare the head on the gem with the archer represented on a steatite vase from Knossos of Late Minoan II times, illustrated and discussed by Sir Arthur Evans.[11] The trunks worn by that figure, resembling those we find worn by the hunters in the lion-hunt composition on the dagger blade from Grave V, may indicate that the man on the steatite vase is also a Mycenaean.

The same could not be stated for the mask (Fig. 50). There can be no doubt that in it we have the general appearance of a bearded

[10] It recalls the jug found in Grave I: Schuchardt, *op.cit.*, fig. 166.
[11] *Palace of Minos*, III, p. 106, fig. 59.

man. Its size (maximum height 0.21 meters, maximum width above eyebrows 0.175 meters, minimum bottom of chin 0.037 meters) would correspond well to a face, but the features seem too generalized. A small hole is apparent beyond the side of each ear, 0.02 meters from the left ear, 0.012 meters from the right, apparently used for holding the mask in position. The holes were not made by a nail driven through the metal and the evidence available would not suggest that this mask was nailed on a wooden coffin, as believed by Staes and Persson. Unfortunately, it was not found covering any face, as seems to be the case with the masks found by Schliemann.

Grave Delta, located to the southeast of Grave Beta, is similarly cut in the rock, but is much shallower, measuring only 1.60 meters in depth, 3.25 meters in length, and 2.55 meters in width. At its floor it measures only 2.50 by 1.38 meters. Ledges left in the rock around the four sides, instead of a wall, served to support the beams of the roof. In the fill of the grave were found many potsherds and animal bones, as well as a fragment of a bronze sword which later was found to belong to a sword uncovered on the floor. This again demonstrates the carelessness with which the gifts of a previous burial were treated. On its floor of pebbles three skeletons were found in an extended position lying southeast to northwest (Fig. 52). A bronze bowl and a well-preserved and decorated vase were found in the northwest corner, while a painted jar was found at the northeast. By the bronze bowl seventeen stone arrowheads were found bundled together; apparently they were kept in a leather bag, traces of which were also found. The most interesting finds from this grave are two swords, illustrating the two forms usual in the shaft graves, one found along the east side and the other not far from the west. The former has a broad and ribbed blade, slightly horned shoulders, and a rather long and strong tang with flanged sides to hold the haft, apparently of wood, which was topped by an ivory pommel. The latter is a magnificent weapon worthy of any king. Its blade, long and rather narrow with a central rib, is 0.945 meters in length and is decorated on both sides with a series of engraved griffins. Its shoulders are rounded and exhibit a small tang over which was placed its haft, apparently of wood; this was covered by a sheathing of gold, made of two plates front and rear, similarly decorated. The sheathing, of very thin gold sheet, is so worked around the shoulders of the blade as to give the impression of a winged type, and was attached by small gold nails, a few of which can still be seen. Its decoration is in repoussé and of great delicacy: the cylindrical part is covered with triple spirals, while the ends, on either side of the blade, are terminated by two snub-nosed heads of lions (Fig. 51). Their manes are graphically rendered by means of triangular incisions, while a pellet bears the triangular eyes with a central dot. On each of the two horn-like projections of the sides, we find engraved the head of a smaller animal, having lozenge-shaped eyes with a dot in the center. Could this be the head of a goat and the entire composition a harbinger of the chimaera notion? Above a gold ring we have the regular ivory pommel of Mycenaean times, badly frayed but still keeping its original shape and dimensions; the pommel measures 0.10 meters in maximum diameter, while the length of the gold sheath is 0.125 meters and its maximum width between the horned edges is 0.085 meters.

The sheathing recalls that found by Schliemann in Grave IV which for a time was considered as the top of a scepter, but now is rightly known as the hilt of a sword.[12] Two daggers, one of which has an ivory pommel, and two bronze knives were also found in this tomb.

Grave Epsilon, adjoining Gamma to the southwest, proved a very instructive tomb. It measures 3.25 meters in length, 2.20 meters in width, and 2.85 meters in depth (Fig. 53). Its northeastern corner is so near the southwest side of Grave Gamma that the rock between them was cut, forming a small opening, enlarged a good deal by the operations and by the continued crumbling of the rock. There can be no doubt that the opening is accidental and cannot be conceived as a means of communication between Graves Epsilon and Gamma because when it was revealed it was at a height above the roof of the latter grave. In the excavation diary I made a special entry regarding the "cut" and also the remark that it was being enlarged constantly by our operations in the course of clearing the two graves. The opening recalls that between Grave I and Keramopoullos' cave in Circle A, already discussed.

The roof of the grave was made of flagstones covered by a thick layer of clay, averaging 0.30 meters in thickness, and was supported by heavy timber resting on low rubble walls. Apparently it had caved in before the cavity of the grave was filled, or even partially filled

---

[12] Schliemann, *Mycenae*, Nos. 451, 452, p. 287; Schuchardt, *Schliemann's Excavations*, p. 250, fig. 250; *Mycenaean Age*, p. 168, fig. 63, Karo, *op.cit.*, pl. 87, No. 294.

with earth seeping into it along with the water; consequently, a good many of the flagstones of the roof were found on the floor itself and on the bones, which were badly disturbed by their fall. By the southwest corner we have the occupant of the grave, a skeleton in a strongly contracted position lying on its right side and with its right hand below the cheek (Fig. 54). A good number of teeth scattered along the east side of the grave seem to indicate that at least two people were buried in the sepulcher, but the position of only the one, in the contracted posture, could be determined. By the skull of that skeleton and in the southwest corner of the grave, a bronze bowl with a very broad opening was found, while in the opposite southeast corner was originally placed a bronze jug with a high swinging handle; only the handle and the rim of the mouth survived, the rest had corroded badly and was found in tiny flakes. Behind the back of the skeleton, and under two flagstones of the roof, a mass of thin gold ornaments was found pressed together (Fig. 54). It will be difficult to forget the impression created by the sudden appearance of these crushed gold ornaments, when the slabs were lifted. We could feel some of the pulsing intensity which characterized the Mycenaean days of Schliemann, and in one instant we were carried back beyond the mythological era of Greece to the days when the greatness of Mycenae was being fashioned by the people whose ornaments were shining brightly once more beneath the rays of a Greek sun.

The gold ornaments are mostly thin bands decorated in repoussé and cruciform rosettes composed of two long bands crossing each other at the center. In a good number of these thin gold sheets, holes for attachment are to be seen at the ends and in the center, while their edges are curled over bronze wire. Why were all these ornaments found in a massive block behind the skull and back of the skeleton? Were they piled there intentionally, having been removed from the parts of the body which they decorated originally? And yet the skeleton, though disturbed by the fallen slabs, seemed to be lying in its original contracted position with all the ornaments at its back. Because of the position of the bones it is impossible to maintain that the skeleton was brushed to the side and that its ornaments were in the same manner removed. Were the ornaments originally placed like a sheet over the torso, face, and head, and were they thrown backward by the impact of the falling roof? Perhaps this may prove the only possible explanation. That they were not placed over a wooden coffin is certain. In the excavation diary I especially recorded the fact that no traces of wood were found near or around the skeleton.

Across the pebbly floor of the grave and in its northwest corner was lying on its side a bronze crater some 0.76 meters high, excellently preserved, and within it was found a bronze jug, some 0.44 meters tall, equally well preserved (Fig. 53). Both are similar to those found by Schliemann in Grave IV,[13] and what is more interesting, they were found in exactly the same relative arrangement—the jug in the crater. It is not yet ascertained whether the bronze vessels from Grave Epsilon are made of copper in the same way as those found by Schliemann. By the bronze vessels, and ranged along the north side of the grave, three large clay vases were found crushed. No weapons were discovered in the grave, which is sometimes called the "Grave of the Bronzes," and this as well as the presence of the massed thin bands of gold makes one wonder whether in this tomb women alone were buried. In Grave IV, where similar bronze vases were found, two women were buried along with men; and yet in four other instances of graves of women, in Circles A and B, we have no bronze vessels of any kind. Perhaps Dr. Angel's final report will clear the matter.

In the summer of 1952 Graves Zeta, Eta, and Theta were also cleared. All three are comparatively small shafts (one could call them cists), cut in the rock, and recall strongly the cist burials of the Middle Helladic period. The contents of Grave Theta were destroyed when the channel of the modern aqueduct was constructed in 1946. A bronze sword is reported to have been found in it, but it was badly smashed by the laborers opening the channel.

Grave Zeta measures at its floor only 1.90 meters in length, 1.10 meters in width, and presents an average depth of 0.60 meters. A single skeleton in a strongly contracted position was found in it, lying on its right side and facing north. Seven clay vessels and a bronze knife with an ivory pommel were placed in front of his torso. Of the vases, three were goblets and cups of Middle Helladic Shapes, one a spouted jug, and the last one a small prochous.

Grave Eta is another cist cut in the rock, measuring 1.10 meters in length, 0.75 meters in width, and 0.62 to 0.65 meters in depth. A single skeleton was found in it, in a strongly contracted position and on its right side (Fig. 55). A bronze knife was found in front

[13] Schliemann, *Mycenae*, Nos. 436, 437, pp. 274-275.

of the body and with it five clay vases of which two were goblets of the Middle Helladic type, the third a spouted jug, the fourth a smaller jug and the fifth a bowl. The three cists in construction and in contents are inferior to the shaft graves and recall the small graves found in Grave Circle A by Stamatakes. They are located in the northwest section of Grave Circle B and are almost adjacent to the modern road which leads to the Citadel. Beyond them to the west and almost under the pavement of the road were located Graves Omicron and Pi.

The channel of the village aqueduct crossed Grave Omicron and, as a matter of fact, exactly over it had been built a small concrete cistern or settling tank. During these operations the stele which was standing over the grave apparently was found and was thrown aside. We found it in pieces where it had been thrown away; unfortunately, it could not tell us anything of its original arrangement. It is made of poros, is rectangular in shape, and the preserved fragment measures 0.74 meters in length, 0.84 meters in width, and 0.19 meters in thickness, and it is not sculptured. A fragment of the base on which it originally stood was also found. Some 1.30 meters below the level of the stele, the remnants of the roof began to appear. Its material and construction are clear: flagstones covered by a deep layer of clay *plesia* supported by wooden beams, abundant traces of which survived, resting in turn on walls of rubble which line the sides of the grave. At the level of the roof a few shattered vases were found, but only a few sherds came from the fill, which consisted of reddish and brownish earth filled with small stones and pebbles. From under the fragment of the base of the stele, however, we have a fragment of a cup of the Vaphio shape, decorated with spirals and possessing a plastic ring around the base—certainly a Late Helladic I product—and a few animal bones. The floor of the grave, covered with pebbles, was reached at a depth of 3 meters from the surface. Along the east side of the grave the skeleton of a woman was found lying in an extended position from south to north, while beyond her left side and against the west side of the grave were disclosed the packed remains of another skeleton. No objects were found with the bones, but the extended burial, apparently the last, yielded a good assortment of gifts. A little beyond and above the right side of the crushed skull two gold bands decorated in repoussé were found lying on each other, but bearing different designs, and immediately below

them with points almost touching the right shoulder, two pins, of
bronze with a head of rock crystal, and another of silver with perhaps
a wooden head covered with gold sheathing (Figs. 56 and 57c). By
the side of the former was found a ten-petaled rosette made of fine
thin gold leaves, kept in place by a central pin, whose head is well
preserved. Over the chest area, and especially over the right side and
the right arm, were found a good quantity of beads of amethyst and
of cornelian, and with them two oblong pieces of ivory with embossed
design. Above and beyond the left shoulder were found a number
of small objects in gold: bird-shaped beads, spirals in filigree work,
perhaps forming parts of bracelets, while a good many beads of
amber were found, especially over the pelvic area. Two gold ear
clips of a very modern design should also be mentioned (Fig. 58).

On the middle of the chest, the crystal head of a third pin was
found (Fig. 57a). This time the crystal ball is ribbed and its bronze
pin was directed toward the upper left arm bone. The crystal heads
remind one of those found by Schliemann in Grave III, a grave of
women, and believed by him to have been scepters.[14] Also, the rock
crystal balls from the same grave, mentioned by Schuchardt, one of
which was hollow inside, must have belonged to pins of our variety.[15]
As a matter of fact, the articles found in this grave remind one
strongly of those found in Grave III. There can be no doubt that
these articles were somewhat displaced when the roof caved in, but
it seems to us that their position clearly suggests the original arrangement. It is probable that the two bands, with the repoussé work, were
placed on the head and perhaps crosswise, the wider one below from
temple to temple and the narrow band across it from front to rear;
that the pins found below the bands were originally holding the
garment over the right shoulder; that the rosette was a decoration
worn over that shoulder, while the pin with the ribbed crystal head
secured or decorated the garment over the left shoulder. The neck-
laces of gold and stone beads were of course worn around the neck.
Is it possible to assume that the small spiraliform and stylized birds
were parts of bracelets placed beside the body?

The impact of the caving in of the roof on the objects contained
in the tomb can be sensed from the condition in which were found
the vases which once lined the walls of the lower half of the grave;
they were completely smashed. Along with those found over the

[14] *Ibid.*, p. 200 and Nos. 309 and 310.   [15] Schuchardt, *op.cit.*, p. 194, fig. 173.

roof they now form a fine collection of about thirty pieces. Against the north side of the grave was placed, among others, a beautiful four-handled jar, about 0.65 meters high, and decorated with crossed zigzag lines placed in three horizontal zones (Fig. 59). With its fragments was found the most interesting single object from the grave, broken, however, in four or five pieces: a magnificent bowl of rock crystal in the form of a duck (Figs. 60, 61). The body of the duck forms the bowl, its tail a flat spout at one end, while the neck and the head, which is turned backward in a most elegant manner, is used for a handle. The mastery with which the bird-form was adapted to the shape of the bowl, the exquisite workmanship, the definite and grace-ful contour lines, and the thinness of its walls, make this rock crystal bowl an outstanding work of art. Although such bowls are known, especially from Egypt, this is the first example of its type unearthed in Greece.[16] It measures only 0.135 meters in extreme length, and is in excellent preservation. Because of the number of objects of rock crystal found, this grave is often called the "Grave of Crystals."

In contrast, Grave Pi is a small and unpretentious rock-cut cist 1.80 meters in length, 0.95 meters in width, and 0.98 meters deep. On its floor the extended skeleton of a youth was found and beyond its feet four clay vases, three of which are stemmed goblets of the Middle Helladic variety.

Farther to the northeast of Graves Omicron and Pi, along the perimeter of the northern section of the Circle, the small Grave Xi was uncovered. Its exploration was very instructive. The area of the grave was originally covered by a layer of small stones mixed with reddish earth and terminated by larger stones which seemed to follow roughly the outline of the grave. Almost in the middle of the area thus outlined we had a clear arrangement of stones measuring 0.65 by 0.63 meters. Perhaps it was the σῆμα, or marker, of the grave. Immediately below this were found a number of animal bones, the remnants of the funeral meal. Below this point the fill was composed of brownish earth mixed with crumbled rock and a few sherds. At 0.54 meters from the surface the ledge for the roof beams formed by the walls lining the sides was revealed, going around the four sides of the grave, which is oriented almost from north to south. Its floor,

---

[16] For a duck fragment of a duck-vase of ivory from Asine see Frödin-Persson, *Asine*, pp. 388 and 391, fig. 254. For two ivory pyxides with a duck-lid from Ras Shamra see *Syria*, 1932, p. 6 and pl. VIII, 2. Also see Furtwängler and Loeschke, *Mykenische Vasen*, p. 14 and fig. 3 for a find from tomb 31 of Ialysos, Rhodes.

with its usual pebbles, was found at a depth of some 2 meters from the surface, and since the grave is a small one, measuring 1.95 by 1.38 meters, it gives the impression of a rectangular well. In its northwest corner were found the remains of a person who seems to have been originally placed in a contracted position and who later, even before the complete decay of the flesh had taken place (hence the relative position of the leg and thigh bones), was pushed aside to make room for the next occupant of the grave (Fig. 62). The skeleton of that occupant was found in its original position stretched from almost the center of the grave to its southeast corner. Around it were found some ten vases, stemmed goblets, jugs, and a large matt-painted amphora which originally stood in the northeastern corner of the grave. The skeletal remains prove that the person buried last must have been five or six years of age, a small girl who was laid to rest in this deep grave with a good assortment of vases and precious ornaments. Around the skull, found almost below the fallen fragments of the amphora, there was placed a diadem made of a gold band on which were secured at short intervals three cruciform rosettes of thin gold decorated in repoussé. All were kept in place by means of bronze pins. Along the temples were suspended beads of rock crystal, cornelian, and amethyst arranged in a semicircular formation, while thin and narrow gold bands coiled in small rings kept her curls in position. Around her neck was found a necklace made of rock crystal beads with a rectangular pendant of bluish faïence decorated with lozenge-shaped elements, reminiscent of the Masonic emblem, and parallel small bars along its short edges (Fig. 63). A pair of simple earrings and a ring of coiled wire around one of the small fingers of the left hand completed her decor.

One more object should be noted: a small gold, hollow, nut-shaped article, with a ribbed outer face. In it apparently were placed a few small articles, perhaps pebbles, so when shaken the object makes quite a noise. Could it be a Mycenaean rattle, a toy which a loving mother placed in the grave as a parting gift? The exploration of Grave Xi gave us a few sentimental hours, and the small, pathetic-looking bones of the tiny girl—of our little princess, as we called her—brought home the sense of helplessness which lies upon the human race when the hour of death arrives. Today the visitor will find but a deep hole in the ground when he visits Grave Xi, but when on its floor were still lying the remains of our little princess, decked in her ornaments and surrounded with vases, it presented a striking picture of the life and customs of a remote and forgotten past.

In the earth between Graves Xi and Pi, was found the burial of a child. Its skeleton is quite well preserved with the exception of the feet, which were destroyed when the channel of the aqueduct was built. The child was lying on its right side and in a strongly contracted position from north to south, with the head turned to the west. In front of it were placed four small vases. They, as well as the burial, recall the find of Schliemann above and to the side of Grave III.

In the north section of the Circle and to the west of Grave Xi, along the perimeter of the enclosing wall, lies Grave Nu. The location of that grave was indicated by the discovery, in the first week of the 1952 campaign, of the lower part of a stele standing on its original base. Its excavation, however, was postponed until the summer of 1953 because the channel of the village aqueduct was crossing its area and it had to be rerouted before the excavation could be resumed. The stele is of shelly sandstone, but so little of it is preserved that it is impossible to state whether or not it was sculptured; however, its faces were turned east and west. Beyond the stele, a group of stones was found as usual marking the outline of the grave below. They must have retained the earth which was poured over the shaft and which in this instance was proved to form a small conical mound rising some 0.35 to 0.40 meters above the surface at the top of which the stele was set. In 1918, Professor Keramopoullos suggested that a small individual mound was formed over each of the shaft graves of Circle A, and his suggestion is now being proved correct by the evidence preserved in the new Circle.[17]

Below the stele and for some 0.40 meters, the fill was of reddish earth and clear of sherds and other objects. Apparently it was the earth which had been poured to form the small mound of the grave. But below this layer the fill became brownish and contained stones and sherds and a quantity of bones of animals. Interestingly enough, animal bones and sea shells were found almost in a thick layer in an area only some 1.10 meters square, corresponding to the ground occupied by the stele and its base. There can be no doubt that the bones are the remnants of the funeral meal, after the completion of which they were thrown together in the central area over which the stele was later erected. The fill below the layer of bones was of

[17] *Ephemeris*, 1918, p. 58.

brownish earth mixed with stones and containing sherds and a few pieces of boar's tusks known to have been used to cover or adorn helmets. The roof of the grave originally stood 1.05 meters from the base of the stele. It was made, as usual, of flagstones covered with clay and supported by wooden beams, traces of which were brought to light. Along the edge of the roof, and on the west side of the grave, a group of 8 vases was disclosed arranged in two rows (Fig. 65). Originally they were standing on their bases, but they were found on their sides as they fell when the roof collapsed.

The walls and the shelving lining the sides presented signs of alterations, indicating that the grave was opened and used more than once. But on its floor, when it was first cleared, only one skeleton was found *in situ*. The area of the floor, because of side margins of clay, was reduced to only 2 meters in length and 0.95 meters in width.[18] The skeleton found on it was lying on its back and in an extended position from north to south (Fig. 67). The head had rolled down and to the side a little, perhaps an indication that it was originally slightly raised. The arms stretch beyond the body, the elbows are bent, and the lower arms are inclined sharply toward the abdominal section. The legs are lying apart in a bow-formation recalling the position of skeleton No. 1 in Grave Gamma. In clearing the skeleton we were particularly careful to see whether any traces of wood or leather could be detected which would indicate that the sprawling attitude was due to a shield held by hands and legs, or to the possibility that the body had been lowered on a wooden litter or a sofa-like contraption. No traces of leather or wood were found over the bones, and it seems certain that the position of the bones was not caused either by a sofa or by a shield, nor because the person was a rider. Perhaps a simple interpretation will be nearer the truth. It is evident that the body was placed on its back with arms bent at the elbow and palms resting on either side of the pelvic area. The feet were not laid completely extended but were pulled up slightly with knees bent upward and the heels resting on the floor. Before complete decomposition occurred, but when advancing decay loosened the tendons and the flesh, the feet could no longer stay in that position but gradually fell to the sides, giving the bow-legged appearance to the lower limbs. We may now note that under the skeleton,

[18] The grave measures 3.90 m. by 3.10 m. on the surface and at the top of its lining 2.70 m. by 2.20 m.

and between it and the pebbles of the floor, was revealed a thin layer of dark, oily substance which was found covering not only the area under the body but almost the whole extent of the floor. There can be little doubt that it is the remains of an unworked piece of leather, apparently a skin on which the body was placed and perhaps by means of which it was lowered to the floor of the grave. Beyond the feet, against the south side, were found four jars, three of which were walled in by clay and were set in a slanting position.

Over the collar bones and under the fallen jaw, a gold band was found (c. 0.40 meters in length) decorated in repoussé work, broad at the center (about 0.07 meters), narrowing to the corners, where it extends only 0.01 meters in width. There can be little doubt that it decorated the upper edge of the garment in which the body was buried. Below the right elbow of the skeleton were found a bronze, single-handled, wide bowl and almost on top of each other two bronze swords, the one below with an alabaster pommel, the other on top with an ivory pommel found crushed by the roof slabs. Another sword, No. 3, in a leather scabbard, traces of which were still to be seen on its blade, was revealed laid diagonally to the swords mentioned, with its point hidden below the margin of clay along the west side. The removal of that margin revealed the packed bones of a skeleton and a good number of offerings (Fig. 66). The sword in the leather scabbard certainly belonged to this earlier burial. Below it was found a spear point of the well-known Mycenaean type enveloped in cloth (Fig. 68b); in addition, around its long socket, remains of cord were preserved, ending below in a primitive tassel. Apparently the cord was used to tie and decorate the wooden shaft of the spear, traces of which were found in the socket. To the left of the spear point, a narrow bronze blade and a pair of bronze tweezers of a late Middle Helladic type were found, while to its right and covered by the sword lay a short and broad knife enveloped in cloth, or in a scabbard made of cloth. Among the packed bones and near the west side of the grave a small, one-handled gold cup was found with its sides elaborated in wide parallel grooves disposed in two superposed zones and its bottom with a dot and leaf design (Fig. 69). In it were found some gold trimmings, apparently belonging to the leather scabbard of sword No. 3, and a long coiled gold band in the inner face of which traces of wood were noticeable (Fig. 66). There can be little doubt that the coiled band once decorated the wooden shaft of the spear and when that was pushed aside its trimmings along with those of the sword were placed in the gold cup. By the cup there was once a bronze vase of which only part of the handle and innumerable tiny fragments survived. Above the gold cup were found the remnants of an ivory pommel, apparently belonging to sword No. 3 and by it a number of gold bands decorated in repoussé, and a completely corroded silver cup (Fig. 66). Between the bands and the bronze cup of the main skeleton was found a triangular bronze dagger whose gold-plated bronze rivets once secured a handle of perishable material; its wooden scabbard was covered with cloth. We must also mention a few pieces of boar's tusks which were found among the packed bones and recall that in the fill of the grave similar tusks were found. Perhaps all belonged to the same helmet which, along with the swords and knives, was pushed to the side when the grave was rearranged to receive the body of the second and later occupant. To him belonged the swords noted lying by his skeleton. Under them came to light a dagger excellently preserved (Fig. 68a). Finally, we must note that in the northwestern corner of the grave and under the margin of clay was found a cylindrical alabaster vessel some 0.12 meters high.

The number of metal objects found with the packed bones seems to indicate that the first occupant of the grave, a man, was of considerable importance. Yet, when a second man came to be buried, the bones and gifts of the first were brushed to the side and perhaps his vases were taken out of the grave. The boar's tusks found in the fill may indicate that some of his offerings were not packed neatly but were broken and dispersed.

Along the perimeter of the Circle and to the east of Nu, Grave Iota was discovered. No stele was found over it, but again its outline was marked by somewhat loosely placed stones and below its center, where a stele might have been standing originally, animal bones and some seashells were found. The grave measures 3.20 meters in length, 2.05 meters in width, and had a depth of 2.85 meters. Its length and width, however, were reduced to 2.55 meters and 1.30 meters at its floor by the shelves left all around to support the roof beams. Traces of these were found across the width of the grave and resting on the shelving. On its pebbly floor was found the skeleton of the person buried last (Fig. 70). The bones of its legs were disturbed by the fallen roof, but the body apparently was laid on its back with a slight turn toward the right side. The head, originally kept higher by an arrangement of pebbles below it, finally rolled in that direction. The hands were stretched along the body with the palms turned toward the pelvic area. Along the right side were laid a bronze sword with an ivory pommel, a bronze pair of tweezers, and a broad knife of bronze with a short tang above its shoulders. In that was fitted and glued a tiny cylindrical handle (0.03 meters in length) of rock crystal. Around the wrist were found four triangular gold bands decorated in repoussé, two around each wrist. Along their broad side tiny attachment holes are evident (Fig. 72). Two other narrower gold bands ending in circular pendants, reminiscent of the vertical bar of the "garter type" ornament (Gamaschenhälter), were found in the abdominal area (Fig. 72). Could they have decorated a belt?

Beyond the sword and almost parallel to it were found a number of vases, stemmed goblets of the Middle Helladic type, and matt-painted pots, while beyond the feet were found four large matt-painted jars and three smaller vases. Of these at least one, decorated in black matt-paint with solid triangles suspended from their base and from a band going around the neck, seems to have contained oil. Nothing of its contents of course survived, and only at its bottom did the earth found in it have an oily feel, but its body was so impregnated with oil that when its pieces were being put together and their joints were heated for the purpose, the odor of oil filled the small laboratory. The second jar seemed to contain flour, but its contents have not as yet been analyzed by a chemist. By the southwest corner of the grave the packed bones of an earlier burial were found and among them a well-preserved, fluted, single-handled cup of silver (Fig. 71).

By the north side of Grave Alpha and between it and Iota a small rectangular area about 1.50 by 1.30 meters outlined by a row of loose stones was found and investigated. Its floor was reached at a depth of 2.10 meters, but nothing was revealed on it. The stray human bones found in the fill, and the sandy earth which filled the shaft above its shelves, indicate that this was a grave whose contents had been removed in the past.

On the west side of Grave Alpha and between it and Grave Delta another small grave was found measuring 0.80 by 1.50 meters and oriented from east to west. We call it Grave Alpha 1. Its eastern side was cut away when Grave Alpha was being constructed and apparently during that operation the head of the skeleton was destroyed, for we found a well-preserved skeleton lying in Alpha 1, but without its skull. The person to whom it belonged was laid in a contracted position on its left side, with the right hand lying toward the pelvic area; the left, under the left side, is bent and brought toward the left cheek. No offerings were found, but perhaps they had been removed earlier.

A bundled burial was found at a short distance from Grave Alpha 1 and to the southwest of it toward Grave Delta. A few Middle Helladic sherds were revealed among the bones, but nothing else, and it is doubtful that the sherds belong to the bones.

The north sector of the Circle was thickly occupied by graves, as was the eastern sector along the wall of the Circle. The central area of Circle B, however, contained no graves. We hoped that there we might find the most important grave, or a structure of some kind, such as an altar, used for the funeral rites, but it was found empty. Evidence of attempts to cut the rock was observed and a good section of the area toward Grave Rho was found filled with earth and stones which apparently had been taken out of that sepulcher, but no traces of an actual grave were revealed. Why was this central area never used? Was it because by the time its turn for use was at hand a new type of tomb, the chamber tomb and the tholos tomb, came into use? We shall never know. The fact remains that no tombs were found in the central area.

That area is separated from the southern section by walls of rubble which apparently served to stop any movement of earth from the center and high point of the Circle to the sloping south side. A group of interesting graves was found in the southern sector, although the objects they yielded could not compare with those from the corresponding northern sector. At its southernmost point, not far from the line of the encircling wall which has not survived, a large rectangular excavation was revealed immediately below the surface some 3.90 meters in width and 2.70 meters in length. But further excavation revealed that this area was divided into two sections by a central wall made of unexcavated rock. The section to the east, called Kappa 1, proved to be a grave which measured at its floor 2.22 meters in length and 1.60 meters in width. The remains of a single skeleton in an extended position were found on the floor, lying from north to south, with only four vases placed in two groups along the western side of the grave. One of these is a jug with striking geometric polychrome decoration (Fig. 73), while another is a large hydria with an unusual band decoration. Some 0.60 meters above the floor and toward the northeastern corner of the grave, an arrangement of stones was found, apparently standing as a marker for the grave, and under it bones of animals.

The west section, known as Kappa 2, was not used as a grave. By its western side, and some 0.62 meters below the surface, a horseshoe-shaped enclosure made of mud brick was disclosed, measuring roughly 1.15 meters in maximum outside length and 1.08 meters in maximum outside width.[19] A thin layer of ashes and a few pieces of bones were found on its floor (Fig. 74). Some 0.25 meters below this and 0.17 meters to the north apparently existed a similar arrangement not so well preserved. The structure is puzzling; it could be taken as a hearth belonging to a dwelling which antedated the construction of the Grave Circle. However, around it, on the face of the excavation of the rock and on its floor, no signs of intense and continued burning were found, as one would expect to be the case, and only a thin layer of ashes remained on its floor. Why, then, did the people who built the presumed hearth for a dwelling lower it almost 0.60 meters below the surface when in the process they had to dig away a lot of rock? Usually dwellings are constructed on the surface of a site.

Beyond the northern edge of Kappa 2, the area presents problems which cannot be discussed in this preliminary report. A narrow strip covered by cobblestones comes first, limited on the north by a weak rubble wall. Beyond this an area which we may call the "boulder area," 3.70 by 3.10 meters, was apparently excavated but abandoned (Fig. 75). A large boulder, obviously fallen in from the west side after that side was cut, fills part of the north half of the area, and the balance of that half is taken by a small grave, 1.13 meters in length and 0.63 meters in width, known as Lambda 1, which was partially excavated in the rock and whose eastern end cuts through the western wall of Grave Lambda. In Lambda 1 were found the contracted remains of a skeleton and two vases, one a two-handled cup and the other a jug with a zonal decoration of circles alternately filled in black and red color. The southern half of the area disclosed

[19] The bricks measure 0.35 m. by 0.16 m.

no remains, but at its extreme south line, below the rubble wall which limits the cobblestone area, what seems like a fireplace was disclosed, filled with ashes and black soot among which were fragments of two vases belonging to the Middle Helladic period. This "fireplace" presents problems hard to determine at this particular point. At the southwest corner of the area intrudes a wall made of *plesia* clay. What purpose was served by the so-called "boulder area" is hard to determine. I believe that workers started cutting a shaft and before the work was completed it was abandoned for reasons unknown, perhaps after the boulder fell in from the side, and then the area was filled in. It was used later only for the construction of the small Grave Lambda 1.

The solid *plesia* wall which intruded in the southwest corner of the "boulder area" was proved to be part of the eastern side of Grave Mu. It is a rather shallow grave cut in the slope of the hill, measuring 2.90 by 2.08 meters, and it contained the skeleton of a young girl laid in an extended position and in the characteristic bow-legged attitude seen in Graves Gamma and Nu (Fig. 76). Along the west and north sides, and especially in the northwest corner of the grave, some twenty-two vases were uncovered and, between the two vases revealed in the northeast corner, at least two bone pins were found, one of them broken in two, similar to those used today for knitting. Among the vases, bones of a child were revealed, proving that the girl whose skeleton was found was but the last occupant of the grave.

On her breast were found some ten beads, of semi-precious stones, arranged in a circle and apparently forming a necklace; in the middle of the circle was located a biconical bead of carnelian, perforated on its long axis, bearing on it a design carved in intaglio (Fig. 80). A large tree with spreading branches, perhaps a palm, grows out of a spherical form which looks almost like a vase with two handles on either side of its neck. At a little distance to right and to left of it we have branches framing the central element. The spherical object could be interpreted as a "flower-pot," but it will be better to think of it as a boulder and symbolic of the earth from which the tree grows. Rendering of boulders in this fashion is common in Minoan-Mycenaean art; it was used extensively by the gem carvers.[20] What

[20] See, among others, the disc-shaped bead from central Crete, illustrated by Sir Arthur Evans, *Palace of Minos*, II, 2, p. 494, fig. 299, and the cornelian from near Kritia, *ibid.*, IV, 2, p. 488, fig. 417 a, b.

seem like handles are the lower two branches of the tree whose tips touch the boulder. One might perhaps see here the "returning to earth" branches of the Anatolian "Tree of Life."

To the east of the "boulder area," and beyond the northeast corner of Kappa, Grave Lambda was discovered and explored in the summer of 1953. It is one of the larger graves, measuring 3.65 meters in length and 2.68 meters in width. Grave Lambda has contributed particularly to our knowledge of the roof construction of the shaft graves. Apparently the roof had caved in before the area over its floor was filled in and we uncovered it lying on the floor or slanting down the sides (Fig. 77). The layer of greenish clay of *plesia*, averaging 0.15 meters in thickness, was still on the flagstones which formed the roof, proving that the roof was horizontal. As usual, it was supported by wooden beams, traces of which were clear in the whole area of the grave, resting on rubble walls averaging 0.45 meters in thickness, going around the four sides of the grave.

By the east side of the grave we found the packed bones of a skeleton. Among and under these bones were disclosed a bronze knife and three complete bands of gold (one of these was broken in two) decorated in repoussé (Fig. 78). At both ends of the bands, holes for attachment are noticeable. The skeleton of the last person buried was found, crushed, in the center of the grave, but absolutely nothing was disclosed on or around him. It was evident that his funeral offerings had been removed. Above the north end of the western side a hole was found (0.70 by 0.55 meters) caused by the makers of Lambda 1, and through that hole the grave was certainly entered and despoiled. Immediately under the hole, by the edge of the side, we found a small pile of earth and stones evidently formed when the side was cut and when people entered Lambda through the resulting hole. When the pile of earth and stones was removed, we found below it a number of weapons which had luckily escaped detection. The most conspicuous of these was a bronze sword over the upper part of which were piled a broad knife with a handle of ivory apparently in a wooden scabbard, a triangular dagger whose handle seems to have been decorated in silver, a spear point of bronze in the round socket of which were found remnants of its wooden shaft, around the top of which a narrow gold band was coiled, and then the sword (Fig. 79a). Under its shoulder was a triangular ornament of gold foil; a little below its middle was another elongated oval ornament of gold with twisted gold bands at its end, and around the tip outlining it a thin gold cord.[21] All these gold ornaments decorated the leather scabbard of the sword (Fig. 79b). The handle was gone, but the gold ring, in two sheets, which formed the connection between the handle and the ivory pommel, as well as the pommel, was found. A band of gold, in two sheets, was also found near the handle, perhaps forming the decoration of the *telamon* or baldrick, from which the sword was suspended. Near the pommel were disclosed twenty-four stone arrowheads, twenty of which are of obsidian, grouped together as if they were originally held in a bag.

Only one or two pots, completely crushed, were found at the southwest section of the grave, but over the roof a number of vases were found in a layer along its south side. Among them are vases with two-colored decoration of birds and arrowheads (Fig. 81).

Grave Lambda was apparently dug in an area where older graves were located. Thus, during its construction the west side of Grave Tau must have been disclosed and the contents of that grave, lying immediately to the east of Lambda, were cleared out and its shaft filled with stones and earth. In a similar manner the north side of Grave Lambda cuts through the south side of a small grave, known as Lambda 2, whose contents were spared. Lamba 2 is only 1.10 meters in length and 0.73 meters in width. It contained the bones of an individual piled against its north side and the complete skeleton of a young boy laid on his back with legs sharply flexed. A small cup and a prochous were found by its skull, while a matt-painted vase was disclosed at the northwest corner of the grave near the packed bones.

To the east of the southeastern corner of Lambda, Grave Sigma was cleared. It is a comparatively small but carefully cut shaft with a shelf in the rock going around the four sides. It measures 1.65 by 1.40 meters on the surface, but 1.15 by 0.80 meters at the floor. A single skeleton in a sharply contracted position was found in it, lying on his right side and facing north. No funeral offerings were found, but between the lower right ribs and the iliac crest two green-brown, faceted and polished "stones" came to light: "they are gall-stones, suggesting a rich and perhaps truly 'Homeric hero' diet." The man seems to have suffered also from arthritis.[22]

[21] These gold ornaments find exact parallels in the gold articles found by Schliemann, *Mycenae*, p. 253, nos. 367-370; Karo, *op.cit.*, pl. 83.

[22] I am indebted to Dr. Angel for the information.

Grave Sigma completes the discussion of sepulchers found in the southern section of Circle B. To the eastern section belong Graves Alpha, Rho, and Upsilon. We have already discussed Grave Alpha, and we shall now describe Grave Upsilon.

It is a rather shallow grave, over which we found as usual a σῆμα, or marker, composed of a pile of stones. Its perimeter was indicated by a row of stones, loosely lined. It is oriented approximately from north to south and measures 1.95 meters in length and 1.37 meters in width. On its floor, paved with pebbles, lay extended the skeleton of a woman. Around her, nine vases were found, of which at least four were typical Middle Helladic stemmed goblets; one is a matt-painted prochous and one a small matt-painted askos (Fig. 82). The skull had rolled over the left shoulder, but on the area of the right temple were still to be seen three leaves of gold decorated in repoussé, once forming a head ornament (Fig. 82). Apparently they were supported by a narrow bronze band which went around the skull and were held in place by three bronze pins found in their original position. Over the left shoulder, another decorated gold band was found; originally it perhaps held a braid over that shoulder. A great number of small beads made of semi-precious stones, of gold, and of silver, and some amulets of faïence, similar in decoration and shape to the one found in Grave Xi, formed a large double necklace around her neck. Under each temple a circle made of silver was found, apparently her earrings, while to the right of the skull, and between it and the matt-painted prochous of the southwest corner, came to light three bronze rings and five pins, two of silver and three of bronze. One of the latter possessed a beautifully grooved rock crystal head. Indeed, this grave, the last to be excavated in the closing days of the campaign of 1954 (July 30 to August 6), although not as rich as others, yielded invaluable evidence for our understanding of the burial customs of the closing years of the Middle Helladic period to which it belongs.

Grave Rho, excavated in July 1954, takes up a good part of the eastern section of the Circle and was just missed by the builders of the Tomb of Clytemnestra (Fig. 87). Its excavation gave us perhaps the most exciting hours of our experience at Mycenae. The southwest corner was located first, and it looked as if we had another normal shaft grave. Yet when we tried to determine its length we were led on and on and when at long last we located its northeastern corner it was found that the shaft had a length of almost 7 meters: the longest shaft grave found thus far! Its width was not so great, indeed almost normal, some 3.10 meters. The earth which filled it presented us with the first puzzle. Its quality and contents differed in the two halves of the grave: in the southern half it was more or less firm and contained some stones and a few sherds. At a depth of 1.20 meters, it exhibited a layer of poros chips not found before in any grave. The fill of the northern half was even more puzzling. It was loose and contained sand and pebbles. It presented a number of striations and a variety of slanting layers clean of any sherds or remains. The distinction of the one fill from the other came at about the center of the long axis and it was so sharp that it looked as if a regular wall of earth terminated the southern end and against this the loose fill of the northern end abutted.

At a depth of 1.50 meters below the surface, we found the shelf, made by narrowing the width of the shaft, cut in the rock which usually served to support the beams of the roof. The shelf ran along the long sides of the shaft. But toward its southeastern end a small area on the top of the shelf had been scooped up and in the resulting cutting, 1.25 by 0.41 meters, human bones were found packed together; and along with them were found fragments of the usual stemmed goblet of the closing years of the Middle Helladic period and a two-handled cup. The area of the bones was limited by stones, and flagstones overlaid with clay covered the bones themselves. Some 0.40 meters below the level of the shelf and in the center of the short axis of the grave we found two adjacent poros slabs horizontally placed with their joints still filled with *plesia*. They caused great excitement because at that depth they had to belong to the roof of the grave. Their discovery made me write in the excavation diary, under date of July 12, 3 p.m.: "Do we have the roof slabs in their original position and intact? I cannot believe my eyes. That will be too much to hope, but everything is possible in an excavation, and especially at Mycenae."

Meanwhile, the puzzle of the northern end with its loose, sandy fill continued. But a day later at the north end of the shaft we struck poros blocks and at the side of the northernmost block we found fragments of pottery on which and between which appeared gold foil. What did it mean? The same day an opening was detected below those same poros blocks. Hopes mounted skyward, and the village of Mycenae celebrated that night. There could be no doubt that an unusually large grave had been located, and to the villagers the fragments of gold foil were considered the harbingers of a discovery of important and rich relics still within the sepulcher. To us, these fragments along with the fill were warnings that all was not well with this large grave. For days the excitement and anxiety went on. First the top of a passage was disclosed, then a doorway with an arched top leading beyond to a roofed room. None of us will ever forget the moment when, lying on our stomachs, we could peer through the arch of the door into the room beyond and by using a torch light tried to see its contents! Perhaps it should be stated right away that when the grave was finally cleared it was found empty of contents; apparently it had been denuded in the past, and almost nothing was found in it. Nevertheless, its importance and value are great.

When the grave was entirely cleared it was proved to be a unique example of funereal architecture, unparalleled in Greece: a large rock-hewn shaft within which a sepulcher was built of well-worked poros blocks. The narrow spaces between the poros walls and the sides of the shaft were filled in with loose stones. The built sepulcher is composed of a passage measuring 2.65 meters in length and 1.22 meters in width at its center, leading to a burial chamber 2.99 meters in length, 1.29 meters in width at its center, and 1.85 meters in height (Fig. 83). The door to the chamber is 0.80 meters wide at the floor and measures 1.83 meters in height (Fig. 85). The roof of the burial chamber is completely preserved, but that of the passage was removed, no doubt when the grave was entered into and its contents removed. It is interesting to note that a quantity of gold foil was found along the west side of the passage, which proves that the contents were carried out of the grave over that side. Furthermore, in the fill beyond the northwestern side of the grave toward the center of the Circle, in 1952 and 1953, more foil was found, fragments of vases, a few belonging to three large palace-style amphorae, pieces of ivory, among which were an almost complete ivory rosette, fragments of vessels made of alabaster, a small piece of lapis lazuli, and the like. In the course of the clearing of the grave it was found that the fragments of pottery, discovered at the northwestern corner of the grave and alongside the first poros blocks discovered there, joined the fragments of the three palace-style amphorae found in the fill beyond the grave (Fig. 86). Thus it was proved that these sherds, gold foil, and ivory were part of the contents of Grave Rho. Dr. Papademetriou tells me that at the laboratory he found the lapis lazuli to be an Egyptian carved scarab.

Four rows of poros stones form the walls of the passage. The lowermost rises vertically above the floor. The second row inclines slightly inward and is reminiscent of the curvature of the tholos tombs. The third and fourth rows incline a good deal, thus reducing the area to be spanned to only 0.80 to 0.70 meters. That span was apparently covered by slabs which had been removed when the grave was emptied and were never replaced in their original position. A single slab remained over the extreme northern end of the passage. This end was walled up by means of four blocks of poros, corresponding in height to the courses of the side walls, but set vertically on the floor and cut to fit the inward inclination of the sides. The south end of the passage abutted against the door-opening without being bonded with it. The joints of the blocks of the passage are filled with *plesia* to make the walls watertight.

The blocks forming the doorway to a height of about 1 meter above the floor were set vertically; above that, they inclined inward, forming an arch over the apex of which projects the edge of the first roof slab like a cornice terminating the façade (Fig. 85). One feels that the arched upper part of the door-opening corresponds to the relieving triangle of the façades of the tholos tombs, and the projecting cornice recalls the endings provided in the Treasury of Atreus and the Tomb of Clytemnestra. The face of the doorway is covered with solid red color. The side walls of the chamber are made up of poros blocks built in four horizontal courses and in good ashlar style. The two lowermost are vertically set, the third and fourth, exhibiting unusual curvatures, incline inward leaving an opening between them of some 0.29 meters. That is covered by flat slabs of poros which form the roof of the chamber (Fig. 84). The rear, or south wall, is built of poros blocks corresponding in height to the courses of the sides and are cut to fit the inward inclination of the side walls. All joints of the blocks used for the construction are filled with water-resisting clay; over this, strips of stucco were laid and on that stucco were painted broad bands alternately red and black in color. Thus the ashlar construction is brought out pictorially. The floor of the chamber, though cut in the rock, is paved with poros blocks. In the northeastern corner of that floor and in a worn-out spot of the poros was found a bead of reddish chalcedony bearing a carving in intaglio which represented a large horned animal running, with head turned backward. A tiny fragment of a skull was the only bone found in the chamber.

On the strength of the evidence we have secured in our excavation we can reconstruct the story of Grave Rho. A shaft grave was constructed toward the end of the Middle Helladic period in which one person, perhaps, was laid. For centuries after that burial the grave was left undisturbed. But after many years it was found by someone who was anxious to make his grave in that area. The bones of its early occupant were removed from the floor and were carefully packed against the side of the grave and on top of the shelf. Of the offerings the shaft grave might have contained, only one broken goblet and a cup were stacked with the bones; the rest were taken away or thrown out of the grave. Then the shaft was enlarged and within it was built in poros the grave with the passage and the chamber. Within that chamber a person of means was placed and around him were arranged perhaps rich funeral offerings. The roof slabs of the passage were secured and the shaft was filled with earth. Later again, someone dug up the northern half of the grave—the half over the passage—removed its roof slabs, descended into the grave, and emptied its chamber. Then that part of the shaft was filled again, and so it remained until our times.

One would naturally ask why the grave was emptied. The answer to that is not so easy. Perhaps its contents were removed to another sepulcher, to a tholos tomb, by the descendants of the person buried in the poros tomb when they attained greater wealth and power. Perhaps it was robbed when its site was accidentally found. The first interpretation seemed correct to the excavators. However, the excellent workmanship and the elaborate decoration certainly indicate that the poros grave was not meant to serve as a temporary place of rest, that its builder did not anticipate a transference of the remains and the offerings to another and more impressive tomb at a later time. But if the grave was robbed, why was it emptied of its bones as well? Could we assume that the robbers wanted to make sure that nothing was left of the gold foil ornaments covering the body and that consequently they took them out to the light before they removed their decor? And could we further assume that in the bundle burial between Graves Alpha and Delta, the only burial of its kind found in Circle B, we have the bones of Grave Rho placed there after their ornaments were removed? These are questions which will remain unanswered, but which will open up a rich field of imaginative speculation.

Let us consider the date of Grave Rho. The original shaft grave and its burial certainly belong to the closing years of the Middle Helladic period. The date of the poros tomb within it can be established within limits. The poros construction, the use of *plesia* for the joints, and the covering of them with stucco, find parallels in the later façade of the Tomb of Aegisthos and in the construction of the Lion Tomb. In the latter the joints are not only filled with *plesia* but are covered with stucco. In it also we find a pit cut in the floor and lined with poros blocks. The Lion Tomb is later than the Tomb of Aegisthos and belongs to Professor Wace's second group of tholos tombs. The construction of the poros Grave Rho, its doorway with its arch which recalls the relieving triangle, the projecting edge of the roof slab forming a terminating cornice, the depth of the doorway, and the painted decoration, are advanced structural elements which will necessitate our placing the grave in a transitional period between the first and second group of tholos tombs, and to about the middle of the fifteenth century B.C. or in the second half of that century.

The palace-style amphorae from the grave will also place it in that period. One of these amphorae with the so-called "necklace" pattern (Fig. 86) finds an almost exact parallel in a fragment found in the fill from the tholos of the Tomb of Aegisthos.[23] In the latter, however, we do not find the "sponge print" pattern which decorates the vertical handle bands of our amphora, and this will perhaps indicate that our amphora should be placed in the later years of the Late Helladic II A period. To the same years belongs our second amphora with a magnificently painted octopus on its surface, while the third amphora with its horizontal zones decorated with a "rock" pattern should be placed somewhere in the Late Helladic II A to Late Helladic II B periods. Consequently, the nature of the pottery and the structural considerations indicate that the poros grave was constructed around the middle or in the second half of the fifteenth

[23] Wace, *BSA*, 25 (1921-1923), pp. 302, 309, pls. 50, 51; *Mycenae*, fig. 60 and p. 39.

century B.C. When was the grave emptied of its contents? It is impossible to determine that date; or whether it was robbed or its contents transferred to a tholos tomb or other tomb by the descendants of the deceased.

In Greece, Grave Rho has no parallel. The cist in the Lion Tomb presents some similarities, but it lacks the dromos, the inclination of the walls, and the saddle roof. Beyond Greece striking parallels are to be found in the subterranean built graves of Ras Shamra and of Minet-el-Beida.[24] Of course, absolute equation is not possible, since the latter possess steps in the dromos, niches and windows in the chamber, and exhibit different details in the construction of the roof. But there can be no doubt that they present striking similarities. For instance, Professor Schaeffer pointed out that the Ras Shamra examples are never provided with a stone wall blocking their entrance, a feature so typical of the Mycenaean graves; however, Grave Rho also lacks the blocking wall. At the time of his publication he could not find parallels in Greece and with good reason suggested that the type of architecture exhibited by his graves was unknown in the Mycenaean mainland. The graves in Cyprus, which could be used as parallels, come down in date to the eighth and seventh centuries B.C. and certainly could not be conceived as the prototypes of the sepulchers of Ras Shamra and of Minet-el-Beida that belong to the fourteenth and thirteenth centuries B.C. Now we have Grave Rho, dating from the fifteenth century B.C., proving that at least one sepulcher of the Ras Shamra type was built at Mycenae itself at an earlier date than that represented by the Syrian examples. Can one assume that it gives us the prototype followed in Ras Shamra and Minet-el-Beida? Can one equally well assume that the lonely example of Mycenae was influenced by the Syrian sepulchers? After all at Ras Shamra we have some very old examples of built chamber tombs from which the later examples could have evolved. There can be little doubt that by Late Helladic II close contact existed between Greece on the one hand and Syria and Egypt on the other. Influences from the one area to the other are natural and to be expected. However, the answer to the question of the derivation of the built graves will require further study and perhaps other discoveries. Meanwhile,

[24] Schaeffer, C. F. A., *Mission de Ras Shamra*, II, pp. 30-92, figs. 75-85 and pls. XV-XVII; "Reprise des recherches archéologiques á Ras-Shamra–Ugarit," *Syria*, 28 (1951), pp. 1-21 and especially fig. 1. Also Cf. Bossert, H. Th., *The Art of Ancient Crete*, figs. 493-494.

we can maintain that Grave Rho, in spite of its lack of funeral offerings, is one of the most interesting graves uncovered in Grave Circle B. Recognizing that fact, and at the suggestion of Dr. Papademetriou, the Greek Archaeological Society has built over it a concrete structure which will protect it from rain and other adverse climatic conditions.

Before we end the description of the graves found in Circle B, we should note that below the southern sector of the circle a chamber tomb was built, perhaps in Late Helladic II times, the north side of the rectangular chamber of which was cut almost under the outer line of the encircling wall. The grave was emptied of its contents after its roof caved in, and in Geometric times it became the center of a cult. In that period a round shrine was constructed over the edge of its fallen roof, on the slope of the hillside. Some fragments of gold foil, tops of nails made in gold, some ivory fragments and a vessel of bronze were among the few objects left for us to find. Incidentally, its door-opening was still blocked by a stone wall at the time of its excavation.

The general description of the graves found in Grave Circle B will permit certain generalizations to be made; final conclusions will be possible only after the thorough cleaning and study of the objects found and the completion of all architectural plans. Thus the generalizations offered should be considered as preliminary and subject to revision and correction.

There can be little doubt that Grave Circle B was built in the second and closing half of the Middle Helladic period. It seems that it was purposely built to enclose an area to be used for burials and not as a wall to surround the area already occupied by graves. A parallel to the practice of placing graves within a circle we find in the cemetery discovered at Leukas by Dörpfeld.[25] Perhaps the Early Minoan to Middle Minoan ossuaries of Mesara will give us earlier examples.[26] But it seems to us that in the stone walls which separated the grave areas of the cemetery of Aghios Kosmas we have the forerunners of the circles.[27] We noted above the suggestion that these grave circles provided the prototypes of the tholos tombs and how

[25] Dörpfeld, *Alt-Ithaka*, pls. 35-41.
[26] Xanthoudides, St., *The Vaulted Tombs of Mesara*, 1924.
[27] Mylonas, "Excavations at Haghios Kosmas," *AJA*, 38 (1934), p. 270.

in Late Helladic III times they reappear in some important graves in the cemetery of Eleusis.

Grave Circle B must have had an entrance. Unfortunately, no information can be obtained from its preserved fragments. However, a study of the plan of the Circle, with all its graves properly placed, will indicate that no entrance could have existed on the northern, eastern, or southeastern sectors (Fig. 87). Graves almost completely occupy those sectors and definitely block any passage. The western, including the southwestern, section, seems to be the only sector in which such an opening could have existed. Unfortunately that part is almost completely gone and no evidence has survived to tell us what it once contained. The positions of the explored graves seem to indicate, however, that the suggestion already advanced by Professor Marinatos,[28] that the entrance to the Circle was on its west side (including southwest and northwest), was correct. Between Graves Epsilon and Mu there is an empty space not used for burials. Could we see in it a passage which led from the entrance to the center of the Circle? To that entrance the stelai seem to have been turned, and close to that probable entrance and its passage we find the strange horeshoe-shaped brick construction in Kappa 2. Could that construction have any connection with the funeral rites observed in the Circle before, during, and after burial, and could it have been used in a manner similar to that served by the small chapel of the burial ground of Mallia, of the Chrysolakkos?[29]

The central area of the Circle was found unoccupied. The traces of rock cutting attempted in that area and in the area of the "fallen boulder" seem to indicate that the area may not have been used because of the difficulties the rock presented, or because of some accident that might have taken place when the boulder slid from the edge of the intended grave to its cavity.[30] One thing, however, appears to be certain: the central area was not used for the construction of a chapel or shrine for burial rites or for a cult. As a matter of fact, no evidence whatever was obtained for the existence of a cult of the dead in Grave Circle B. We focused our attention on that question during the excavation. The so-called channels to be seen on

[28] Marinatos, *Geras*, pp. 55-56.

[29] Demargne, P., *Fouilles exécutées á Mallia, Explorations des Nécropoles*, fasc., 1, pp. 35-38, and pls. L-LI.

[30] We have also suggested that the appearance of the tholos and chamber tombs might have caused the abandonment of the Grave Circle before it was completely filled, *supra*, p. 153.

the rock to the south of Grave Beta—originally mentioned as used for libations and the burial rites—by their extent, meandering course, and smoothed walls are certainly proved to be natural grooves made over the centuries by the roots of shrubs which grew over the area in imposing numbers even when we started the exploration of Grave Circle B in 1952.

The construction and the burial customs of the shaft graves are now clear. A vertical shaft was cut through the earth of the surface and the rock below it. The sides of the shaft in the rock were often lined up to a height of 0.70 to 1.25 meters with walls; sometimes the walls lining the short sides were of mud brick. In some instances the shaft was narrowed some 0.80 meters above the floor and thus a rocky shelf was produced running around the sides. Shelf or walls were used to support wooden beams placed at a short distance from each other across the width of the grave. On these beams flagstones were often placed horizontally to form the roof, and they in turn were covered with a thick layer of the water-resisting *plesia*. Sometimes instead of flagstones a matting of leaves and branches was used for the roof and this matting was covered with clay. Thus the roof of the grave stood at least 0.70 meters from its floor. The deceased were not covered with earth. In accordance with an ancient Middle Helladic custom, the floors of the graves were covered with pebbles. The bodies were laid on it in a more or less extended posture; on rare occasions the old contracted position was kept and sometimes the bodies were laid on their backs in an extended position but with legs pulled up a bit, a posture which resulted in the strange bow-legged attitude observed. In the small rock-cut cists the contracted attitude was followed.

Sometimes only one person was buried in the shaft grave; more often, more than one, four being the maximum found in Grave Gamma. Around the bodies their funeral offerings, or *kterismata*, were placed. When there was more than one body in a grave, we often found that the bones of those previously buried were swept aside toward the side or the corner of the grave and their funeral offerings were dispersed with but few things left with the bones. Sometimes the vases belonging to older burials were put out of the grave and on the roof along one or the other of the sides. Sometimes they were merely thrown out of the grave and their fragments were mixed with the earth-fill of the shaft. No traces of cremation were found in the graves, and there can be no doubt that only inhumation was practiced at the time. No evidence for embalming was obtained, nor was there evidence indicating the use of wooden coffins. The bodies were laid on the pebbly floor dressed in garments, sometimes on animal pelts.

Professor Marinatos has already described the procedure followed in the use of the grave for repeated burials.[31] After the first occupant of the grave was laid on its floor, the roof was constructed and over it earth was poured almost to the height of the rock level. Then a funeral meal was held in which libations may have been poured or a toast offered to the deceased in a manner illustrated by Achilles' actions by the pyre of Patroclos.[32] Perhaps the goblets used for this purpose were smashed over the grave. Then the bones of the animals consumed were thrown onto the middle area of the sepulcher and more earth was poured over it to form a small mound rising some 0.30 to 0.50 meters above the surface. On top of that mound a stele was erected or a σῆμα, a marker of stones, was piled and the outline of the grave was indicated by stones. When the grave was to be used for a second burial, the stele or the marker was removed, together with the earth over the roof; the roof itself was broken through; and the body lowered to the floor. If there was not sufficient room, the bones of those previously buried were pushed aside and their offerings were piled in the corner, or were scattered or even carried away. Then the funeral gifts were arranged around the newcomer. Finally, the roof was built again, the shaft above it was filled with earth, and the funeral meal and the erection of the stele or the marker followed. This process was repeated as many times as necessary, as many times as the grave was reused.

The procedure corresponds to that followed in the burials of the chamber tombs, whose use follows the era of shaft graves. The types of offerings also parallel each other, although the opportunity to remove valuable or useful objects was greater in the case of the chamber tombs—and was often taken. What is even more striking is the similarity of ideas underlying the burial customs of the two, especially to be noted in the indifference toward the remains of ancestors, evidenced by the brushing of bones to the side and by scattering or destroying older funeral offerings. The evidence obtained in the new shaft graves certainly proves that the burial customs

[31] *Geras*, pp. 64-65.   [32] *Iliad*, XXIII, 218ff.

they represent evolved from the Middle Helladic, as the shaft graves evolved from the cist grave, and that no changes in burial customs occurred in the years which saw the appearance of the chamber and tholos tombs.

In Graves Epsilon, Mu, Omicron, and Upsilon at least, skeletons belonging to women were found, while in Grave Xi we have that of a very small girl. However, in Grave Gamma the skeleton of one woman was found with those of three men, and in almost all the other graves bones of earlier burials, brushed aside, were disclosed but in such a state of decomposition that identification of the sex was impossible. They, could of course, have belonged to women. Therefore the evidence in favor of separate graves for women is not conclusive and seemingly both men and women were buried in the same grave. Interestingly enough, the unsculptured stelai found in Grave Circle B stood over Graves Omicron and Gamma. In the latter a woman was buried along with three men; in the former at least the person buried last was a woman. Although the examples found are too few to be determinative, they seem to add support to the suggestion made long ago by Schuchardt that unsculptured stelai were placed over the graves of women. Certainly they seem to indicate that Heurtley's suggestion that unsculptured stelai were erected at a later period, to replace sculptured ones previously destroyed, is not tenable.

Vases constitute the most numerous class of objects found in the graves of Circle B; of these, most common are goblets and jugs for holding liquids. Gold and silver cups are rather rare; they were found in Graves Gamma, Iota, and Nu, but clay cups and goblets are most common. It is worth noting that cups were the only objects found in the earlier graves of Eleusis, which belong to the last half of the Middle Helladic period.[33] They seem to be the first type of funeral offerings placed in the grave when, perhaps under Minoan influence, the custom of placing gifts in the graves was again adopted in the mainland of Greece. They bring to mind the fact that drinking cups are the indispensable and often the only equipment of pilgrims, mendicants, and traveling monks even today. Were the cups and liquids placed in the graves to be used in the long and dreary trip to the lower world? The evidence seems to indicate this. Again, we may recall that in the Orphic doctrine, drinking water from the fountain

[33] *PAE*, 1952, p. 64.

of Mnemosyne or Lethe, before entering Hades, was part of the process of the trip to the lower world.[34]

Weapons are very common, as we have seen. Bronze swords, knives, daggers, at least two spear points, a number of stone—but no bronze—arrowheads are among the funeral offerings. These weapons are made of strong bronze and therefore they could be used in reality. Perhaps they were the actual weapons used in their lifetime by the people in the graves, and were placed in the grave because of the primitive belief that the departed wanted to take with him personal objects which he valued in life.[35] The swords are of the two types distinguished by Karo in his study of the weapons from the shaft graves explored by Schliemann. The type with rounded shoulder is the longer, averaging some 0.94 meters in its blade. The type with the horned shoulder has a shorter blade not exceeding 0.70 meters. Both have a central rib which is sometimes toothed. The handles were of perishable material and were sometimes covered with gold sheathing, but they always seemed to be topped by pommels of ivory or alabaster. It is instructive to note that a good knife or dagger is always found with the sword and to recall that Agamemnon carried a knife beside his trusted sword.[36] Was it a Mycenaean custom to carry the two together, a habit which lasted to Homeric times?

The gold ornaments are as a rule made of gold leaf which might have proved too flimsy for use in actual life. Perhaps they were made for the grave. Most common are bands decorated in repoussé with embossed circles with a margin of dots, lines, or leaves, and the cross-rosettes. Some are crude, others more delicately worked. Apparently bands and cross-rosettes, or even sheets cut in the form of leaves, were used as head ornaments for women. Bands and triangular sheets of gold were used as garment ornaments for men as well. No gold band was found near a male skull, which would suggest its use as a diadem. An analysis of the motifs employed and of the technique of the bands will have to await the complete study of the material. We may only note here that bronze wire was often used to strengthen the edges of the bands and keep them in shape in a manner noted in the finds from the shaft graves in the Citadel. Further study of the death mask will be required before any valid conclusions are

[34] Cf. the Petelia gold plate: Guthrie, W. K. C., *Orpheus and Greek Religion*, pp. 172ff.
[35] Cf. Percott, Peru, I, 4th ed., p. 31; Strabo, 503.
[36] *Iliad*, III, 271-272; XIX, 252-253.

drawn. It is clear, however, that the example from Grave Gamma was not attached to a wooden coffin. As we have seen, wooden coffins were not used for the burial of the people in Grave Circle B. Very few gems were found, but one of these gives us the portrait of a Mycenaean.

We noted above that no evidence was found indicating the existence of a cult held in honor of the people buried in Grave Circle B. It seems that the bones and grave offerings of the ancestors were treated by their descendants with the same indifference and carelessness which characterizes the burial habits of the Mycenaeans of later times. It also seems certain that toward Circle B the people and rulers of Mycenae did not feel the respect which they seem to have felt toward Grave Circle A. We have seen how one of its shaft graves, Rho, was opened, enlarged, and used for the construction of a grave and the burial of a body at least a century after it was sealed and the entire Circle area was no longer used for burial. Again, we find that the tholos of the Tomb of Clytemnestra encroaches decidedly on the Circle. A good deal of the eastern section of the wall of the Circle was destroyed when the shaft for that tholos tomb was cut. This would not have taken place if the area of the Circle was considered sacred. Not even in later Geometric times, a period when ancestral respect and worship seem to have reached a high point, was the Grave Circle area respected. This is proved by the lack of Geometric relics in its area and the existence of a Geometric circular structure, an altar or a shrine, over the ruined top of the chamber tomb built below the southern edge of the wall of the Circle. That shrine was built when the grave was revealed by a caving in of its roof. If a tradition had survived, or if the Grave Circle showed above ground level, or if its stelai were to be seen in Geometric times, we should expect to find similar evidence of respect and worship in some part of its area as the one found over the adjacent chamber tomb.

We may now recall that Professor Wace suggests that a mound of earth, with a radius of at least 25 meters, was piled over the tholos of the Tomb of Clytemnestra. The splendid wall of poros ashlar Professor Wace uncovered to the east of that tholos is, according to him, the retaining wall of the mound. Furthermore, he suggests that the mound over the tholos is what Pausanias calls the "Tomb of Atreus," in which case the mound must have still existed in his day.[37]

[37] Wace, *JHS*, 74 (1954), p. 170.

If that view is correct, then a good part of the area of Circle B was also covered by the mound of the Tomb of Clytemnestra.

There is another bit of evidence worth noting. The area to the north of Grave Circle B exhibits a thick layer of white-yellowish chips and dust of what was thought to be poros. At first it was believed that in the area were cut the poros blocks used for the construction of the Perseia fountain uncovered by Professor Wace. However, the Circle area is rather at a distance from the fountain, a fact involving the necessity of transportation, while the blocks could be cut almost on the spot. Also, I am not sure that the layer is formed of remains of poros. I think that it was made of the dust and broken chips of the "almond stones," of the conglomerate, used for the construction of the Tomb of Clytemnestra. A good many of those blocks were shaped to size by sawing, and the thin, dust-like quality of the fill and the small pebbly chips it contains would naturally be produced by such a process. Also, the area next to the tholos cutting and by the side of the road which led from the plain, and the quarries, to the Citadel would have been the right place for the final dressing of the stones to be used in the construction of the tomb. It should also be added that all the sherds found below the "white-yellowish" layer are exclusively prehistoric, with no sherds of the historic period, and the latest of them seem to belong to Late Helladic II-III times. Of course, it will be necessary to study the sherds more fully and completely before final conclusions are reached, but a brief examination, while the excavation was in progress, seems to justify the statements made. A petrological analysis will be required to determine this point.

If it were proved that the layer in question was made up of poros chips and dust, even then we should be forced to consider it as the result of the dressing and cutting to size of the poros blocks employed for the construction of the heavy wall which supported the mound of the Tomb of Clytemnestra to the east. What is of added interest is that we found traces of that layer over the top of the wall of the Circle and even in the northern sector of the Circle to a distance of at least 1.50 meters of its wall. That would indicate that the top of the Circle was already covered up or was in the process of being covered up at the time when the "white" layer beyond it was being formed. That the layer is found in the Circle may show that stones were worked in that area too, adding another indication to those already mentioned that the Circle area was not an object of respect or reverence. After the construction, that "white-yellowish" layer would have been covered up by the mound, which, according to Professor Wace, covered the tholos. It could not then have been made in Hellenistic times.

These considerations seem to indicate that:

1. the Circle area was not respected in the days of the construction of the Tomb of Clytemnestra;

2. it was covered up at least to the top of its encircling wall when that construction was underway;

3. at least its greater part was buried under the mound formed over the tholos of the Tomb of Clytemnestra, if such a mound existed and if it had a radius of 25 meters;

4. it was not used as the place of a cult in Geometric times; we may assume that it would have been used for a cult if a tradition regarding its important graves had survived to those times;

5. it could not be seen in historic times.

If we should assume that the "white-yellowish" layer was Hellenistic, and that no mound over the Tomb of Clytemnestra had survived, even then we should have to admit that the Circle was filled up to the height of the top of its wall, and that no special respect was shown it, since the white layer, indicative of the presence of a workshop, extended to its interior.

All this reasoning is essential to determine whether or not a tradition as to the existence of the graves could have been kept alive in historic times. As early as 1950, Professor Marinatos, in a lecture delivered in Athens, suggested that beyond the Citadel other shaft graves would be found and that these might be the traditional graves of Aegisthos and Clytemnestra, which according to Pausanias were at a short distance from the walls because those legendary figures "were not considered worthy to be buried within the walls, where Agamemnon himself lies and those who were killed with him."[38] When Grave Alpha was found, in November 1951, Professor Wace in a letter to the then Director of the British School, John Cook, expressed the belief that the new shaft graves were the ones attributed by Pausanias to Aegisthos and Clytemnestra in the same way that the shaft graves within the Citadel were attributed to Agamemnon and his followers.[39] Dr. J. Papademetriou, after the first season's work,

[38] *Geras*, pp. 78ff.

[39] Since then he has expressed this view in "Pausanias and Mycenae," in the *Volume in Honor of Bernhard Schweitzer*, pp. 24-25.

expressed the same opinion and stated further that perhaps Pausanias had seen some of the stelai of Grave Circle B still standing.[40] In view of the facts stated above, I doubt that the Grave Circle was visible in the days of Pausanias or even in the days of the Classical era of Greece. And since the Circle had already been intruded upon at the end of the 13th century B.C. by the builders of the Tomb of Clytemnestra, I doubt that a tradition around it was created which reached the days of Hellanikos and Pausanias. There can be no doubt as to the correctness of the statement regarding the existence of the tombs attributed to Aegisthos and Clytemnestra beyond the walls. But I think that the graves of Aegisthos and Clytemnestra are still to be located or that in the days of Pausanias they might have been identified with mounds which no longer exist—like the mounds which must have existed over the Tomb of Aegisthos and the Lion Tomb. The latter was well known before it was cleared, but the former was discovered by Tsountas in 1892. Its modern name may well have some traditional background.

Whether or not the graves of Circle B were identified by ancient tradition as those of Aegisthos and Clytemnestra, the fact remains that none of them was actually the grave of the two almost legendary figures. They belong to people who will have to remain unknown and unnamed; but there can be no doubt that they belong to members of the ruling class of Mycenae, perhaps to members of a royal family, and most of them to mighty warriors, as can be surmised from the weapons buried with them. Dr. Angel, who is studying their skeletal remains, has kindly written me that "they had massive as well as tall bodies, since both the vertebrae and the thickness of all long bone shafts are extra large." They average 1.706 meters (5′7⅛″) in height, "over 0.06 m. taller than Middle Bronze Age commoners," and at least three of them, in Graves Gamma, Zeta, and Nu, were over 1.80 meters (about six feet) tall. Perhaps we have the appearance of one of them in the gem from Grave Gamma, and maybe a general indication of features in the death mask from the same grave. All the available evidence proves that they do not belong to the Minoan type, that they are Greeks, in the historic sense of the word, descendants of the early Indo-Europeans who found their way into the mainland of Greece at the beginning of the Middle Bronze

[40] *ILN*, Sept. 27, 1952, pp. 505-507.

Age. They certainly belong to the group of people who laid the foundations of the greatness of the Mycenaean state.

The discussion of the date of these graves was intentionally left to the end. Dating prehistoric graves is a difficult operation, and it should be based upon a complete study of all the evidence obtained in excavation. Since the study of all the objects found in the course of our excavation has not been completed as yet, dates for the graves cannot be given now. It may be suggested that the graves of Circle B as a group seem to be somewhat earlier than the graves explored by Schliemann. Those graves are usually placed between 1580 and 1500 B.C. The older graves of Circle B antedate the upper chronological limit of the group in Circle A and they must be placed in the last half of the Middle Helladic period, in the seventeenth century B.C. The latest burials in some of the graves of Circle B may be contemporary with burials of Circle A. Beyond this statement we cannot go at present with any degree of certainty. It seems evident from the statement made that for some time at least the two Circles may have been used concurrently. Professor Marinatos has made the interesting suggestion that such a use may indicate the existence of two branches in the royal family, reflecting the practice of the succession of the kingship from brother to brother and then to the son of the first.[41] An example of this in Mycenae itself is given in the *Iliad*: Atreus is not succeeded by his son Agamemnon, but by his brother Thyestes, after whose death Agamemnon became the king. At any rate, both sets are graves of the ruling families of Mycenae of the seventeenth and sixteenth centuries B.C.

EPILOGUE

The excavation of the new shaft graves of Mycenae has contributed considerably to our knowledge of the mythical world of Greece and has added many works of art to our collections. To us, who were privileged to take part in this exploration, the excavation gave an experience never to be forgotten. The final study covering the work will contain a complete description of the graves and objects unearthed, the observations made, and the conclusions reached. It will give little indication of the thoughts which kept crowding our minds as the excavation proceeded and of the feelings which increased the beat of our hearts. Objects fashioned centuries ago, weapons which

---

[41] *Geras*, pp. 83-86.

gave victory to their bearers, vases which contained nourishing food or priceless ointments; and with them the bones of those who used them! Who were they? What did they think? What were their deeds? We, too, like Menippos of old, anxious to see and learn, felt helpless in the world of the shadows. Lucian's Dialogues of the dead have a new meaning for those who looked into the depths of the graves, and Hermes' answers to Menippos become our answers.

MENIPPOS: Where are all the beauties, Hermes? Show me round; I am a new-comer.

HERMES: I am busy, Menippos. But look over there to your right, and you will see Hyacinth, Narcissos, Nireus, Achilles, Tyro, Helen, Leda,—all the beauties of old.

MEN.: I can only see bones, and bare skulls; most of them are exactly alike.

HER.: Those bones, of which you seem to think so lightly, have been the theme of admiring poets.

MEN.: Well, but show me Helen; I shall never be able to make her out myself.

HER.: This skull is Helen.

MEN.: And for this a thousand ships carried warriors from every part of Greece; Greeks and barbarians slain, and cities made desolate?

HER.: Ah, Menippos, you never saw the living Helen; or you would have said with Homer,

> Well might they suffer grievous years of toil
> Who strove for such a prize.

We look at withered flowers, whose dye is gone from them, and what can we call them but unlovely things? Yet, in the hour of their bloom these unlovely things were things of beauty.

—Lucian: *Dialogues of the Dead*, XIX; translation F. G. Fowler

ABBREVIATIONS AND GLOSSARY

ABBREVIATIONS

AA   *Archäologischer Anzeiger*
AASOR   *Annual of the American Schools of Oriental Research*
AJA   *American Journal of Archaeology*
Annuario *Annuario della R. Scuola Archeologica di Atene*
Ath. Mitt *Athenische Mitteilungen*
BCH   *Bulletin de correspondence hellénique*
BSA   *Annual of the British School of Archaeology at Athens*
CJ   *Classical Journal*
Deltion   'Αρχαιολογικὸν Δελτίον
Ephemeris 'Αρχαιολογικὴ 'Εφημερίς and 'Εφημερὶς 'Αρχαιολογική
Geras   Γέρας 'Αντωνίου Κεραμοπούλλου, Athens, 1955
Hesperia *Hesperia*, Journal of the American School of Classical Studies
            at Athens
IG   *Inscriptiones Graecae*
ILN   *Illustrated London News*
Jahrbuch *Jahrbuch des K. deutschen archäologischen Instituts*
JHS   *Journal of Hellenic Studies*
PAE   Πρακτικὰ τῆς ἐν 'Αθήναις 'Αρχαιολογικῆς 'Εταιρείας
PAPS   *Proceedings of the American Philosophical Society*
RA   *Revue archéologique*
REA   *Revue des études anciennes*
TAPA   *Transactions of the American Philological Society*
See also the Bibliography for full titles of books and year of publication.

GLOSSARY

Abacus: Rectangular block forming the uppermost member of the capital.
Aethousa: A portico or porch through which one entered the Megaron.
    The front part of the Megaron. Usually it was in antis, i.e. in its
    front it had two columns placed between the projecting lateral walls.
Aniconic: Not in the form of a human being.
Anta: The end of a lateral wall. In later times it was in the form of a
    slight projection or a pilaster terminating the lateral wall and usually
    served as a respond to a column. Plural: antae.
Capital: The uppermost member of a column.
Cist graves: Graves made of four slabs placed vertically so as to enclose a
    small box-like rectangular shape. Characteristic type of grave of the
    Middle Helladic period, *c.* 1900-1580 B.C.
Clamp: Link of metal used instead of mortar to bind together blocks of
    stone.

Corbel vault: A false arch or vault constructed in horizontal courses, so that each course projects slightly above the one below it, thus gradually reducing the area to be spanned. All thrusts are vertical. In the Greek Prehistoric structural system it has an inverted V shape.

Cyanus: A dark blue paste (enamel-like) used for the decoration of architectural friezes and of other articles.

Cyclopean construction: Massive masonry made up of large stones piled on each other without regard to a horizontal arrangement. They are held together by their own weight and no mortar is used as binder. The interstices, or spaces left between blocks, are filled with small stones and earth.

Dado: Term given to the lower portion of a wall when faced with wood or marble or when colored differently from the upper part of the wall.

Domos: The main room of the Megaron. It usually contained the hearth.

Dowel: Metal attachment used to secure blocks of one course to those below them.

Dromos: A long and narrow passage cut in the hillside and serving as an approach to the doorway of a chamber or tholos tomb.

Echinus: The convex part of a capital (Doric capital in the historic period) met immediately below the abacus. The name is derived from the sea urchin whose shell, when deprived of its spine, the convex part resembles. Plural: echini.

Electrum: A natural alloy of gold and silver.

Enceinte: An area enclosed by fortification walls. Usually applied to an enclosed shrine or an acropolis.

Entablature: The part of the superstructure carried by the columns; it includes the architrave, the frieze, and the cornice.

Fascia: An architectural term given to a flat projecting band.

Fillet: A narrow, flat moulding.

Heroon: Shrine of a hero, or a precinct dedicated to a hero.

In situ: Archaeological term used to indicate that certain objects or stones are in the original position in which they were laid by their owners or the original builders.

Jamb: The vertical lateral member of a door frame. Usually it supports the lintel.

Kourotrophos: A terracotta figurine in the form of a woman holding a baby in her arms. Plural: Kourotrophoi.

Kterismata: Gifts and offerings placed in the grave along with the dead.

Lintel: A beam, in prehistoric times a block of stone, placed horizontally to span the opening of a doorway.

Megaron: A long and narrow unit of the Mycenaean palace, to which one entered through an open front portico placed on one of its short sides.

By crosswalls it was divided into a front portico (*aethousa*), a vestibule (*prodomos*), and the main room (*domos*), where the hearth was located.

Peribolos wall: A fortification wall built to enclose an acropolis or the top of a hill.

Pithos: A large, clay storage vessel. Plural: pithoi.

Plesia: A greenish, waterproof clay.

Polygonal masonry: Wall construction in carefully cut and fitted stones of small dimensions and of polygonal shapes. It is characterized by an accurate adjustment of adjacent stones and a smooth face.

Poros: A soft and porous limestone, in color ranging from creamish white to brown, often filled with fossil shells.

Prochous: jug.

Prodomos: The second section of the Megaron. A small compartment or vestibule between the porch entrance (*aethousa*) and the main room (*domos*) of the Megaron.

Propylon: An entranceway building, with one doorway. Often a porch is added on either side of the door opening. Simpler structure than a regular Propylaeum.

Ramp: A sloping causeway.

Relieving triangle: A false arch or triangular form, constructed on the principle of corbelling and over the lintel of doorways to relieve it from the weight of a regular wall. It was usually blocked by a slab, often decorated.

Rhyton: A funnel-shaped vase. When used for ritualistic purposes, it had a hole in the bottom. Rhytons in the form of an animal head were also made and used in the ritual of the Mycenaean period.

Rosette: A circular floral ornament with petals. In Mycenaean times, half rosettes, elongated in form and alternating with triglyphs, were employed to fill bands or friezes.

Saddle roof: A roof constructed on the principle of the inverted V type of corbelling; however, the sides stop before coming together to a point and the distance between them is spanned by a single slab: ⟋⟍

Sema: A marker of a tomb; a tombstone.

Shaft graves: Large graves of rectangular shape cut vertically in the earth and rock. Entered into by means of their roof, usually to be found some feet below surface.

Steatite: Very soft stone; soapstone. Usually greenish in color.

Stele: A stone slab placed in an upright position over a grave to serve as its marker. Often one of its sides is covered with reliefs. In historic times decrees and public accounts were also inscribed on slabs known as stelai. Plural: stelai.

Stephane: A wreath-like small cap usually placed on the heads of the Mycenaean figurines.

Stomion: A deep entranceway of a tholos or chamber tomb.

Talent: A commercial weight and also the value represented by the corresponding weight of gold, silver, or bronze. Used in bartering in prehistoric times (instead of money which did not exist then).

Temenos: A sacred precinct.

Tholos: A circular enclosed and roofed area. A building composed of one circular room. Plural: tholoi.

Triglyph: A motive used in the decorative scheme of the Mycenaeans, usually composed of three vertical grooves. Employed along with the elongated rosette with which it alternates.

Tympanon: The part of the façade of a tholos tomb above its lintel.

Ushebtis: "Answerers." Small figurines used in Egypt and placed in the graves of the nobles and Pharaohs to serve them in the lower world. They were there to answer all demands of the buried master.

CHRONOLOGY; MYCENAEAN HISTORY AND MYTHOLOGY

CHRONOLOGY

HELLADIC   The art and culture developed and produced in the mainland of Greece during the Bronze Age from about 2500 B.C. to *c.* 1100 B.C.

HELLADIC PERIOD   The period during which that art and culture were being produced, i.e., the years from *c.* 2500 to *c.* 1100 B.C. The period is usually subdivided into the following sub-periods:

Early Helladic (I, II, III), from *c.* 2500 to *c.* 1900 B.C.

Middle Helladic (I and II), from *c.* 1900 to *c.* 1580 B.C.

Late Helladic I, from *c.* 1580 to *c.* 1500 B.C.

Late Helladic II, from *c.* 1500 to *c.* 1400 B.C.

Late Helladic III A, from *c.* 1400 to *c.* 1300 B.C.

Late Helladic III B, from *c.* 1300 to *c.* 1200 B.C.

Late Helladic III C, from *c.* 1200 to *c.* 1100 B.C.

The sub-periods are abbreviated EH, MH, and LH.

MINOAN   The art and culture developed and produced in the island of Crete during the Bronze Age from about 2800 B.C. to about 1100 B.C.

MINOAN PERIOD   The period during which that art and culture were being produced, i.e., the years from *c.* 2800 to *c.* 1100 B.C. The period is subdivided into the following sub-periods:

Early Minoan Period and Art, c. 2800 to 2100 B.C.

Middle Minoan, c. 2100 to 1580 B.C.

Late Minoan, c. 1580 to 1100 B.C.

The sub-periods are abbreviated: EM, MM, and LM.

MYCENAEAN HISTORY AND MYTHOLOGY

B.C.

c. 2500-1900   Earliest occupation and settlements of Mycenae. Inhabitants a non-Indo-European people racially related to the tribes inhabiting the Cyclades and Crete.

c. 1900   Arrival of the First Indo-European tribes at Mycenae. First Indo-European settlement on the Acropolis.

c. 1900-1700   Gradual expansion of early Indo-European settlements. Increased wealth and power.

c. 1650-1550   Grave Circle B; excavated 1952-1953-1954; proves increasing prosperity of Mycenaean settlement.

c. 1600-1500   Grave Circle A. Excavated by Schliemann in 1876. Perhaps earliest primitive palace built on top of Citadel.

c. 1350-1330   Perseus becomes king of Mycenae and builds the first peribolos walls in the Cyclopean style.

c. 1350-1250   Perseus and his descendants, the Perseid dynasty, rule Mycenae.

c. 1250   Atreus, son of Pelops, becomes the ruler of Mycenae. He built the Lion Gate, expanded the Acropolis area, and erected the so-called Treasury of Atreus. Perhaps during his reign Mycenae attained greatest expansion, prosperity, and renown.

c. 1250-1200   Rule of Atreus and Thyestes.

c. 1200   Agamemnon rules over Mycenae, during whose reign the Trojan War takes place.

c. 1183   Traditional date for the fall of Troy and shortly after that the return of Agamemnon and his death.

c. 1183-1175   Death of Clytemnestra and Aegisthos. Orestes becomes king of Mycenae.

c. 1175-1100   Rule of Orestes and his son Tisamenos.

c. 1100   Destruction of Mycenae perhaps by the Dorian tribes. End of her glory and her role as the leader of the Greek world and as a focal point of culture.

480   Mycenaeans take part in the battle of Thermopylae.

479   Mycenaeans take part in the battle of Plataea.

c. 468   Mycenae destroyed again by people of Argos.

c. 300   Mycenae reinhabited by people of Argos and becomes a township.

A.D.

c. 160   Pausanias visits Mycenae.

c. 300   Mycenae, as a small village, survives still.

After A.D. 300 we have no news of Mycenae.

1800-1818   Her ruins are pilfered by art collectors.

1840   The Greek Archaeological Society cleared the Lion Gate.

1874   Schliemann tested the Acropolis of Mycenae by means of exploratory trenches.

1876   Schliemann's great discovery of the royal tombs of Mycenae: Grave Circle A. Stamatakes' work.

1877-1902   The Greek Archaeological Society, through Ch. Tsountas especially, excavated a good part of the Acropolis of Mycenae and many of her graves. The Palace of Agamemnon was then discovered and cleared.

1920-1923   The British School of Archaeology at Athens, through Professor A. J. B. Wace, continued the exploration of Mycenae and her graves.

1939   Professor Wace began the exploration of the houses of the city of Mycenae.

1940-1950   Interruption of the work by World War II.

1950   Professor Wace resumed his excavations.

The Greek Archaeological Society through J. Papademetriou and F. Petsas began the exploration of Mycenaean houses.

1950-1955   Professor Wace continued his excavations of the houses and early cemetery of Mycenae.

1951-1955   The Greek Service for the Restoration and Preservation of Monuments, under the direction of Professor A. Orlandos and E. Stikas, restored the Tomb of Clytemnestra, the Cyclopean walls around the Lion Gate and the Palace on the Acropolis of Mycenae.

November 1951   Discovery of second Grave Circle of Mycenae.

1952-1954   Exploration of the second Royal Circle by the Greek Archaeological Society through the ephor of the district, John Papademetriou, and Professors Keramopoullos, Marinatos, and Mylonas.

BIBLIOGRAPHY

Belger, C., *Beiträge zur Kenntnis der griechischen Kuppelgräber*, Berlin, 1887.

Bennett, E. L., "The Mycenae Tablets," *PAPS*, 97 (1953).

——, *The Pylos Tablets*, Princeton, 1951.

——, *A Minoan Linear B Index*, New Haven, 1953.

Blegen, C. W., *Korakou, a Prehistoric Settlement near Corinth*, Boston and New York, 1921.

——, *Zygouries, a Prehistoric Settlement in the Valley of Cleonae*, Cambridge (Mass.), 1928.

——, *Prosymna, the Helladic Settlement Preceding the Argive Heraeum*, Cambridge (Mass.), 1937.

——, "The Roof of the Mycenaean Megaron," *AJA*, 49 (1945).

——, Excavations at Pylos, 1952, 1953, and 1954, *AJA*, 43 (1939); 58 (1954); 59 (1955).

——, "The Halberd from the Sixth Shaft Grave," Ἐπιτύμβιον Χρ. Τσούντα. *See also* Wace and Blegen.

Boethius, C. A., "Hellenistic Mycenae," *BSA*, 25 (1921-1923).

Bossert, H. T., *The Art of Ancient Crete*, London, 1937.

Chadwick, J. See Ventris, M. and J. Chadwick.

Cook, J. M., "The Agamemnoneion," *BSA*, 48 (1953).

Desborough, V. R. d'A., "Mycenae, 1939-1953. Four Tombs," *BSA*, 49 (1954).

Dinsmoor, W. B., "Notes on Megaron Roofs," *AJA*, 46 (1942).

Dörpfeld, W., "Kretische, mykenische, und homerische Paläste," *Ath. Mitt.*, 30 and 32 (1905 and 1907).

Durm, J., "Über vormykenische und mykenische Architekturformen," *Jahresh. Oest. Arch. Inst.*, 10 (1907).

Dussaud, R., *Les Civilisations préhelléniques dans le bassin de la mer Égée*, 2nd ed., Paris, 1914.

Evangelides, D., "Ἐκ τῆς Μυκηνῶν γεωμετρικῆς νεκροπόλεως," *Ephemeris*, 1912.

Evans, Sir Arthur, *The Palace of Minos at Knossos*, I-IV, London, 1921-1935.

——, *The Shaft Graves and Beehive Tombs of Mycenae and Their Interrelations*, London, 1929.

Fimmen, D., *Die Kretisch-mykenische Kultur*, 2nd ed., Leipzig, 1924.

Frödin, O., and A. W. Persson, *Asine, Results of the Swedish Excavations, 1922-1930*, Stockholm, 1938.

Furtwängler, A., and G. Loeschcke, *Mykenischen Vasen*, Berlin, 1886.

Furumark, A., *Mycenaean Pottery, Analysis and Classification*, Stockholm, 1941.

Furumark, A., *The Chronology of Mycenaean Pottery*, Stockholm, 1941.
Heurtley, W. A., "The Grave Stelai of Mycenae," *BSA*, 25 (1921-1923).
Holland, L. B., "Primitive Aegean Roofs," *AJA*, 24 (1920).
——, "Architectural Commentary," *BSA*, 25 (1921-1923).
Holland, M., and M. S. F. Hood, "The Perseia Fountain," *BSA*, 48 (1953).
Hood, M. S. F., "A Mycenaean Cavalryman," *BSA*, 48 (1953).
Karo, G., *Die Schachtgräber von Mykenai*, Munich, 1930-1933.
——, "Die Perseia von Mykenai," *AJA*, 38 (1934).
Kavvadias, P., Προϊστορικὴ ᾿Αρχαιολογία, Athens, 1909.
Keramopoullos, A., "Περὶ τῶν βασιλικῶν τάφων τῆς ᾿Ακροπόλεως τῶν Μυκηνῶν," *Ephemeris*, 1918.
Kourouniotes, K., "Porosskulpturen aus Mykenai," *Jahrbuch*, 16 (1901).
Lamb, W., "The Palace Frescoes," *BSA*, 25 (1919-1923).
Marinatos, Sp., " 'Numerous Years of Joyful Life' from Mycenae," *BSA*, 46 (1951).
——, "Περὶ τοὺς νέους βασιλικοὺς τάφους τῶν Μυκηνῶν," Γέρας ᾿Αντωνίου Κεραμοπούλλου.
——, "Μικραὶ ἔρευναι ἐν Μυκήναις," *Ephemeris in Memoriam G. P. Oekonomos*.
——, "Der 'Nestorbecher' aus dem IV. Schachtgrab von Mykenae," Festschrift Bernhard Schweitzer, Stuttgart, 1954.
Meurer, M., "Der Goldschmuck der mykenischen Schatzgräber," *Jahrbuch*, 27 (1912).
——, "Form und Herkunft der mykenischen Säule," *Jahrbuch*, 29 (1914).
Müller, K., "Fruehmykenische Reliefs," *Jahrbuch*, 30 (1915).
Müller, V., "Development of the Megaron in Prehistoric Greece," *AJA*, 48 (1944).
Mylonas, G., "Homeric and Mycenaean Burial Customs," *AJA*, 52 (1948).
——, "Οἱ βασιλικοὶ τάφοι τῶν Μυκηνῶν καὶ ἡ ᾿Αθηναϊκὴ παράδοσις," ᾿Επιτύμβιον Χρ. Τσούντα.
——, "The Cult of the Dead in Helladic Times," *Studies Presented to David Moore Robinson*, I, St. Louis, 1951.
——, "The Figured Mycenaean Stelai," *AJA*, 55 (1951).
——, "Μυκηναϊκὰ εἰδώλια," ᾿Επετηρίς, School of Philosophy, University of Athens, 1954-1955.
——, "Τὰ τείχη τῶν Μυκηνῶν," *ibid.*, 1955-1956.
Mylonas, G., and J. Papademetriou, "The New Shaft Graves of Mycenae," *Archaeology*, 1952.

————, "The New Grave Circle of Mycenae," *Archaeology*, 1955.

Nilsson, M. L., *The Minoan-Mycenaean Religion and Its Survival in Greek Religion*, 2nd ed., Lund, 1950.

————, *Homer and Mycenae*, London, 1933.

————, *The Mycenaean Origin of Greek Mythology*, Berkeley (Calif.), 1932.

Noack, F., *Homerische Paläste*, Leipzig, 1903.

Oekonomos, G. P., *Volume in Memoriam G. P. Oekonomos, Ephemeris*, 1953-1954.

Palmer, L. R., *Achaeans and Indo-Europeans*, inaugural lecture, 4 November 1954, Oxford: Clarendon Press, 1955.

Papademetriou, J., "'Ἀναστηλωτικαὶ ἐργασίαι ἐν Μυκήναις," *Ephemeris*, 1948-1949.

————, "'Ἀνασκαφαὶ ἐν Μυκήναις," *PAE*, 1951, 1952, and 1953. See also Mylonas-Papademetriou.

Pendlebury, J. D. S., *Aegyptiaca*, Cambridge (Eng.), 1930.

Perrot, G., and C. Chipiez, *Histoire de l'art dans l'antiquité*: VI. *La Grèce primitive, l'art mycénien*, Paris, 1894.

————, *Art in Primitive Greece*, London, 1894.

Persson, A., *Royal Tombs at Dendra Near Midea*, Lund, 1931.

————, *New Tombs at Dendra Near Midea*, Lund, 1943.

————, "Legende und Mythos in ihrem Verhältnis zu Bild und Gleichnis im vorgeschichlichen Griechenland," *DPAGMA Martino P. Nilson Dedicatum*, Lund, 1939.

Philadelpheus, A., "'Ἀνόρυξις θαλαμοειδῶν τάφων ἐν Μυκήναις," *Deltion*, 1919.

Picard, Ch., "Sur un groupe d'ivoire de Mycènes," in Ἐπιτύμβιον Χρ. Τσούντα.

Pryce, F. N., *British Museum Catalogue of Greek and Roman Sculpture*, I, Part I, London, 1928.

Reber, F. v., "Beiträge zur Kenntnis des Baustiles der heroischen Epoche," *Sitzb. Mün. Akad.*, 1888.

Reichel, W., *Homerische Waffen*, 1901.

————, "Die mykenische Grabstelen," *Eranos Vindobonensis*.

————, "Die schachtgräber-Terasse von Mykenai während Schliemanns Ausgrabung," *Antike Denkmäler*, II, pls. 46, 49.

Robertson, D. S., "New Light on the Façade of the Treasury of Atreus," *JHS*, 61 (1941).

Rodenwaldt, G., "Mykenische Studien I. Die Fussböden des Megarons von Mykenai," *Jahrbuch*, 34 (1919).

————, "Die Wandgemälde von Tiryns."

————, "Fragmente mykenischer Wandgemälde," *Ath. Mitt.*, 36 (1911).

Rodenwaldt, G., "Votivpinax aus Mykenai," *Ath. Mitt.*, 43 (1918).

——, *Der Fries des Megarons von Mykenai*, Halle, 1921.

Rowe, K. R., "Mycenae, A Possible Middle Helladic Fortification Wall," *BSA*, 49 (1954).

Schliemann, H., *Mycenae: A Narrative of Researches and Discoveries at Mycenae and Tiryns*, New York, 1880.

Schuchardt, C., *Schliemann's Excavations*, London and New York, 1891.

Smith, E. B., "The Megaron and Its Roof," *AJA*, 46 (1942).

Stais, V., *Collection Mycénienne du Musée National*, Athens, 1911.

——, "Περὶ τῆς χρήσεως Μυκηναϊκῶν τινων κοσμημάτων," *Ephemeris*, 1907.

——, "Das silberne Rhyton des vierten Grabes der Burg von Mykenai," *Ath. Mitt.*, 40 (1915).

Steffen, Captain H., *Karten von Mykenai*, Berlin, 1884.

Stubbins, F. H., "Mycenae 1939-1953. A Bronze Founder's Hoard. A Winged Axe Mould," *BSA*, 49 (1954).

Thiersch, F., "Die Tholos des Atreus zu Mykenai," *Ath. Mitt.*, 4 (1879).

Thomas, H., "The Acropolis Treasure from Mycenae," *BSA*, 39 (1938-1939).

Tsountas, Ch., " 'Ανασκαφαὶ Μυκηνῶν," *PAE*, 1886.

——, " 'Αρχαιότητες ἐκ Μυκηνῶν," *Ephemeris*, 1887.

——, " 'Ανασκαφαὶ τάφων ἐν Μυκήναις," *Ephemeris*, 1888.

——, " 'Εκ Μυκηνῶν," *Ephemeris*, 1891.

——, "Γραπτὴ στήλη ἐκ Μυκηνῶν," *Ephemeris*, 1896.

——, "Μῆτραι καὶ ξίφη ἐκ Μυκηνῶν," *Ephemeris*, 1897.

——, "Κεφαλὴ ἐκ Μυκηνῶν," *Ephemeris*, 1902.

——, "Μυκῆναι καὶ Μυκηναῖος Πολιτισμός, Athens, 1897.

——, "Zu einigen mykenischen Streitfragen," *Jahrbuch*, 1895.

——, 'Επιτύμβιον Χρήστου Τσούντα, Athens, 1941.

Tsountas, C., and J. I. Manatt, *The Mycenaean Age*, London, 1897.

Ventris, M., and J. Chadwick, "Evidence for Greek Dialect in the Mycenaean Archives," *JHS*, 73 (1953).

——, *Documents in Mycenaean Greek*, Cambridge, 1956.

Wace, A. J. B., "The Date of the Treasury of Atreus," *JHS*, 64 (1926).

——, "Chamber Tombs of Mycenae," *Archaeologia*, 82 (1932).

——, "The Treasury of Atreus," *Antiquity*, 14 (1940).

——, "Middle and Late Helladic Pottery," 'Επιτύμβιον Χρ. Τσούντα, Athens, 1941.

——, *Mycenae. An Archaeological History and Guide*, Princeton, 1949.

——, "Excavations at Mycenae, 1939," *BSA*, 45 (1950).

————, "Mycenae, 1939-1952," *BSA*, 48 (1953).

————, "The Mycenae Tablets. An Introduction," *PAPS*, 97 (1953).

————, "Mycenae, Preliminary Report on the Excavations of 1953," *BSA*, 49 (1954).

————, "The Tholos Tombs at Mycenae: Structural Analysis," in Persson, A., *Royal Tombs at Dendra*.

————, "Chronological Note," introduction in Ventris-Chadwick, *Documents in Mycenaean Greek*.

Wace, A. J. B., and others, "Excavations at Mycenae," *BSA*, 24-25 (1919-1921 to 1921-1923).

Wace, A. J. B., and C. W. Blegen, "The Pre-Mycenaean Pottery of the Mainland," *BSA*, 22 (1916-1918).

————, "Middle Helladic Tombs," *Symbolae Osloenses*, 9 (1930).

————, "Pottery as Evidence for Trade and Colonisation in the Aegean Bronze Age," *Klio*, 1939.

Wace, A. J. B., and F. H. Stubbins, "The Grave Circle," *BSA*, 49 (1954).

Wace, Elizabeth B., "Mycenae, 1939-1953. The Cyclopean Terrace Building and the Deposit of Pottery Beneath It," *BSA*, 49 (1954).

Weinberg, S., "Aegean Chronology," *AJA*, 51 (1947).

Wurz, E., *Der Ursprung der Kretisch-mykenischen Säulen*, Munich, 1913.

INDEX

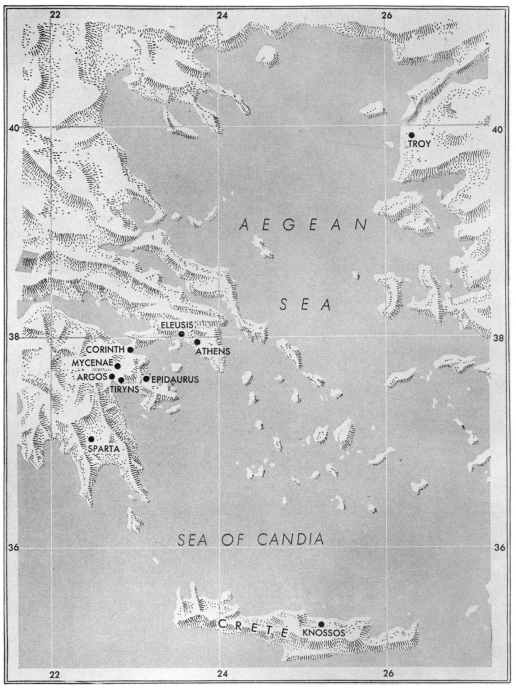

TROY

AEGEAN

SEA

ELEUSIS
CORINTH
MYCENAE
ATHENS
ARGOS
EPIDAURUS
TIRYNS

SPARTA

SEA OF CANDIA

CRETE KNOSSOS

1. Map of Greece showing location of Mycenae

2. General view of Mycenae from the west. Prophet Elias on the left, Zara on the right. Citadel of Mycenae in the center. Grave Circle B in the foreground, where the excavators are seated. Modern road (left) leads to Citadel

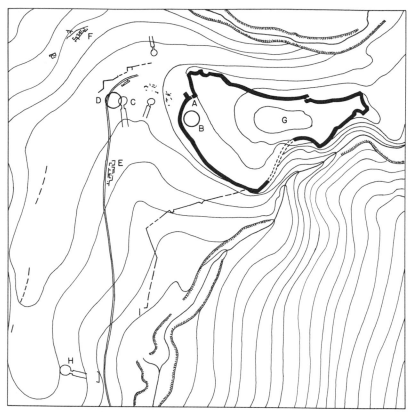

3. Topographic sketch of the Citadel and its environs. A. Lion Gate. B. Grave Circle A. C. Tomb of Clytemnestra. D. Grave Circle B. E and F. Mycenaean houses. G. Palace. H. Treasury of Atreus

4. Cyclopean wall of Mycenae

5. Corner of the bastion guarding Lion Gate and behind it polygonal wall, perhaps built in the third century B.C., when the walls were repaired. Restored by the Greek Service for the Restoration and Preservation of Ancient Monuments

6. The Lion Gate as it looks today after restoration. To the right, the bastion. Note how the east wall is founded on the rock and how the rock is used as part of the wall

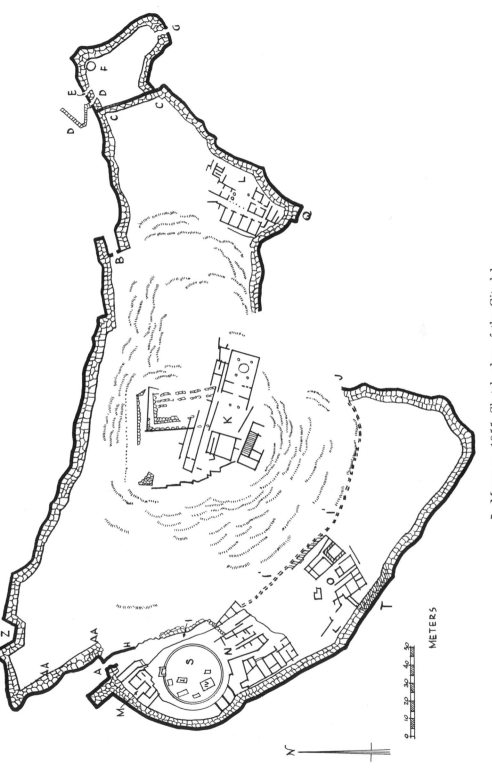

METERS

7. Mycenae, 1955. Sketch plan of the Citadel

9. The relief of Lions over the Gate

8. The Lion Gate after the restoration of its façade. Through
can be seen Wall II and the Ramp I which led to the

11. Sally port in the northeast extension of the walls of the Citadel

10. Threshold of the Lion Gate. Scale in centimeters: 0.50 m.

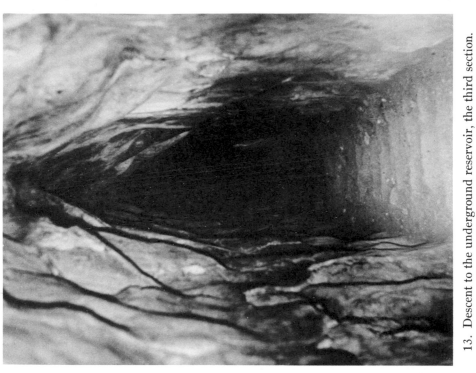

13. Descent to the underground reservoir, the third section. Note walls covered with plaster

12. Oblique passage through the wall to the underground reservoir

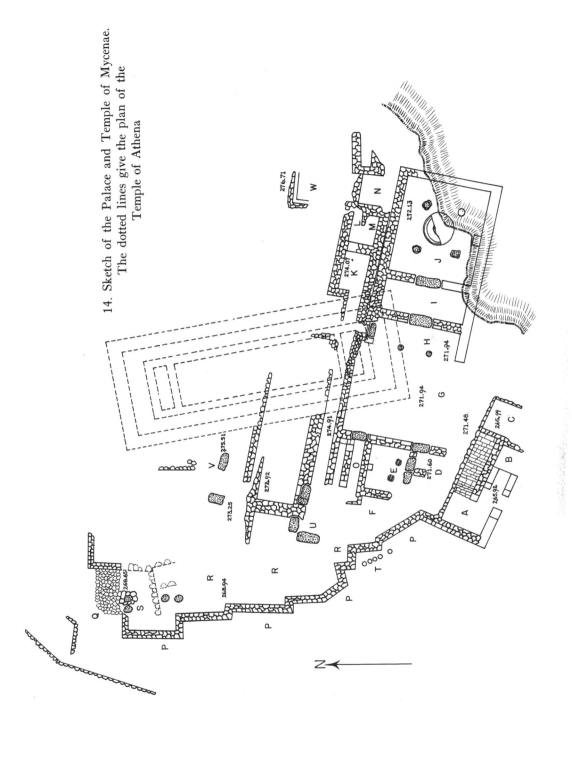

14. Sketch of the Palace and Temple of Mycenae.
The dotted lines give the plan of the
Temple of Athena

15. The Grand Stairway of the Palace

16. The Grand Stairway as restored. B and C, rooms under the second flight
of steps

17. Remains of the Megaron before restoration. The Court in the foreground. In the middle of the picture, walls separating the portico and vestibule

COURTESY OF DR. E. STIKAS

18. The Megaron and its Court (in foreground) after restoration

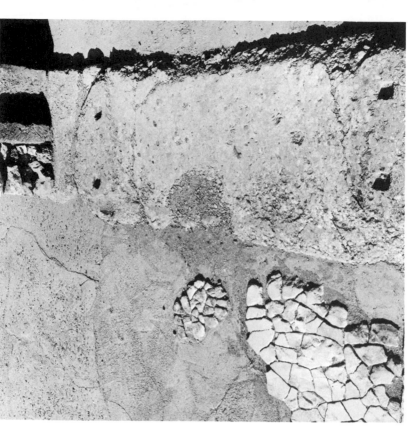

20. Large threshold block from the portico to the vestibule. To the left, remnants of gypsum slab on the floor of the vestibule as restored

19. Column base *in situ* and fragments of gypsum slab as restored in the portico of the Megaron

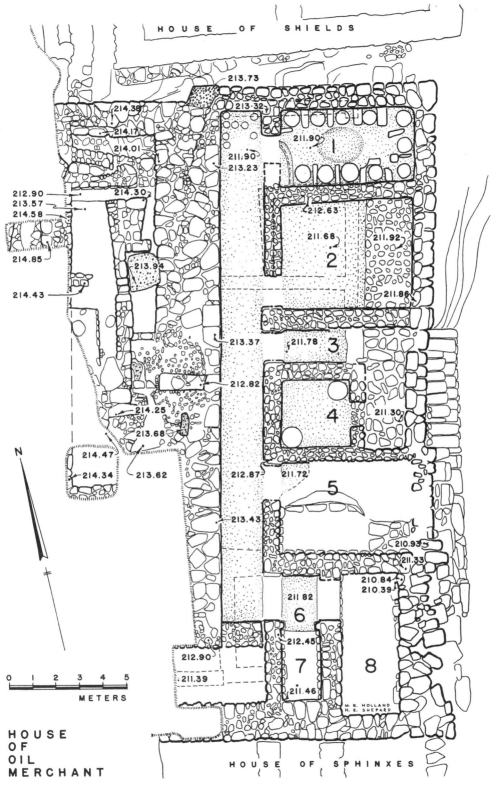

21. Basement rooms of the House of the Oil Merchant

COURTESY OF DR. A. J. B. WACE

23. Mycenaean clay tablet with inscription in Linear Script B from the House of the Oil Merchant. Scale in centimeters: 0.10 m.

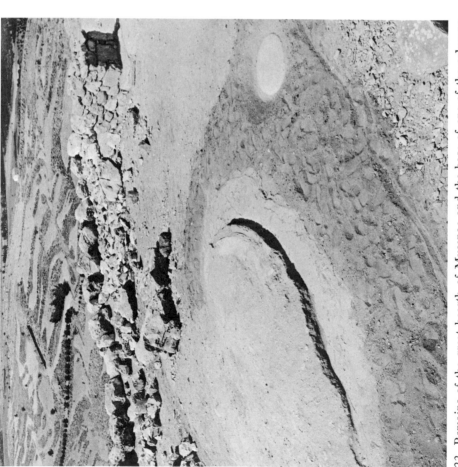

22. Remains of the great hearth of Mycenae and the base of one of the columns of the inner room. By the hearth can be seen a segment of the original floor covered with lime-cement. The photograph was taken in the course of restoration work in the summer of 1954

25. Door leading to the side chamber of the Treasury of Atreus

24. The façade of the Treasury of Atreus

26. Façade of the Treasury of Atreus. Restoration of its decoration, based on
Wace's and Marinatos' restorations

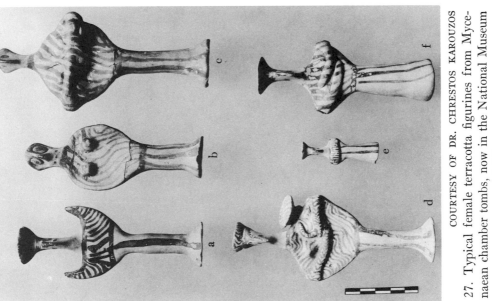

28. Remains of the Hellenistic theater across the passageway of the Tomb of Clytemnestra

27. Typical female terracotta figurines from Mycenaean chamber tombs, now in the National Museum of Athens

29. The Tomb of Clytemnestra after its restoration

30. Fluted base by the doorway of the Tomb of Clytemnestra

32. The tholos of the Tomb of Clytemnestra in the course of restoration

31. The upper façade of the Tomb of Clytemnestra

34. The restored vault of the Tomb of Clytemnestra

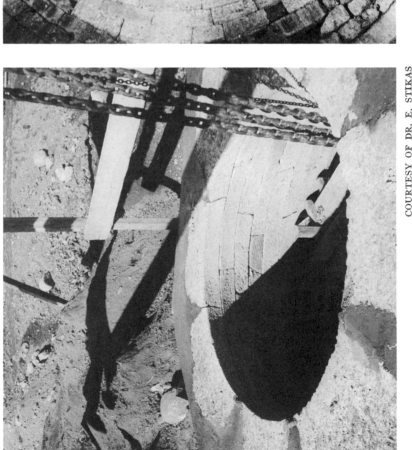

33. The tholos of the Tomb of Clytemnestra in the course of restoration

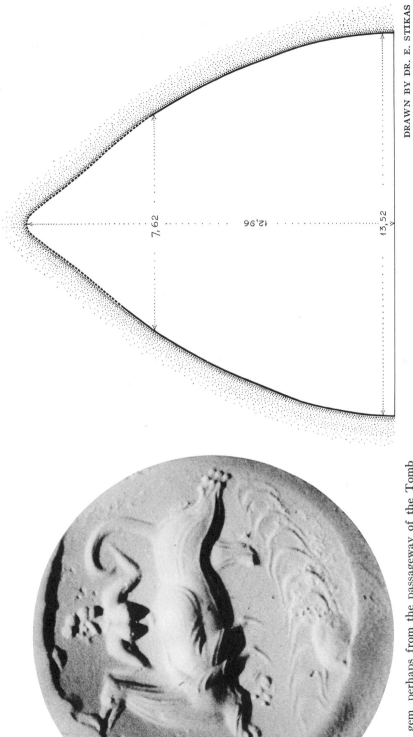

7,62

12,96

13,52

DRAWN BY DR. E. STIKAS

36. Section of the Tomb of Clytemnestra

35. Engraved gem, perhaps from the passageway of the Tomb of Clytemnestra

38. Entranceway and parapet of Grave Circle A. In the background, the remains of the Granary and the rear view of the Cyclopean wall. Beyond the doorway at the edge of the parapet, Shaft Grave VI

37. Grave Circle A, discovered by Schliemann within the Citadel

MYCENAE
SKETCH RESTORATION
OF GRAVE CIRCLE
WITH FIRST STAGE OF GRANARY

COURTESY OF DR. A. J. B. WACE

39. Grave Circle A. Drawing by George Dexter and Piet de Jong.

40. North section of Grave Circle B

41. Stele, tombstone, over Grave Alpha

42. Gold ornament from Grave Alpha. Scale in centimeters: 0.05 m.

a   b

43. Painted vases from Grave Beta

45. Stele from Grave Gamma, later transformed into a base

44. Contents of Grave Beta. a. gold band around left arm. b. bronze dagger. c. gold bands

46. Contents of Grave Gamma. Scale in centimeters: 0.50 m.

47. Jug with spiral decoration from Grave Gamma. Scale in centimeters: 0.10 m.

48. Grave Gamma. Gold bands found below jug of Figure 47 and gold cup in position

49. Amethyst bead with portrait of a Mycenaean

51. Detail of sword from Grave Delta. Haft covered with gold sheathing, pommel of ivory on top

50. Electrum mask from Grave Gamma. Scale in centimeters: 0.05 m.

53. Contents of Grave Epsilon. Scale in centimeters: 0.50 m.

52. Contents of Grave Delta. Note sword in lower left corner. Scale in centimeters: 0.50 m.

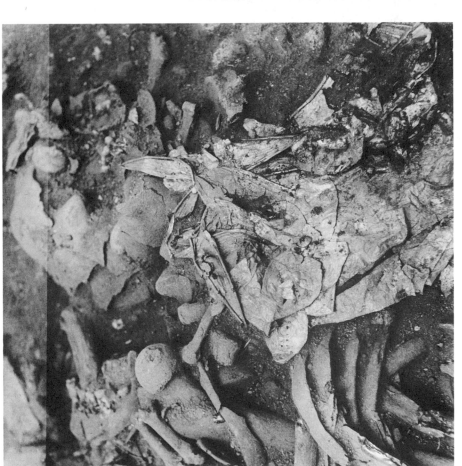

54. Detail of the gold bands found massed behind back of skeleton in Grave Epsilon

55. Contents of Grave Eta. Scale in centimeters: 0.50 m.

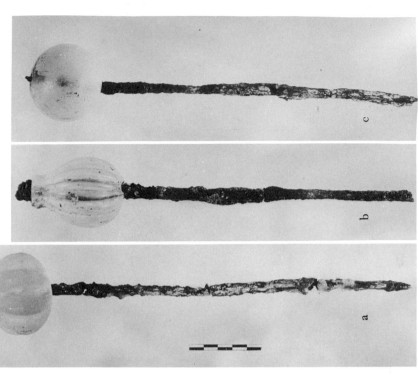

57. Pins with rock crystal heads from Grave Omicron. Scale in
centimeters: 0.05 m.

56. Grave Omicron. Gold bands, pins with crystal head, rosette,
and beads of amber

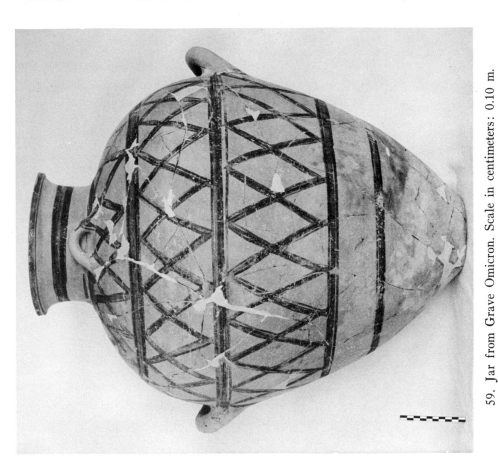

59. Jar from Grave Omicron. Scale in centimeters: 0.10 m.

58. Gold ear clips, beads of semi-precious stones, and gold buttons from Grave Omicron. Scale in centimeters: 0.05 m.

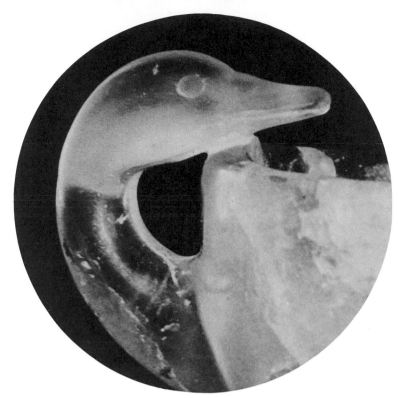

60. Detail of rock crystal bowl from Grave Omicron

61. Rock crystal bowl in the form of a duck from Grave Omicron

63. Gold ornaments from Grave Xi. Scale in centimeters: 0.05 m.

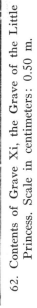

62. Contents of Grave Xi, the Grave of the Little
Princess. Scale in centimeters: 0.50 m.

64. Painted vases from Grave Nu. Scale in centimeters: 0.10 m.

65. Vases over roof of Grave Nu

67. Contents of Grave Nu. Scale in centimeters:
0.50 m.

66. Gold cup with gold bands from Grave Nu.
Below, handle of bronze vase. Scale in centimeters:
0.10 m.

68. Bronze dagger and bronze spear from Grave Nu. Scale in centimeters: 0.10 m.

69. Two views of gold cup from Grave Nu. Scale in centimeters: 0.05 m.

71. Silver-ribbed cup from Grave Iota. Scale in centimeters: 0.05 m.

70. Contents of Grave Iota. Scale in centimeters: 0.50 m.

73. Polychrome jug from Grave Kappa. Scale in centimeters: 0.05 m.

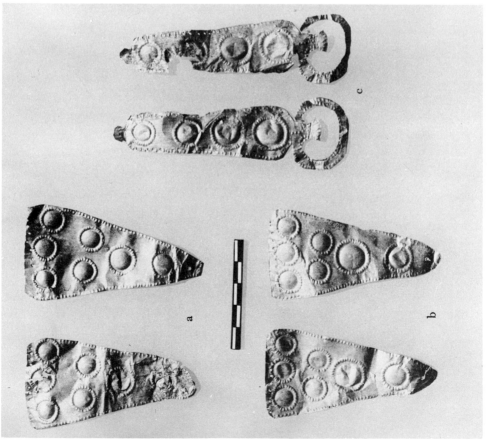

72. Gold band ornaments from Grave Iota. a. from right wrist. b. from left wrist. c. from abdominal section. Scale in centimeters: 0.05 m.

75. Boulder area, Grave Circle B. Right, the break to Grave Lambda. Under it, Grave Lambda 1 (Λ). Scale in centimeters: 0.50 m.

74. Brick structure in Kappa 2. Scale in centimeters: 0.50 m.

77. Roof slabs of Grave Lambda as found. Scale in centimeters: 0.50 m.

76. Contents of Grave Mu

a

b

79. Bronze sword by the northwest corner of Grave Lambda. a. the sword. b. remains of leather scabbard. Scale in centimeters: 0.10 m.

78. Gold bands from Grave Lambda. Scale in centimeters: 0.05 m.

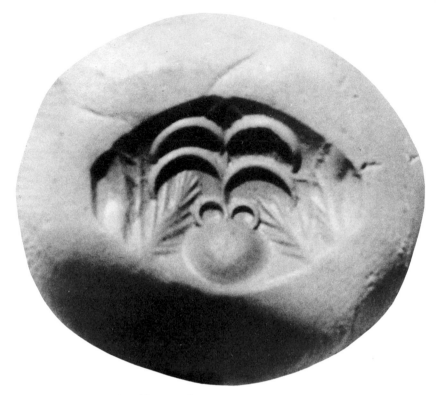

80. Engraved gem from Grave Mu

81. Painted vases from roof of Grave Lambda. Scale in centimeters: 0.05 m.

82. Contents of Grave Upsilon. Scale in centimeters: 0.50 m.

84. Interior of burial chamber, Grave Rho. Scale in centimeters: 0.50 m.

83. Grave Rho

85. Doorway to burial chamber, Grave Rho. Scale in centimeters: 0.50 m.

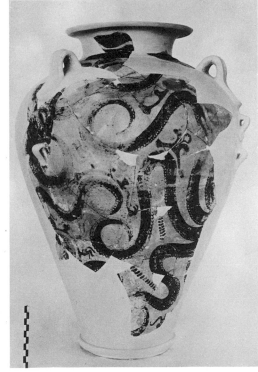

86. Palace style amphorae from Grave Rho. Scale in centimeters: 0.10 m.

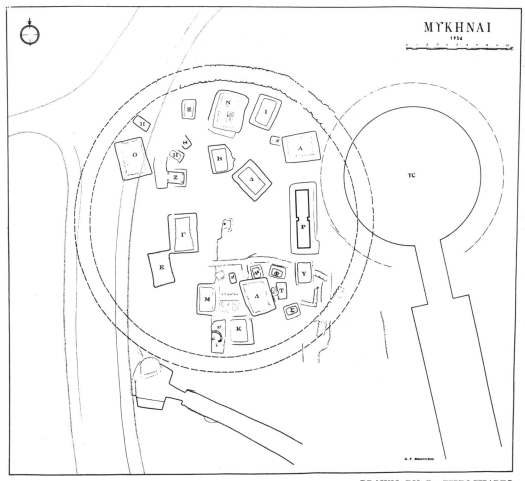

MYKHNAI
1954

87. Plan of Grave Circle B. TC, Tomb of Clytemnestra.